ZEN AND NOW

ZEN AND NOW

ON THE TRAIL OF ROBERT PIRSIG
AND THE ART OF MOTORCYCLE
MAINTENANCE

Mark Richardson

Alfred A. Knopf

New York / Toronto

2008

THIS IS A BORZOI BOOK
PUBLISHED BY ALFRED A. KNOPF
AND ALFRED A. KNOPF CANADA

Knopf, Borzoi Books, and the colophon are
registered trademarks of Random House, Inc.

Knopf Canada and colophon are trademarks.

Library of Congress Cataloging-in-Publication Data
Richardson, Mark, [date]
Zen and now : on the trail of Robert Pirsig and
the art of motorcycle maintenance / by Mark Richardson.
p. cm.
ISBN 978-0-307-26970-6 (alk. paper)
1. Pirsig, Robert M. Zen and the art of motorcycle maintenance. 2. Pirsig,
Robert M.—Criticism and interpretation. 3. Fathers and sons—United States.
I. Title.
CT275.P648R53 2008
917.304'9290922—dc22   2008017156

Library and Archives Canada Cataloguing in Publication
Richardson, Mark, [date]
Zen and now : on the trail of Robert Pirsig and the Art of Motorcycle Maintenance /
Mark Richardson.
ISBN 978-0-307-39747-8 (bound)
1. Richardson, Mark, [date]—Travel—United States. 2. Pirsig, Robert M.
3. Pirsig, Robert M. Zen and the art of motorcycle maintenance.
4. Motorcycling—United States. 5. United States—Description and travel.
6. Motorcyclists—Canada—Biography. I. Title.
E169.Z83R53 2008
917.304'931092   C2008-902503-2

Manufactured in the United States of America
First Edition

For RMP,

who started it all,

and for Wendy,

who never stopped believing

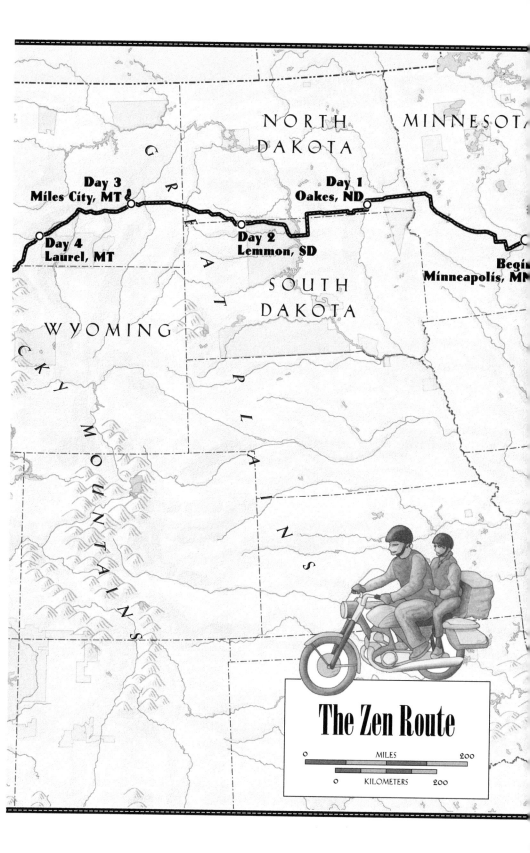

NORTH DAKOTA

MINNESOTA

G R E A T

Day 3
Miles City, MT

Day 1
Oakes, ND

Day 4
Laurel, MT

Day 2
Lemmon, SD

P L A I N S

Begi
Minneapolis, MN

SOUTH DAKOTA

WYOMING

CKY MOUNTAINS

The Zen Route

0	MILES	200
0	KILOMETERS	200

CONTENTS

ZEN AND NOW

CHAPTER ONE

Minnesota

I CAN TELL from the sign by the bank, without turning my head from the road, that it's nine thirty in the morning. The sign flashes to show it's 80 degrees, and the heat's already coming through my jacket. It's going to be hot today. That's okay—on a motorcycle, heat is always welcome.

The small town passes, and I'm back among the fields. The bike's running well this morning, and both of us are stretching out a little, starting to relax on the road now that this trip's finally under way. You'll have to excuse me if I think of her sometimes as if she's a person. It's just me now, me and my old bike.

I'm on Highway 55, the original road that runs up from Minneapolis toward Minnesota's northwest. This is an old road, made from concrete with flattened stones in the mix for hardness and ridges every few dozen feet that set up a *clickety-clack* sound like a locomotive on its tracks.

There aren't many cars on this stretch of highway because anybody who's really trying to get somewhere is on the interstate that runs alongside a couple of miles away. Sit on the interstate and you don't need to stop till you run out of gas. In fact, on the interstate, if you didn't have to pull over every few hours and pay at the pump, there'd be no reason to ever slow down or even speak to anyone. Truckers do it all the time. Stay awake for long enough and you'll be at the coast by Wednesday.

Not on this road, though. Trucks stay off this road. *Clickety-clack.* There's been a track here for centuries, paved sometime in the 1920s or '30s to better link farmers with their markets, Bible salesmen with their customers, children with their schools. This is the kind of road on which life happens, connecting other roads and streets and driveways and communities, not a thruway that picks you up here and throws you off there. It meanders around properties and makes way for the marshes that breed the ducks and red-winged blackbirds that take flight as I ride past. *Clickety-clack.*

The only way to truly experience a road like this is to be out in the open—not shut up in a car but riding along on top of it on a motorcycle. It's tough to explain to someone who's only ever traveled behind a windshield, sealed in with the comforting *thunk* of a closing door. On a bike there's no comforting *thunk.* The road is right there below you, blurring past your feet, ready to scuff your sole should you pull your boot from the peg and let it touch the ground. The wind is all around you and through you while the sun warms your clothing and your face. Take your left hand from the handlebar and place it in the breeze, and it rises and falls with the slipstream as if it were a bird's wing. Breathe in and smell the new-mown grass. Laugh out loud and your voice gets carried away on the wind.

At least that's how it is on a warm, sunny day like this Monday morning. Some rain a couple of days ago was a struggle, but I won't think about that now. There'll be plenty of time for that later.

Clickety-clack. Somewhere beside the road near here should be a rest area with an iron water pump. Nearly four decades ago a couple of motorcycles stopped here, and their riders took a cool drink from the pump. Should be coming up on the left and—here it is. Just like in the book. This road really hasn't changed much at all.

There's a place to park the bike near some picnic tables under a shelter, and the grass drops down to a stream behind the trees. To one side is the iron hand pump that's mentioned in the book. It still draws cool water. The spout is opposite the pump, so I have to dash around with my hands cupped to catch the gushing water. I capture just a trickle—I have no proper cup. The Zen riders would have brought a cup. Besides, there were four of them—enough for one to pump and another to drink. I'm on my own today.

Those Zen riders—they're why I'm here. Robert Pirsig and his eleven-year-old son, Chris, on Pirsig's old 28-horsepower, 305-cc Honda Superhawk CB77, and Pirsig's friends John and Sylvia Sutherland on their new BMW R60/2. They were making a long summer ride back in 1968, and then Pirsig went and wrote about it and his book became a best seller. *Zen and the Art of Motorcycle Maintenance* is still in bookstores, and of the five million copies sold, two are in my saddlebags.

One of those two books is an early edition, liberated from the bookshelf in my aunt's living room years ago because it had a picture of a motorcycle on its pink cover; the other is the twenty-fifth-anniversary edition, larger and a little revised. And now here, at the first stop mentioned in the book, it's the pink edition I pull out and read awhile, lying back on the grass.

I've always been curious about this book, although it took years for me to read it all the way through. I pulled it from that bookshelf one quiet afternoon, settled on the sofa, and was captivated by its first pages, by the evocative description of these ponds and marshes and the riders' gentle progress. It tells the story of a man and his son, ostensibly Pirsig and Chris, on a vacation trip to San Francisco by motorcycle from their home in the twin cities of Minneapolis/St. Paul. This is the framework for a multilayered, intricately structured narrative that is far more about their personal struggles with inner demons than it is about getting to the coast. It's also the platform from which Pirsig explores and explains his philosophy. Only a few pages in, the narrator wanders from his road trip to lament the lack of quality in his modern-day America, and that's when my teenage attention tuned out. I took the book home anyway. There was something about that illustration on the back cover—a guy standing with his son, beside a motorcycle, looking away to the horizon.

A few years later, halfway through Philosophy 101 and getting nowhere, I found the book again and gave it another try. Reading slowly but steadily, I made it to the mountains of Montana before the term ended and other courses overwhelmed me. Something had clicked, though. Maybe it was Pirsig's luggage list, his rhyming off of the same sweaters and gloves and rain gear that I'd grown accustomed to packing for frantic weekend trips to the mountains on my sport bike. More likely it was the items on the list that made us different: rope when I carried bungee cords; goggles instead of a full-face helmet; a cold chisel, a taper punch, and point files for those mysterious workings inside the bike's engine, when I carried just a pair of Vise-Grips. Both of us were looking for the same thing from our travels, just using different tools.

It wasn't until last summer that I picked up the book for a third time, looking for something to read on the first vacation in five years during which I could relax from some of the responsibilities of parenthood. That time, reading with a whole new perspective, I sailed right through. The guy *got* it! He wasn't just looking for a nice vacation; he wanted to figure out "quality" as a thing in itself, not just a description—a noun, not an adjective. He wanted to learn what's needed for his life—my life, everyone's life—to move up a notch, to be the best it can be, truly harmonious in a world swamped by so many improvements that they buckle under the weight of their time-saving intentions. As a busy parent juggling work with family, that perspective struck close to home.

But it's showing its age, this book. It's written in a folksy style that reminds me of my parents, and it refers constantly to the paraphernalia of a previous generation. Just a few pages in, reading now on the warm grass of the travelers' pause at this exact place, I come to Pirsig's description of Sutherland going through his luggage here and finding a pair of shoelaces and their joking about his overpacked bike. Shoelaces! These days, in 2004, my kids don't even know how to tie shoelaces—their footwear uses Velcro.

If I want to update the journey, I must find out more about the people who forged it and follow their tire tracks for myself. The ultimate truth about the world is biography, wrote Pirsig much later, and while my tools will be different, the reward could still be great. Perhaps some of its lessons will rub off along the way.

Beyond the rest area the road is straight and predictable, rising and dipping through fields and swamps, bordered by blue and yellow wildflowers in the uncut verge. Every small pool I pass seems to have a heron at one end, eyeing the fish or the frogs and waiting to see which of them can stay more still, and ducks at the other end, paddling softly around the shoreline's reeds. Such slow and lazy movement, while on the road itself the concrete stretches on and on, *clickety-clack,* as I ride steadily northwest and the hot sun slips across the sky.

At the side of the road up ahead there's a dead animal, well picked over by predators and no longer recognizable for whatever it used to be. The road may be hot and sultry, but it is not kind. It's hard and noisy and can kill anything in a blink if it's not understood and treated with respect.

Back in Wisconsin a couple of days ago, riding to Minneapolis to start this journey, I passed through a national forest, and there, lying beside the road, was a bald eagle, huge and glassy eyed, its neck twisted. The bird's feathers were scattered across the lane— a vehicle must have struck it as it swooped down for prey. I rode past, then doubled back and looked more closely, peering into its unseeing eyes and studying its sharp talons and perfect beak. Even in death it was intimidating.

A few miles on, as I was half watching wakeboarders on a river that flowed alongside the highway and was heading into the curves a little faster than usual, the tires hit a series of expansion joints filled with lines of slippery black bitumen. The leaning bike slid into the oncoming lane before I could correct it. *Whoa!* There was no one else on the highway and it was no big deal, but this anonymous roadkill here in Minnesota is a reminder of the road's potential treachery.

After a while now there are railway tracks on the left and a train up ahead. The bike's moving at maybe 60 miles an hour while the train is pressing along at ten less than that, so in a few minutes I catch up with it and begin to pass. The boxcars are covered in graffiti, and it's tempting to watch every carriage as it slides by, reading the graffiti artists' names. Eventually I reach the front and look across to the driver, who's looking across at me. We wave to each other. Looking back, I see a blackbird flying alongside on the right. Its red-tipped wings blur against the blue sky.

I take my feet off the pegs and skim them along the road, stretching my stiff legs. Holding the handlebars for balance, I lean into the wind, and it's as if the bike is flying. The bird soon goes away and the train soon drops behind, but the feeling stays there as the miles roll on, *clickety-clack,* reluctant to fade.

At its heart, *Zen and the Art of Motorcycle Maintenance* is a simple tale that praises basic values and decries ugly technology. Pirsig tells his story while riding the secondary roads across the Dakotas to the mountains, touching Yellowstone National Park before a pause in Bozeman, Montana. From there, he crosses into Idaho and over to Oregon before dipping down into California and reaching the Pacific coast and San Francisco. Pretty good trip, really.

In keeping with the theme, Pirsig's bike was a simple one that he maintained himself along the way. He was a capable mechanic who had made his living writing technical manuals for computers and military hardware, and who took great pleasure in doing a precise job properly. He'd strive to achieve excellence—*quality*—in everything he did, applying exactly the correct amount of measured pressure to a nut to ensure it was tight without becoming burred, or spending those extra few minutes dripping oil on the bike's drive chain to make certain it was properly lubricated. He couldn't bear machinery that was not well tuned, be it an engine or a faucet, and he'd spend as much time as necessary to make sure a problem was fixed properly. Like my bike, his was a simple machine that responded well to simple care. For a man able to explain guided missile launch systems to their operators, the dissection of a two-cylinder motorcycle engine came easily.

Mind you, everything he learned came through trial and error. He tells of breaking down on a motorcycle trip with Chris up to Canada when the boy was probably about eight. It was raining hard, and the bike just stuttered to a halt. He checked all he could think of on the engine, shook the bike to hear the gas sloshing in the tank, pulled out the plugs, and eventually gave up. The two of them hitched home and returned with a trailer for the bike. Two weeks later, checking it over at home, Pirsig found the problem: he'd run out of gas. The sloshing was in the reserve tank, which he hadn't switched on because he'd assumed he had plenty of gas and the rain was the cause. From then on, he didn't assume anything and took the maintenance of his bike very seriously.

Most certainly he didn't trust that others would invest the time and care that a problem deserved. There's a lengthy diatribe in *Zen and the Art* against the mechanics who failed to diagnose the reason his bike's engine seized and who butchered the motor in the process, rounding the bolts of the tappet covers with a wrong-size wrench and smacking a hole through the aluminum cover with a chisel. These were guys who listened to the radio while working, and Pirsig would have none of it. He eventually found the cause himself through a painstaking disassembly, and used the example to demonstrate the lack of concern for quality in many people's lives—and, by extension, how a job's worth doing properly.

Back then there was often a simple solution. If the bike broke down somewhere, you'd just unwrap the Honda tool kit and pull the engine apart to the piston rings right beside the road. If the electrics were flickering, you might wrap some foil from a cigarette pack around the contacts and be on your way; if the suspension collapsed, you could hike to a nearby farm and barter with the farmer for an old length of tractor spring to do the job till you got home. Maybe you'd even stay the night in the barn because it had gotten late and the farmer's beautiful daughter would keep you company.

Not today, though. Today's machines are filled with wizardry so that they're more powerful, more responsive, and more reliable—so that they get you wherever it is you're going even faster. They still break down, but their high-tech parts often can't be fixed without a software patch; all you can do is hope a nearby shop will be able to replace the piece. You never get to search for a strip of foil from a cigarette pack or for a tractor spring, and you never meet the farmer's daughter.

He's well into his seventies now, Robert Pirsig. He lives in New England and works hard to remain a recluse. He's written only one other book since *Zen and the Art,* an autobiographical novel called *Lila,* which delves even more deeply into the modern search for quality and morals, and which some, including Pirsig himself, consider the superior work, but although it's sold more than half a million copies, it has not been a blockbuster.

I wrote to him and asked for a meeting, and he wrote back right away. "The best place to meet an author is on the pages of his book," he wrote kindly, turning down the request. "Anywhere else is a disappointment, believe me."

After all, the narrator of *Zen and the Art,* who is not Pirsig himself but a character who shares his name and many of his foibles, is ultimately quite unpleasant. Pirsig admits at the opening of the book that "although much has been changed for rhetorical purposes, it must be regarded in its essence as fact." As he tells it, in making the ride to Bozeman in 1968, he was reliving a part of his life that had been erased several years before. For he had once taught there, at Montana State College. With an IQ of at least 170, he was a tortured genius whose intellectual restlessness drove him insane at age thirty-three; he spent Thanksgiving of 1961 in a mental hospital and fluttered in and out of schizophrenic madness for two years. Finally, his wife and father had him committed to a psychiatric ward, where—according to the narrator—his memory was damaged by electric shock therapy and from which only fragments of his former self could be recalled.

"He was dead," wrote Pirsig.

Destroyed by order of the court, enforced by the transmission of high-voltage alternating current through the lobes of his brain. Approximately 800 mills of amperage at durations of 0.5 to 1.5 seconds had been applied on twenty-eight consecutive occasions, in a process known technologically as "Annihilation ECS." A whole personality had been liquidated without a trace in a technologically faultless act that has defined our relationship ever since. I have never met him. Never will.

Pirsig called his former personality Phaedrus, and much of the conflict takes place between Phaedrus and the narrator as they struggle for control over the father's mind and, in turn, for control over the son. Young Chris Pirsig is caught in the middle, remembering the affectionate father he once knew and the father who now wears that man's face. But he rarely sees the face. For the many hours that they're riding on the little Honda, the narrator is in front, with the sun and wind and rain on his chest and the controls at his fingertips, master of the motorcycle, while Chris is behind, unable to see much, unable to speak or be heard, alone with his thoughts, sometimes crying, yearning for the father he lost six years before, who has been replaced by the broad back of this tyrant.

I could not write to Chris. In 1979 in San Francisco he was stabbed to death outside the Zen Center, where he had been studying. He was about to turn twenty-three.

It's getting even hotter now. The farmland is widening, and the ground is drying—fewer trees, and the few there are have been planted to protect the farm buildings from the wind. The bike's going to need gas soon. She doesn't go that far on a tank.

When I first began planning this trip seriously, I traded a few brief letters with Pirsig, and later with Nancy, his wife at the time, and his surviving son, Ted. It didn't take long to find addresses for two of the other characters in the narrative: John Sutherland of Minneapolis, who rode with his wife, Sylvia, alongside the Pirsigs for the first week of their journey to Montana, and Gennie DeWeese, who hosted the Pirsigs and Sutherlands for a few days in Bozeman before the travelers split up to complete their vacations separately.

Both Sutherland and DeWeese wrote to say they'd be pleased to meet with me. They're used to such requests, for each year several "Pirsig's pilgrims" make the same trip and seek out the elements of the book.

Arriving in Minneapolis just a couple of days ago, I called John Sutherland, and we met up yesterday morning. He's separated from Sylvia, although they remain close friends. I asked if she'd speak with me about the book, and he was emphatic that she would not. She didn't like the book and wants to forget about it, he said.

That is because the two of them come across as shallow—they're supposed to represent the carelessness and sloppiness of modern life. Pirsig's acknowledgment that he's taken some liberties in his portrayals must be small consolation to Sylvia. Sutherland, though, says he's not bothered about being portrayed as an affable drunk who can't fix his bike or even a dripping faucet. Worse than that, in Pirsig's view he doesn't *care* about the dripping faucet. He lives now in a bungalow near downtown Minneapolis (with all the faucets tight) and was pleased to talk about the good old days, although he has no souvenirs from the '68 trip. It wasn't that big a deal at the time, he explained.

Sutherland later became a pro photographer, but he hadn't taken any pictures back then—the few that survive are from Pirsig's camera. They're on the Internet now, those dozen pictures, and I'd printed some copies for just such a meeting as this. Sutherland has no computer and was pleased to accept the prints, even if he was none too sure of their primitive color. "Color photos give you exactly what you see," he said. "Black-and-white still has a mystery about it." Here he is with Sylvia, posing with young Chris at a mountain pass and again somewhere on the prairie. Here he is with Bob Pirsig, hoisting Chris between the bikes. The three of them leaning against a hay bale. You've probably got family pictures just like them.

I showed him some of the photos I'd taken on the road to Minneapolis, and he peered into the little digital screen on the back of my camera and muttered something about today's technology. There were a dozen photos just of the dead eagle, and I flipped through them quickly to find the best. "It's a lot easier when you don't have to develop them all, isn't it?" said Sutherland. "When you don't have to pay for all the paper and chemical?" But there was no good photo of the eagle; every picture just showed a dead bird, ants crawling through its feathers.

Sutherland's favorite photographs are framed and presented on tables throughout his small home or stored in flat boxes on the bookshelves. He looks good in his old pictures, as he does in Pirsig's photos from the trip. These days his dark hair has thinned, his gut has filled, and his hearing requires a visitor to use a loud voice, but he seems fit for a man in his late seventies and keeps active. Most days he heads over to his wife's apartment, or visits one of his four daughters. So after some coffee we drove around awhile to see the Twin Cities and to take a look at Pirsig's old house in St. Paul.

It's a good-size family home on a quiet, leafy street, with white siding and green-shuttered windows and a large sheltered front door. A thirtysomething woman was tending the flower garden in front, and we introduced ourselves. Her name was Susan Nemitz, and she was thrilled to meet us.

"John!" she called to her husband. "We've got visitors interested in the Pirsigs!"

For Sutherland, stepping through the front door on that sunny Sunday afternoon into the shade of the dark wood hallway, it was the first time he'd been back in the house since his friends had moved away.

"These people know about the Pirsigs and are interested in the house," Sue said to her husband as he came downstairs. "And this is John Sutherland, the same John Sutherland who's in the book and who rode with them for a while."

John Curry, her husband, knew all about *Zen and the Art* and was impressed to meet Sutherland, who in turn was rather tickled to receive the attention. We were offered Coke and Fresca and Welch's grape juice, and Sutherland's memory was tapped for his recollections of the trip. After all, Sue and John had each read the book before they bought the house and were pleased to move into a home once lived in by a famous genius and his family.

"I remember cocktail parties in here," said Sutherland, looking into the paneled living room. "Bob was the quiet one, but Nancy was much more lively and was such a great host. Always plenty to eat and always plenty to drink. The kids were upstairs in their rooms, and we were down here drinking and eating. Those were great parties."

Looking up the dark wood stairs, he remembered his girls going up there to hang out with the Pirsig boys while their parents visited.

"The boys had guinea pigs, and my girls, who were a few years younger, loved to come over to see them and play. We stayed down here and talked about politics, the university—all kinds of things."

"And how would you describe yourself now?" asked Sue.

"Well, I'm a social worker, a jazz musician, a photographer, and a recovering alcoholic."

"Ah," she exclaimed, and then, to lighten the suddenly somber mood, "a Renaissance man!"

Sutherland smiled at her graciousness. He hasn't had a drink since his family surprised him with an intervention in 1979, but alcohol runs through the *Zen and the Art* journey. Sutherland's probably the worst of the travelers, always propping up a bar somewhere, stopping for beers at lunch and a nip of something in the afternoon, followed by late-night liquors, but his wife and friends aren't too far behind. One of the things that date the book is all the breaking for booze before getting back on the bike.

Sutherland took another sip from his Fresca, and Sue asked about the Pirsig boys. Like me, she's been in touch with the surviving younger son, Ted, who lives in Hawaii and maintains no contact with his father but has fond memories of the house in which he grew up.

"Ted and Chris really didn't get along," Sutherland said more quietly.

"If one boy was in a room and the other walked in, that boy would get up and leave. On the trip, Chris was kind of a drag, always whimpering. But I think we helped Chris, helped him to get away from the whole father-son thing. They tried—Nancy would do something with Ted one year, then Bob with Chris— but there wasn't too much emotional togetherness in that whole crew."

The room was quiet. None of this was news to Sue and John, for they'd corresponded with Ted, but it was hard to hear it in this house, in which they're now making a life with their own young daughter. Before they'd bought the house eight years ago, with Sue pregnant and the two of them looking for a happy family home, they'd almost purchased a property that seemed perfect, but it was being sold because of a divorce and they eventually shied away from its "bad karma."

"We thought this would be a happier place," said Sue, "but we learned afterward that they weren't really all that happy here. So now we think of it as a creative place. And we've made it happy."

The rooms and layout are still as the Pirsigs would recognize them. The original workbench remains in the basement, well constructed and solid, its drawer still sliding reliably on the wheels from the boys' roller skates. When Ted wrote to tell them of a secret walled-up room under the front stairs, where he and his brother would hold up a mirror to look through a gap high in the paneling to see only blackness, John Curry had gone down there to look for himself.

With mirror and flashlight in hand, he took me downstairs to see it. There was a small hole in the wall above where a mosaic of his daughter's artwork had been pinned to the panels. John shone the flashlight through the hole and angled the mirror beside it to show me the interior. The reflection on the silvered surface was dark and unclear, and the space there, probably five feet square, remained obscure.

"I think there are skeletons in there," he said with only a half smile. "Lots of skeletons."

After we left the Pirsig house, Sutherland drove us past the house on Clarence Avenue in Minneapolis where Maynard and Harriet Pirsig had lived most of their days, raising their son, Robert; their younger daughter, Jean; and later, an adopted daughter, Wanda, whose unmarried mother had lived next door. Harriet had cared for Wanda as a baby while her mother went to work; when the mother went to California to find a better job, she left her eight-month-old behind, planning to return for her when she became established, but she never reclaimed the child. For the rest of their lives, Harriet and Maynard considered her their own.

We passed the campus where Sutherland had met Pirsig in the mid-'60s while attending lectures on Eastern philosophy. Robert had been involved with the university from early in his life. In kindergarten, being already able to read and write, he was promptly bumped up to the second grade, where, as the smallest child in the class, he was bullied and picked upon. It didn't help that his teachers made him write with his right hand when he was naturally left-handed and that he developed a stammer. So his parents enrolled him in a school for the children of university faculty, where his classmates were his own age and he was allowed to write with his left hand, and he excelled. From there he went on to the university high school and then to the university itself, studying chemistry when he was just fifteen years old. He was an otherwise normal teenager, enjoying chess and keeping a wild squirrel in his bedroom; he called it Gus, and the rodent chewed on his wooden chess pieces. But at eighteen, with the rapid academic progression being all too much too soon, he was expelled from the university for failing grades, inattention to his studies, and overall immaturity.

"Here I am a child prodigy," he told a journalist many years later, "and I'd like to discover—I know this is a childish dream—the secret of life, to know everything there is to know, to be an intellectual master of things. And they're trying to seal me into Wrap and Wax for the rest of my life." And as he also once wrote, pure science should be a search for truth, not for profit.

Unwilling to go to work for the local waxed paper manufacturer with the university's chemistry grads and unsure of his calling, Pirsig joined the army and was sent to Korea for fourteen months; in Asia he discovered ways of thinking that went far beyond the rigid rationalism of Western tradition. "I told the Koreans one time the most marvelous thing about the English language is that in 26 letters you can describe the whole universe. And they just said, 'No.' That was what started me thinking."

After his discharge he returned to the University of Minnesota to study philosophy and pursue a why-are-we-here ideal that he called "the ghost of reason," but it eluded him. On earning his bachelor of arts, he went to India with money from the GI Bill and enrolled at Banaras Hindu University to study Eastern philosophy, but he spent more time traveling around than poring over books; in his own words, "nothing much happened," and he returned to Minnesota to take up a more practical pursuit—the study of journalism.

His parents expected a lot of him, for they had both risen from a poor midwestern farming background to affluent success through a combination of intelligence and sheer grit. Maynard had spoken only German until he went to school and then became the first person in his town to go on to college; at the University of Minnesota Law School he earned the highest grades ever recorded and eventually became its dean and one of the most respected—and toughest—lawyers in the region. "I used to have many enemies in this state," he once told an audience. "I'm pleased to report to you that now they're all dead!"

Harriet, the oldest child in a large Swedish family in northern Minnesota, had it harder. Her mother died when she was twelve years old. Her father, a simple man who needed a wife to care for the family and his own needs, claimed a version of Swedish tradition and took Harriet into his bed. Within a year she bore him a child. When the authorities found out, they were horrified: her father was committed to an asylum and the seven children were placed in foster homes around the state. Not Harriet, though, who was devastated to lose the father she still loved. She moved to Minneapolis, where she found room and board in exchange for reading to an old, blind scholar and put herself through high school and then college, where she met Maynard.

Harriet eventually found all her siblings, but the illegitimate baby was lost, its fate never recorded. "It doesn't matter to me," Maynard told her, "but don't ever tell anyone about it." Which she did not—until the day more than thirty years later when Robert Pirsig was visiting his parents' home and answered the ringing telephone; a state official was on the line, asking permission to perform surgery on Mr. Sjobeck, the grandfather he'd always believed was dead. The sordid story came out when he confronted his parents, but it would still not be spoken of outside the family.

.   .   .

On the way home we drove by the house of one of Sutherland's daughters, and when he saw her out walking with her children, we stopped for a chat through the car window.

"I told them about how you'd go upstairs and play with the guinea pigs," he said about the day's visit.

"Dad!" And she grinned. "We hated those guinea pigs. We thought they were creepy!"

I left from outside the Pirsig house this morning. John Curry came out with a cup of coffee for me and a pat on the gas tank for the bike to wish us both well. This journey had to start somewhere, and the place might as well have been accurate. Whenever possible, I plan to stick to the same route and the same rest stops and see how much remains. Pirsig was sometimes vague about names but always precise in description, so I expect to find the way. He left in July, and today's July 18; the journey should take two weeks, ending in San Francisco on my birthday.

As a guide, I have a GPS unit fixed to the bike's handlebar—worth more than the old bike herself—and it's been loaded with waypoints that were sent to me by a tech-savvy Pirsig fan. I'm not the first to travel this road and sure won't be the last, but all that really matters right now, as the heat bears down and the landscape begins to flatten, is that the front tire stays true to the west. The rest will follow.

CHAPTER TWO

Into North Dakota

I T'S 91 DEGREES in Elbow Lake, still in Minnesota, and time to stop for lunch. Most people ate a couple of hours ago, but I'm on my own time here, stopping when I want, riding when I want. It's time to cool off now and eat something.

The Pirsigs would have had a proper meal, so the Heartland Café seems about right, here on Central Avenue, and I park the bike carefully outside the front window. When your luggage is secured only by bungee cords, it's a good idea to keep an eye on the machine. As well, the pavement is very hot, and the weight on the side stand might push it into the asphalt, creating its own little pothole and causing the bike to fall over. That could break a mirror, leak the gas, and—most important—look very uncool.

Inside it's almost cold enough to leave the leather jacket on. The place is about empty in the dull hours of the afternoon, but the young waitress—well, younger than me, anyway—says hello with a smile, points out a booth, and hands over a menu. My hands are stained black from the dye in the gloves, thanks to the sweat from holding the grips.

The choices include chicken gizzards and beef liver and onions—midwestern culture shock for my eastern taste. A club sandwich seems safe. I sit studying the map. There's a detour coming up, where the Zen foursome missed a signpost and didn't make the logical turn west. If their route is to be followed properly, I must also miss the turn and take the longer way around.

"You don't sound like you're from the Cities," says the waitress, bringing the sandwich and fries. Her name tag says Stacey. The overloaded, weather-beaten bike parked outside the window bolsters her opinion of me. And then, "Is that a Harley you're riding?"

Hah! Jackie New, which is my name for the bike, is about the farthest machine from a Harley-Davidson. She's a Suzuki dual-purpose motorcycle—a bit too big for riding easily in the dirt, a bit too small for riding comfortably on the highway. Stacey clearly knows nothing about motorcycles, and I don't want to start trying to explain.

On the other side of the restaurant, the only other diner is a friend of Stacey's from the Family Coalition. Coming into town, I had passed a billboard with a huge picture of a smiling baby wearing a baseball cap and clutching a football, placed there by a group called ProLife Across America. "If you're not ready to be a DADDY, let someone who is," it called out. Then, "2 million couples wait to adopt."

The billboard's a reminder to call home. Well, not home, because nobody's there now. My wife and the boys are visiting her sister in Europe, and I'd better call to let her know the trip's under way. She'd wanted to know when it started.

When the sandwich is finished, I push a tip under the empty plate and head outside to find a pay phone. There's one at the library across the street, where the young but motherly librarian greets me with a beautiful smile and leaves her desk to guide the way down a corridor to the phone. When the call finally connects, there's nobody home there, either. The machine kicks in. I hate machines and leave a curt message: "It's me. I'm fine and the bike's okay and we're on our way west now. You wanted to know. I'll call you later."

That'll do it. She'd said she wanted to know. I hang up and wander back into the sunshine toward the bike, feeling a little angry. On the library lawn a couple is enjoying the coolness of a shady picnic table.

"That looks hot," says one, eyeing my leather jacket and jeans.

"I'll be fine once I get moving." And I will be. Got to look for that signpost and make sure it's ignored.

In *Zen and the Art* the Pirsigs were riding in front; the Sutherlands caught up and told them they missed the turn west into North Dakota. The sign was as "big as a barn door," said Sutherland, but since they'd already traveled some distance beyond it, they just carried on and took the next route west, over the Red River at Breckenridge. The narrator also claimed to be distracted by an impending thunderstorm, though Pirsig admitted later that he'd made up the storm in order to introduce the character of Phaedrus—a flash of lightning lights up the scenery, and the narrator remembers driving the same road years before.

Riding north, I also miss the sign without even trying.

Yes, it's big, at the top of a small rise clearly showing the way to Wendell five miles to the west and the continuation of the highway, but distracted by the farms off to the east, I sail straight on. The farm buildings are shielded on three sides by heavy woods with only the south side exposed. Any wind that might push through that dense foliage would have to be strong and bitter.

In today's heat it's tough to imagine the snow whipping across the fields to drift over the road, or the farmer hunched into the frigid Arctic air, breath freezing into beaded droplets on the outside of his scarf, ice crunching underfoot as the naked trees swing back and forth, their dead leaves long since crumbled or blown away. This is a hard land, with cold winters and long, dark periods of hibernation, the snow protecting and cosseting everything underneath but leaving the surface brittle and cold until the ice begins to melt and the corn and soybean rise, oblivious to the motorcycles that come in the summer and are gone in seconds.

Lost in these thoughts, I take a while to realize I must have passed the sign and so wheel back to the south to go after it. There it is, three miles back down the road, big as a barn door. I swing north again, soon crossing over the interstate and entering another small town. But I make my own wrong turn, and instead of riding through the center of town to cross under the highway again, I'm back at the next junction with the interstate.

Oh, what the hell. It'll be easy to get back onto the road at the next exit. Sorry, Pirsig.

But as soon as the ramp begins to merge onto the four-laner, everything changes. Giant trucks hurl past on the left, their wheels churning up dust and grit. The comfortable 60 miles an hour must be pushed up to 70 and more just to keep pace with the traffic; the engine strains against the stronger headwind, and the clutch slips as the worn plates fight for grip at the hurried speed.

There's no time to look at the scenery and little scenery to see, nothing to smell except diesel, no wind to laugh into, just noise from the tires spinning all around.

A car speeds by with a Manitoba license plate, and a memory comes back: I've been on this road before! This is the route to Winnipeg that I pursued blindly over a long weekend seventeen years ago. I drove this way to find my girlfriend, a woman I loved with the infatuation of youth, who had visited Winnipeg for a week of work in the spring.

The car belonged to another woman, the girlfriend of one of the men Jackie was traveling with, and we both thought it would be a wonderful thing to surprise them so many miles from home. And we both thought they were cheating on us. And we both wanted to let them know we could find them anywhere, anytime. But they weren't cheating on us at all, and our visit was disruptive and unwelcome.

We returned after less than a day, another long drive in the Volkswagen through the night and the day and the night again. Somewhere north of Minneapolis in the middle of the night, the woman asleep in the passenger seat and me exhausted at the wheel, my eyes closed for too long, and the speeding car moved slowly off the interstate onto the wide central verge.

The earth was hard and comparatively smooth, but its ruts jolted me awake to fight the wheel in panic as we swerved through the shallow ditch toward the oncoming traffic. Sawing left and right in the grass, I finally pulled the car back onto the southbound lane and steadied the steering wheel with a grip that just wouldn't release. Adrenaline surged through every vein and artery.

It was clear what had happened and what had almost happened. It was as if it had been lit by a dazzling white light. And it was clear *why* it had happened—because I was too jealous and infatuated and self-obsessed to make the right choice, to just let my girlfriend go off to Winnipeg for a week and achieve her own success.

"What was that?" murmured the woman, woken by the bumps but too sleepy to open her eyes.

"It's okay," I said, staring straight ahead. "I had to swerve for a deer." Eyes wide open, both hands locked to the wheel.

But at least there was the freedom in those days to just drop everything and go wherever, whenever. Not like now, when trips take months, years, of preparation and negotiation. Kids complicate matters.

Long forgotten but no longer far away. Maybe it was right here, north of Minneapolis. There's a wide central verge between the lanes. Two miles later I'm spewed back onto the road to Breckenridge, and I take a deep breath of relief when the pace slows.

The fields are flattening as the Red River valley approaches. Sugar beet's the main crop, growing thick to the horizon on each side as the road leads straight west without a curve. Trucks pass laden with produce and supplies, heading to the interstate as I go into the valley and the border with the Dakotas.

The feeling is different now. Not better or worse, just different. The bike's valves are sounding a little clattery—I'll adjust them tomorrow.

It's still hot, but the afternoon sun seems stronger as I ride toward it, moving off my shoulder and directly onto my face, making my eyes squint behind the sunglasses and the tinted visor. This is the first time today I've headed directly west for more than a few miles, and it'll need some getting used to. I won't be turning away again until the Pacific coast.

The bridge leads from Minnesota into North Dakota, the latest bank sign shows it's 95 degrees, and it would be good to stop for an ice cream. Dairy Queen would be okay, but there's no Dairy Queen. There's a tiny Dairy Delight, but the tables are outside in the direct sun, so I ride back and forth along the main street, even down to the Wal-Mart on the edge of town, to find ice cream. Finally there's nothing to do but park the bike at Burger King and go in for a milk shake.

The girl behind the counter barely looks up as she drops the change into my hand, making sure not to touch the palm that's stained black again. The gloves have lost so much dye by now it's surprising they still have any color in them.

In the corner a television is tuned to *Jeopardy!* Just one person is over here, a tall, thin man with a checked shirt spread loosely over his broad shoulders, and he notices me as I sit down. My T-shirt is sweat stained down the spine and across the chest.

"You look like you're coming from a long way away," he says. When he speaks, the deep lines on his tanned face barely move. "Where are you coming from?"

A bike will always help you strike up conversation. His name's Vince and he's a farmer and he says he's been to every state in the Union except Maine. "Got to get there sometime." He grins. Though he's traveled widely throughout his country, he keeps coming back here, to the town where he was born.

"It was a different place then," he says. "Smaller. Then it grew; then it stopped. It made a big change when they put in the bypass. Not better or worse, just different. There sure was no Burger King back then."

He likes it here in the fast-food restaurant because he can watch *Jeopardy!* in comfort, and sometimes he'll even buy something to eat. Not too often, though.

Vince talks about the various crops and why they thrive here. He asks about Maine, for I mention that I drove through it with my family a couple of years ago. When it's time to leave, he grips my hand with a firm and gnarly shake. "You have a good trip," he says. "Make the most of it."

And now it's the final stretch of the day, eighty miles west and just a little south.

The lonely road arrows through the prairie, and thoughts whir along like a movie reel. Sometimes when you're on a bike in the stillness of the ride, your thoughts are like those at 3 a.m. when you can't sleep, and they can get pretty wild. Here's one that comes now: next week I'll be forty-two years old. Forty-two. The number reminds me of *The Hitchhiker's Guide to the Galaxy,* in which aliens construct an enormous computer designed to give an answer to the Ultimate Question about the meaning of life. After waiting ten billion years, they get their answer: "Forty-two." So now the aliens have to build another computer and wait another ten billion years in order to discover what the Ultimate Question is exactly. Not too enlightening. North Dakota's not the universe, but maybe if I stay on schedule and turn forty-two in San Francisco, I'll discover the meaning of life. Or learn to ask the right questions, at least.

Nancy James was wondering about her life in 1953. She'd been married for two years to a guy she'd met when she was an eighteen-year-old freshman studying journalism at the University of Minnesota. He graduated and promptly joined the navy, and she dropped out of school to be with him in Washington, D.C., and then his ship sailed away and she was alone.

So she moved back to Minnesota, went back to school, and volunteered again for work at *The Minnesota Daily,* the student newspaper, and tried to love a man who was thousands of miles away for months at a time. Instead, she fell under the charismatic spell of the *Daily*'s associate editor, Robert Pirsig.

I wrote to Nancy and asked her how the two of them met. She wrote back:

Everyone I knew in the Daily *crowd, which hung out together after hours as well as during the day, was fascinated by Bob. I was captivated as well. He talked a lot in the group that got together over beers at Stub and Herb's on Oak Street. He told stories about his time in Korea and in India, fascinating stuff about a world none of us knew a thing about. One night he led a group of maybe six of us into a large park at midnight, walking through a light snow cover on the ground, calling out to each other, maybe singing some songs, probably a little drunk, laughing a lot, all feeling as I did, that the world was ours and we were invincible—and happy.*

It may have been at the end of that outing, or some other, that one by one people dropped off and went home until only Bob and I were left. We ended up going to his parents' house around 2 a.m., where he led me to the add-on room behind the kitchen, which held a sofa, some chairs, bookshelves and a TV. We sat on the sofa and he talked for what seemed like hours until he finally ran down and we looked at each other and finally hugged and kissed. We had an attraction for each other, no doubt about it. From then on we were secretly a couple. I could not imagine ever going back to the "boy" I had married. This new thing was my first real love.

Bob thought differently from anyone I ever knew. He was thoroughly unconventional, extremely bright (early on he told me he had an IQ of 170), very articulate, and could be charming. He had had all these worldly experiences and adventures and talked freely about them, piquing my interest in exploring the world. I was quite content to more or less sit at his feet and adore his knowledge and attention. As for what about me appealed to him, I don't know. I just

felt lucky that we seemed to be falling in love, that he cared
for me.

Today's last stop will be Oakes, where the Pirsigs and Sutherlands stayed the night at a motel. The town isn't named in the
book, but it's described fairly clearly. What is named is the town
where they stopped for breakfast the next morning, after riding
for forty-five minutes, so a careful look at the map shows that the
only place where they could have spent the night was Oakes.

There were two motels back then, the A1 on the town's west
side and the E&I on the east. They must have stayed at the A1
because they turned right off the highway onto Main Street and
passed underneath the cottonwood trees for a couple of blocks,
but the place burned down a few years ago. The E&I is still there,
though, and I have a reservation.

I get to Oakes as the sun is low in the sky, turning left and riding a few blocks to the eastern edge of town, and the owner himself is standing outside the motel office. Sidney Berreth looks to
be an intelligent man, his small, clean-cut head out of place on a
very large body. He's come outside to see his son Jeremy, who's
just arrived with his two young daughters.

"You've come a long way," Sidney says, looking at the dirt
bike, scuffed and dusty. "It looks like you could head right over
the mountains with that. You're in room twenty-one—it's got a
good shower."

Sidney Berreth is pleased to talk about his town, which he loves
dearly. We agree to go out for a beer later in the evening, and I
accept his offer to show me around.

He's right that the shower is good, and the room actually com-
prises a kitchenette, living room, and bedroom, with two TVs, all
for $42 for the night. Most of the other rooms are taken by work-
ers staying for weeks or even months at a time. The guy next door
is retired and lives in his room. If I hadn't booked ahead, there
wouldn't have been space for me tonight.

Sidney's pleased to have me here, and with me washed and changed and keen for a beer, he drives us slowly through town in his pickup truck.

He's intrigued by the talk of *Zen and the Art of Motorcycle Maintenance,* which he'd not heard of, and even more intrigued by his son's reaction earlier when I first mentioned it.

"That's a fabulous book," Jeremy had said. "I've read it, like, four times."

Had he finished it?

"Not the first time. I got stuck in it the first time. But then I started again and read it half through. Then the third time, I read it all the way through, and it was great. And I keep reading it. It doesn't age. I didn't know Oakes was in it. I'll have to read it again."

I'd pulled out the pink copy from my saddlebag and checked the reference, and we'd all read the relevant page and agreed the town had to be Oakes. The A1 Motel, which burned down in 2001, must have been the motel they stayed in because there are no cottonwood trees at this end of town. And the description of them sitting outside in the metal armchairs of the A1's courtyard, drinking a pint of Sutherland's whiskey, Pirsig baffling his companions as he argued for the material existence of ghosts, read as if it had happened just last night—a late-night chat with friends over a drink after a hard day.

Sidney parks the pickup in front of Rudy's Bar, and we go inside, where it looks like just about every other bar in America—long and narrow, dimly lit, and mostly empty on this early weekday evening. There are a half dozen people at a table at the far end, and we join them. They're all wearing baseball caps, but that's okay—so are we. They seem like old friends by the way they're speaking, but it turns out Sidney knows only two of them and then only vaguely. That's all you need in rural North Dakota.

Sidney introduces me and somebody buys me a beer and the book is explained and the copy handed around and each person reads the descriptive paragraphs about Oakes's cottonwood trees. Nobody carries on to read about the ghosts.

It comes out that our new friends are truck drivers, intimately familiar with the rigors of the road, and so the talk steers to motorcycles and trucks and cars. Somebody else buys more beer, and the obvious question comes up quickly.

"Are you riding a Harley?"

The question gets asked a lot, and the answer usually disappoints. "No, she's a Suzuki. A dirt bike."

"A dirt bike? Why are you riding a dirt bike?"

A good question. Maybe these truckers will understand.

The 1985 Suzuki DR600 was never a very good bike—the Kawasaki was better, with liquid cooling and an electric start—but I liked her for the basic nature of her traditional air-cooled engine. It was the first year for the big single-cylinder dirt bike, and Suzuki quickly improved it with better brakes and more power. An electric starter became standard sometime in the early '90s.

My bike has the kick start, though, and it became the machine's signature. Because of the bike's large-bore engine, the kick start must be pushed gently until the piston is at an exact point in the cylinder; otherwise it just won't start when you give it that hefty kick for real. Worse, the kick-starter pedal might recoil from the bottom of the stroke. My bike did that once to a cocky mechanic, ramming the young man's leg back up with the power of a cannon, smacking his knee into the handlebar with such force that he was sent to the hospital with a cracked kneecap. He had ignored the trick to starting the bike, which is to pull in a small compressor lever on the handlebar and then fiddle about until it clicks out again.

Remember that and the DR will start with ease every time; forget it and you're going *nowhere*.

I bought her brand-new in 1985 with a plan to quit my job and ride around the world. The choice was between a secondhand Harley-Davidson—to chase the American dream on the American dream machine—and a new dirt bike, a dual-purpose motorcycle designed for exploring gravel roads and gentle trails. The dirt bike won because I figured it would be more practical and reliable for reaching the Arctic Ocean and spanning the jungles of Central America.

I quit the job, but the ride around the world was trimmed back to a year or so of wandering North America, up to Alaska and Canada's Northwest Territories, down to Mexico and Florida, with stops at many points in between. I broke down plenty of times but always managed to fix the bike myself beside the road. I worked at odd jobs for a few days here and there to make money to keep on the road, staying with friends when I could and in hostels when I couldn't, sometimes just pitching my tent in a quiet place and reading for a while. Cops shooed me off the beach in San Diego and threw me in jail in South Dakota; travelers welcomed me at campsites in the Southwest desert and the mountains of New England. Then, broke and windburned, I kept a promise and settled down, and the rest is history.

Yet I also kept my bike, remembering her many flaws and challenges but also her simple nature and familiarity. I called her Jackie Blue for her color and the girlfriend who went to Winnipeg; as well, there's the '70s song "Jackie Blue," in which the singer's Jackie is *"goin' places where you've never been."*

The long-suffering girlfriend left me soon after I sold my first piece of writing, to a motorcycle magazine, which described how I'd named the bike. "She's called Jackie because, like my girlfriend, she's great if only I can get her started," I'd written enthusiastically. "Until then, she just sits around and coughs and costs me money." Understandably, Jackie wasn't amused. I don't know where she is now.

But my bike stayed with me, rotting quietly and sheltering mice. I fixed her up a few times, but she kept leaking oil, and the transmission that years ago shouldn't have lasted the month finally began to slip. Parts became more difficult to find. The plan was to restore her and leave her on display at home, but then I learned of another bike, an identical machine, sitting in a garage in the city and up for sale.

"I haven't ridden her for a few years now," said the owner as he drew open the garage door. The motorcycle had only a thousand miles on her; I could see her clearly, parked in the bike shop with a mechanic doubled up in pain, lying on the floor clutching his knee.

The purchase was a formality, and the bike, called Jackie New, came home with me to continue life's journey. She's outside the E&I now, with many more miles to go.

The truckers nod, but they don't really understand. If it's not a Harley-Davidson, it's just a rice grinder, and machinery that needs to be fixed too often should be discarded. The table's getting crowded with the cans and bottles of Coors Light and Bud, and the dim air's thickening from the cigarette smoke. Cell phones and Bics and Zippos are pressing for space among the water rings and ashtrays.

The conversation switches for a while to politics and the economy, and my mind drifts back and forth with the beer. Pirsig understood the personality of motorcycles—he's still got his little Superhawk in his garage in New England and will never sell it. Sutherland didn't understand. He would buy a new bike every spring and sell it in the fall. But Ollie Foran understands, probably better than anyone.

I met Ollie in Wisconsin on Saturday, just before arriving in Minneapolis. I'd found him through an Internet contact, and I dearly wanted to visit him because Ollie Foran is the man who owns the BMW that John and Sylvia Sutherland rode alongside the Pirsigs.

He's owned it for years, having bought it from an interim owner in the late '70s. Ollie was looking for a BMW and had little money, but as a young architect had saved enough over three months to cough up the $1,150 needed to take it home. "Hey," said the seller as Ollie was about to ride away, "did you ever read that book *Zen and the Art of Motorcycle Maintenance*? This is the

Sutherland BMW!" Ollie had read the book, and suddenly the weight of the world was on his shoulders. He hadn't bought a motorcycle—he'd bought a piece of cultural history.

Still, Ollie loved that motorcycle and rode it to California the next year, leaving Minneapolis in early November and following his girlfriend in her truck. That was a cold ride, forcing a detour toward Phoenix to avoid snowdrifts in the Rockies.

He doesn't ride it so often now, since he's returned to western Wisconsin, but he'll never get rid of it and maintains it with understanding and love. It has its own home in a small shed behind his house, and he showed the bike to me with pride.

At least, he showed it to me with pride through the window of the shed. "I can't open the lock on the door," he said. "It's just seized. I'll have to drill it out."

For an hour, Ollie pressed a succession of ever-larger drills into the lock. Mosquitoes buzzed in the heat; I watched one in fascination as it settled on Ollie's ear and began to drink, undeterred by the shriek and vibration of the half-inch drill.

Eventually the shaft fragmented, the lock fell away, and the door swung open in resignation. Ollie went to fetch a broom to sweep the swarf off the wooden floor.

Inside, the black BMW sat in splendor, the first true relic of the Zen trip I could touch and consider. It had a different seat, from a Harley Sportster that Ollie had fitted many years ago for its marginally enhanced comfort, and the saddlebags were removed and lying off to one side, but it was otherwise exactly as it appears in the photographs from the trip.

Ollie returned with the broom, and I swept away the specks of drilled metal while he wiped the bike down. Then, without warning, he climbed onto the left side and shoved down on the sideways kick start. It started immediately with a *WHOOMP* of exhaust that knocked me backward in the doorway and blew more specks of swarf out the door.

He grinned. "I treat her right, and she treats me right."

We went for a ride together down to the Mississippi River, he and I, and the old BMW kept up a cracking pace. Later, when he let me ride it, I was astonished by the engine's strength, and concerned about the heaviness of the steering. But neither was a worry for Ollie. He's ridden forty thousand miles on the bike in the many years he's had it, and it repays him every time he takes it out of the shed. He's got everything organized to work at its best, even if something needs to be drilled out first. Ollie understands, all right.

My mind's back in Wisconsin, but the truckers are here in North Dakota, and suddenly I'm aware that everyone is staring my way. Darrell, a large man with snake tattoos crawling around his thick sunburned arms, is asking a question.

"Sorry, what was that?"

"What's your route from here?" he repeats. "What roads are you taking west?"

Time to get back to the journey at hand. "Well, pretty much straight across to the Missouri at Mobridge, then through into Montana and over to Billings."

The truckers nod with approval—they know those roads. Probably an easy day's drive from here to Billings, though it will take me three.

"Then I get to the mountains, and that's where the road gets more interesting. I'll go up over the Beartooth Pass into Wyoming and Yellowstone."

"The Beartooth!" exclaims Darrell.

"Yes. You know it?"

"It almost killed me two years ago," he says, and the other truckers look at him with deference. "You be careful on the Beartooth—it's a road that shouldn't be there."

He's right in a way. The twisting route into Yellowstone's northeast was built as a make-work project during the Depression and would never be constructed these days, wriggling and squirming as it does straight up the side of the Beartooth Range. Hairpin bends and steep inclines keep it closed to trucks and commercial traffic, and heavy snowfalls can quickly shut the road at any time of the year, even now, in July.

What was he doing there?

"I was hauling a Sno-Cat to Cooke City, going slow and steady, and around one of those hairpins I guess one of the chains broke holding the Cat down. It started to slide off the trailer, and there was nothing I could do. It slid and it slid and I braked and I steered and it made no difference. It just knocked us sideways. As the truck dragged itself over the edge, I jumped out the cab's passenger window and it went right over and all that was left on the road was me."

The truckers nod again and murmur approval. This is a great story. Probably true, too—Darrell's got all the facts to back it up.

"You can forget about the rig. And the hundred-thousand-dollar Cat on the trailer. They were wrecked. But it cost seven thousand to get four tow trucks to pull it all out of there and four thousand to the EPA to clean up the fuel because it's a national park. Then the troopers fined me twelve hundred for being there in the first place. That one really hurt.

"There was no reason for it, that's all. Weather was good, I was driving slow. Don't matter how good you are or how much you prepare, there's always the unexpected. Watch out for any trace of moisture in the air because that'll be snow on the road at the top. If the Beartooth wants you, it's going to bite your ass."

This story is getting better and better—for everyone except me.

The Beartooth was supposed to be a nice scenic break from the prairies and a welcome to the mountains. Pirsig had written of its beauty, though also of its challenge as a place of summer snowfields and unexpected cold. But Jackie New's clutch is starting to slip when pushed, and the front brakes have been feeling a little spongy as well. No big deal, at least not on normal roads, but my schedule calls for me to be at the pass on Friday, with no time for delay if I'm to make it to San Francisco on my birthday, seven days after that. There's no allowance for a delay by snowstorm.

"Well, I should be okay if I just take it carefully," I say, and the other truckers look to Darrell.

"That's what I thought, too," he says. "Just take it easy and make sure you've got good brakes and a real strong clutch."

Sidney drives us back to the E&I, taking the long way around to show off Oakes's massive grain elevators. He talks with passion of the thick layer of fertile black soil that supports the local farms. He mentions some of the Bible's lessons that could be applied to his world, and looking through the truck's side window, I blink back beer and stale smoke.

Back in the room and in bed at last, I fall asleep quickly, but right away there's something else there. It's looking at me from the shadow of the corner with glassy sightless eyes, strong and intimidating even in death.

CHAPTER THREE

Eastern North Dakota

THERE ARE TWO BEDS in the room at the E&I, and in the morning there's luggage spread all over one of them. It looks like the saddlebags have exploded—clothes and books and paperwork on the duvet, empty white and yellow plastic grocery bags stuffed into one another up by the pillow—but there's order to the chaos.

Packing was the last thing I did before leaving home. I knew what was needed and how much could be carried; the art came in squeezing it into a couple of saddlebags and then stowing it safely on the bike.

Some of it practically sorted itself, anyway. The tent and camping equipment, for example, which until a couple of weeks ago had not been unpacked since the last time I used them, a decade earlier, and then shoved them into a back corner of the garage. I set the tent up in the garden as a test before I left and all seemed well, so I repacked everything—tent, ground cloth and fly, poles and pegs and a hatchet—in a soft black bag that straps to the rear seat. On top of it is a sleeping bag that's rolled into a large waterproof sailor's bag, and a separate "mattress roll" that inflates to provide an insulating cushion between the sleeper and the cold, lumpy ground. They're still unused and packed, lying on the floor.

The bulk of the stuff is carried in two soft expandable panniers that sling over the pillion seat behind. Fully filled, they weigh at least thirty pounds apiece, and it's important for each of them to weigh about the same so as not to throw off the bike's balance.

Weight on a motorcycle is best kept low to the ground, where it moves the least when the bike leans around corners, so the really heavy stuff is at the very bottom of the bags. That would be the tools: a socket set (metric) in one pannier and in the other a grocery bag of wrenches, screwdrivers, electrical connectors, pliers, plugs, and three kinds of tape all wrapped in a couple of small shop towels. If the bike breaks down, I don't want to be stranded for want of a strip of duct tape and a 14-millimeter wrench.

There's also a multitool in a pouch on my belt that includes pliers and a knife and various attachable heads, for quick fixes without having to unpack the bags. A quart of oil and a spray can of chain lubricant are in the right-side bag, wrapped up tight to make sure they don't leak.

On top of the tools are the books and valuable stuff. My aunt's pink-covered copy of *Zen and the Art of Motorcycle Maintenance,* as well as the larger twenty-fifth-anniversary edition (printed in a clearer font) in case I leave the pink copy behind somewhere. There's a copy of *Lila,* Pirsig's other book, and the largest volume of all, *Guidebook to "Zen and the Art of Motorcycle Maintenance,"* compiled by a pair of studious Jesuit university researchers who provide invaluable background and explanations.

There are maps for all the states along the way, although the map of the state I'm in now is folded into my jacket pocket. And then there are handbooks for the equipment that's coming along: a digital camera, the GPS unit, and the motorcycle itself. These are wrapped in resealable plastic freezer bags to keep them from getting wet if rain should leak through the fabric of the panniers.

In fact, almost everything is wrapped and double wrapped in plastic bags to make sure it stays dry in the heaviest thunderstorm—I've yet to find anything more effective than a plastic grocery bag. However, there's also a large, heavy plastic document bag that I found at a camping-equipment shop that's perfect for holding a sheaf of documents and correspondence and Web-site printouts that will help guide the way. It's still unopened.

The pink copy of *Zen and the Art* lives in the left saddlebag, which is where I keep the stuff I may want throughout the day, while the other stuff stays in the right bag. That way I don't have to guess which bag something is in, for the bags open only at the top and are not easy to rummage through. Need it in a hurry, it'll be in the left. Need it at the end of the day, it'll be in the right. Sounds good in theory, anyway.

There's another proviso for packing this motorcycle, which is that anything easily damaged by heat goes in the left bag, for the right bag rests just an inch from the muffler and gets hot enough to cook its contents.

So the toiletries and electronics go in the left side. That would be a plastic freezer bag for soap and toothbrush and shampoo and razor and another one for basic first-aid items. The camera lives in a pouch on my belt beside the multitool, but its spare battery and memory card and charger are in the saddlebag, as is a Palm Pilot (with portable keyboard) that I've not yet brought out because it just looks pretentious. There's a cell phone, too, which rarely gets a signal and is pointless to carry in my pocket because I can't hear it ringing or feel it vibrating while riding— which is the way it should be. All those items are padded and protected by clothing that's sorted into bags of clean and dirty, with the dirty on top to discourage light fingers. Altogether there's a spare pair of jeans, seven pairs of socks and underwear, and four T-shirts, a dress shirt, swimming shorts, running shoes, and a wool sweater.

Next comes the motorcycle equipment, also now scattered over the bed—there as a reminder, as I open my eyes, that this is no easy car trip.

There's the full-face helmet, three years old, with some scratches and dings but quite comfortable. It has a new tinted visor and another new visor, a clear one, that I keep with the sleeping bag, since it's hard and curved in the shape of the rolled-up bag. There's the old leather jacket, light and comfortable, given to me twelve years ago by a friend who'd already owned it for a decade, and a fancy Gore-Tex jacket that should be waterproof but isn't. That jacket comes with a warm inner lining, but it's bulky, so I've left it at home, preferring to wear the leather jacket underneath if the weather gets chilly. And a favorite find, in case the temperature plummets: a thin vest that's electrically heated by the bike's battery and which can be worn under the main jacket. Feeling the warmth run through me on a cool day is like slipping into a hot bath. It, too, is rolled up carefully with the sleeping bag, to protect the slender wires.

There's still more. On the floor are the boots, calf-high leather bike boots, comfortable but satisfying to remove at the end of the day. Somewhere on the bed are the thin, ventilated leather riding gloves, and there are two other, heavier pairs, for cool and cold weather, tucked into the sailor's bag with the sleeping bag. That's also where I keep the waterproof gear so I can pull it out quickly and without rummaging: a pair of water-resistant overpants for muddy or damp conditions, rubber overboots that take forever to pull on and off but do keep my feet dry, waterproof overgloves, and a pair of Gore-Tex inner liners designed for a BMW riding suit, bought cheap from a friend whose suit had fallen apart. If I can get the the inner liner jacket and pants on in time, no water gets past them, but they're a size too large and the sleeves and pant legs tend to flap about. Finally, buried deep in the sailor's bag is a small towel, so I'm not stuck in a cheap motel with a dirty one.

This would be about the right amount of luggage—two saddle-bags, tent, sleeping bag, and sleeping roll—for the average motorcycle journey, except that I'm also carrying a laptop computer. So much for getting back to basics and staying low-tech. I want to be connected to the Internet, post my progress on a Web site, download photos, and maybe get some writing done. So there's a large plastic Pelican case, totally impervious to rain and dust and vibration, which is carrying the laptop and its accessories in a deep bed of dense sculptured foam. Loading up each day, I lock it and lay it directly on the seat behind me and then run a chain through the handle, which is locked in turn to the bike's small luggage carrier, designed by optimistic Suzuki engineers for a light lunch box or perhaps a half case of beer.

I've figured out the system by now: the saddlebags go on first, followed by the computer case, then the tent, and finally, highest and lightest of all, the sailor's bag and sleeping roll. It's all lashed down with ten bungee cords of various lengths, and the poor bike seems to flex like a stoic mule as each heavy item takes its place.

There are a few other things as well, not part of the packed luggage but important nonetheless.

On the floor, ready to be laid on the bike's vinyl seat, is a black velour pad, a Butt Buffer gel seat that provides a bit of extra padding and comfort between the bike and my backside. Motorcycle seats tend to concentrate your weight on a narrower area of the butt than car seats do, so after a while your buttocks start to sting from the vibration and eventually turn numb. Large bikes usually have large seats (as do their riders), and they're quite capable of providing comfortable support for hours at a time, but this midsize dirt bike was never intended for long hauls.

It was a serious concern while preparing for this trip that I couldn't ride much longer than a half hour before my backside would start to hurt. The seat was the original one, and when I told my wife that it should be replaced because the foam inside had finally broken down, she was brutal in her reply. "Actually, dear, I don't think it's the *bike's* seat that's broken down," she said.

Nonetheless, I replaced the foam in the seat, and of course it made no difference.

In the '80s, I rode hundreds of miles at a stretch without feeling uncomfortable; now I need endurance to make it to the store. But I found this high-tech gel pad at a bike show. It goes on top of the refurbished seat, and with a bit of muscle conditioning, I've gotten my nonstop range up to a hundred miles at a time.

On the bike itself, some spare bulbs and fuses are in a plastic box under the seat, padded in foam. A small leather pouch on the gas tank holds a tire-pressure gauge and a lock with an alarm that bolts through the front brake disk when the bike's parked at night. The GPS unit fixes to a mount on the left handlebar and is wired to the battery. In my jacket are spare sunglasses and eyeglasses, a saddlebag pocket holds sunscreen and a bandanna, and there's a bottle of water to be tucked under a bungee, covered by a baseball cap.

My wallet has credit cards and a phone card and various bike and health-insurance documents, my passport's in my inside jacket pocket, and my leather jeans belt has a secret zippered compartment with a complete record of my wallet's contents and $40 in cash, just in case. Also just in case, hidden out of sight, are spare keys duct-taped to the inside of one of the bike's side panels and an American Express card duct-taped to the inside of the other.

Finally, near the bottom of the right bag is an unknown parcel, a small square box wrapped in tissue. It's a present from my family and is not to be opened until my birthday, on the last day of the trip west. I said I wanted a toy, not too big, and I have no idea what it is.

Getting out of bed now and starting to pack the saddlebags, I see it there. I'm tempted to pull it out and mull over it awhile, but I hold off and put the spare jeans on top, hiding it for another day.

She didn't want to see me go but let me go all the same. For weeks, months, I couldn't wait to leave.

The boys got in the way as I fixed up the bike in the driveway. They wanted to help but only distracted. They're too young—I could leave nothing lying around. Once after working on the bike the previous summer, I couldn't find the ignition key. I had only one, and it was gone. Lost an entire morning searching for it. Couldn't get a new key because there was no record of the old key, so eventually there was no choice but to buy a whole new ignition. A month later I found the key at the bottom of the boys' toy box. It sure as hell wasn't me who'd put it there.

I needed to get away. Right now there's a lot I want to get away from. My wife packed their little Pokémon and Hot Wheels suitcases while I packed my saddlebags, and last week we all went to the airport—they flew away to a vacation at her sister's so that Dad could take off on his motorbike for a while. We had some ice cream in the terminal, and then they went to passport control, each boy holding his mother's hand and pulling his red plastic carry-on luggage behind. With a turn and a last wave good-bye, they slipped behind the pale frosted glass of airport security. I could see their shadows fading slowly into white through the screen, and then they were gone.

There was no doubt for Bob Pirsig and Nancy James, star-crossed young lovers in 1953, that they wanted to be together. They'd teamed up that fall to produce the first edition of *Ivory Tower,* the university's literary magazine, both named as editors on the masthead, although Bob was in charge and Nancy was happily subordinate. But she was still married to a faraway husband who would not consent to an uncontested divorce, and the only alternative they knew of was to end the marriage in Nevada. The Silver State's divorce mills cared little for midwestern sentiment.

They left Minnesota early in January 1954 and headed west through the snow, intending to stay at a "guest ranch" outside Reno for the six weeks of state residency a divorce required. But the ranch was too expensive, so they moved into a trailer camp.

To pay the bills, they took jobs at Reno's Nevada Club, Nancy dealing roulette and Bob dealing keno. The casino jobs paid well, and they stuck around after the divorce came through, paying off their student debts and saving for the future. Neither wanted to marry, however—they wanted a relationship on their own terms, which meant no religion to get in the way and no hassle if they should ever decide to part; her divorce had taught them *that* lesson. So on May 10, 1954, Nancy's twenty-first birthday, they went to the Reno courthouse and bought a marriage license; they had wedding announcements printed, declaring them married, which were mailed to friends. To their parents they sent extras, to distribute to whomever they saw fit. Their lives held a promise and excitement that they were happy to share.

Nearly forty years later, after her mother died, Nancy found those announcements still folded and hidden in a desk drawer.

Her mother had never liked Bob (a mutual feeling), and her father, a building contractor, just tried to avoid the whole testy subject. Her older sister had once given her a lecture on the unrealistic expectations of marital happiness. Nancy's divorce was the first in the James family, and the shame had been hard for her mother to bear.

I didn't set the alarm last night. After waking at nine and packing the bags, I check *Zen and the Art* and am reminded that this was a grueling ride for the foursome, nearly three hundred miles across the prairie on a day that began early and cold but became hot and temperamental, not ending until after dark.

Tonight will also be my first night of camping, for the riders pitched their tents to cheer Chris, who loved to sleep under the stars next to the wild beauty of trees and water. The Sutherlands had the right idea in preferring motels, with their box springs and mattresses, flushing toilets, and power outlets, but this South Dakota campsite should get a try tonight. It won't be good to arrive too late, and today's route is a hundred miles longer than I'd remembered.

Damn. The bike's loose valves need adjustment, but it's too late in the morning. They can wait till tomorrow.

I do, however, take the time to pull the motorcycle manual from its place in the right saddlebag to check the adjustment procedure and the correct tolerances. It's been a very long time since this bike has needed more than basic maintenance, but this is a small book, and I leaf through the pages to find the section on valves. And it's not there. I check the index—nothing. I've brought the wrong damn book! This one tells how to put gas in the tank and start the thing but has nothing on maintenance.

How could I have been so stupid? It's because I'd been preoccupied with other stuff and left the packing until the last minute, not checking the manual to be sure it was the right one. Now I'm carting around half a ton of tools and can't remember what to do with them.

Outside it's already hot, and the bike's engine is resting in the retreating shade, dusty and exposed to the elements but still oil-tight and intact.

What's going on in there, inside that cylinder and all its workings, its chains and valves and shafts? For a moment it's as if the engine is running with the oil sliding around everywhere and the large trusty piston pumping slowly up and down, up and down, as I'm picturing it, pushing the rear wheel along. But I'm trying to recall the basic maintenance that will be needed, and there are parts behind the clutch and the alternator that draw a blank. Once I could rebuild the entire engine in a morning because I'd done it so many times, and now I can barely picture even the basic parts of the motor. Still, it was all checked over a month ago at home, and it was running well then, and the valves sounded good and nothing needed to be touched. It's running well now, too, just a bit clattery, that's all.

So much for keeping it simple—I don't want to rip apart any internal gaskets just to see if there's something behind them that might need checking. Maybe it would be better to give up on doing the job myself and just book the bike into a shop, even though this is the most basic of machines. Was it the boys' fault for distracting me in the driveway or my own fault for not finding the time to better organize myself?

It'll be okay. I'll load up the bike and give her a pat on the gas tank. Come on. It'll be okay.

Sidney is in the motel forecourt and waves hello, and we walk into the office to settle the bill. He wishes me well on the route to San Francisco—"Guys kiss guys there, girls kiss girls, and here we think, 'What the hell?' It's a different world. You be careful"—and then I go outside, swing a leg over the bike, kick it to life, and head off for breakfast in the next town.

It had been a very cold start for the Zen riders, who left Oakes at six thirty after Pirsig roused them all out of bed for an early start, the temperature in the 40s.

"I was never one to get up in the morning," Sutherland had told me in Minneapolis, "but Bob loved it. I'd be playing a gig somewhere the night before and sometimes wouldn't get to bed before dawn, but Bob could never let the morning go by."

It had been a late night for me last night, too, drinking with the truckers, and I'm quite content to miss much of the morning. I'd forgotten the day's distance, because when the foursome arrived in Ellendale for breakfast after a half-hour ride, they were so cold that they dawdled in the restaurant for a couple of hours, putting on long underwear and extra clothing and moaning at Pirsig for dragging them through the frigid morning. I thought I had time to spare, forgetting how early they'd begun their day.

It's warm today, though, up in the 80s already, and as the flat fields of corn and sugar beet slide steadily past, I'm listening to the engine and thinking about its moving parts, now whirring and clattering and meshing as the piston kicks up and down a hundred times a second. And something doesn't sound right.

Is this just paranoia because I don't have the manual? No shop will sell it—it must be ordered specially, if it's even still available. Now it's not just the tolerances that have me worried; it's everything. Any decent dealership will give you the correct tolerances if you ask at the counter, but there's other stuff that must be maintained, and if it's missed, the bike will break down. After all, Jackie Blue was clattering so badly in 1987 that something snapped and a valve broke off into the cylinder. She needed a thousand dollars of parts and specialized reboring, back when I was the bike's sole mechanic. What was the thing that needed adjusting back then? I can't remember, but I'm sure I can hear it now.

By the time I reach Ellendale, it's late morning and I'm convinced the bike is doomed, incapable of getting to San Francisco without a professional tune-up along the way. I park outside the Nodak Café, the only place in town where the Pirsigs and Sutherlands would have stopped in 1968, and go into the air-conditioning to consider the problem. Breakfast is still being served, and the coffee and juice will help clear my head. It's a classic café, large and airy, popular with locals and a fine place to order pie.

The coffee does help, and when breakfast arrives, I have a possible solution. The manual's the key, and there's a photocopy of it in my desk drawer at work. I've booked a room on Friday night near Yellowstone and know the address there—perhaps someone in my office can send it through on time. Today's only Tuesday.

Outside the restaurant, there's no signal on my cell phone. The waitress can't give me directions to a pay phone, either. "You know, I don't think we have any in town anymore," she says. "They all got pulled out. Everyone has cell phones now."

She suggests asking at City Hall, and there a woman recommends the Amoco station at the south end of town. There's a phone there, but it doesn't work.

"Yeah, they just let it break," says the manager. "Everyone's got cell phones now. No money in pay phones, I guess. But there's a pay phone at the Fireside Steakhouse on the north end of town."

This is ridiculous. America is known around the world for its superior communications and cheap phone system, but now the pay phones that were once an essential part of that system are being pulled out, their rooted wires replaced by less reliable mobile phones that send invisible transmissions to cellular towers and satellites. It's not like cell phones can be easily fixed, either— they're just another case of throw the broken thing away and get a new one. If it's a matter of life and death, there's nothing to be done but find a private phone with a solid connection and wave around a $10 bill—and it's getting close to that point, but just for the sake of a telephone?

At the Fireside there's no phone. "They pulled it out a couple of years ago. You might try the motel around the corner," says the waitress.

And at the motel there's no pay phone, but at last there's an understanding manager. "If you've got a calling card, you're welcome to use the office phone," he says.

I dial the number on the cordless phone he offers. It doesn't work—the battery is dead. Another phone is found, and the call is placed at last. I leave a message on the machine at work, reciting the Gardiner address and stressing urgency.

"Where are you headed?" asks the manager. He smiles when he hears it's San Francisco. "Ah," he says. "I have a nephew who rode his motorcycle to the West Coast a few years ago, from Boston. He went with his friend, and they both had Suzukis. The friend was a mechanic who worked on Suzuki racing motorcycles, and my nephew told me he was real glad to have him along, in case something should happen to the bikes. But it never did, I guess. They were pretty well prepared." His every word is like a hard poke in the chest with a rigid index finger.

As I ride away to the west, the noise in the engine seems to settle into a rhythmic thrum, and the wind ripples the grass in the fields alongside the road. The tops of the blades are waving to and fro, and it's easy to imagine the valves in the engine rising and falling with them, in sync with nature.

As southeast North Dakota slips by, the fields become drier and sparser, separated by water towers and small windmills and buildings that are sometimes well maintained, sometimes desolate.

Often there's a broken-down house at the corner of the property, with a new home not far away, the owners having just given up on the fixer-upper and started afresh. The landscape is sparse, but the land is good. There's room to breathe and stretch the legs. There's room to see the sky and watch the clouds. Room to run without having to stop.

I'll just keep following the Zen route dead west across the state, along the same road Sutherland's BMW and Pirsig's Honda rode all those years ago. But already, on the second proper day, the itinerary has begun to change.

Strictly speaking, I should have left this morning at six thirty and headed to Ellendale for a crisp start to the ride, but the point of all this is not to copy Pirsig exactly but just to use his trip as a starting point for my own journey. It's undeniable that if his book could open so many readers' eyes to more of life's qualities, then there's a good chance his actual journey can open my own eyes wider still.

There've been many others who have followed this route before me, Pirsig's pilgrims, and they've all had their reasons. Right now there's a pair of Germans, Franz and Gregor, who left a week before me, riding the road on rented Harley-Davidsons. They're taking a month to track the route, staying anyplace that looks comfortable and eating well. We corresponded by e-mail. Franz Schabmueller, who will turn fifty next week in California, said that he's always been fascinated by Pirsig's descriptions of the western landscape; Gregor Schleicher is along for the ride. The two of them have even arranged for German supporters to sponsor their journey, to raise money for charity.

One of the early pilgrims was Gary Wegner, who in 1978 rode with his wife on their Honda 750 as far as Bozeman. He sent me some maps of the route, which I used to first figure out the way-points. "Every spring since '74, I've read *Zen and the Art* for therapy," he told me. "Pirsig is my Beckett and his book has, indeed, helped me these past 30 years. When I open the covers and begin riding back into the country, the tensions begin to disappear along the old roads. And when he whacks Chris's knee and points to the red-winged blackbird, we begin to fly."

This is quite a recommendation from a former English teacher. He explained the book's therapeutic effect:

My favorite line from Zen and the Art of Motorcycle Maintenance *is the line that served as a kind of mantra on my '78 trip and the line that has stayed fresh in my memory all of these years: "We want to make good time, but for us now this is measured with emphasis on 'good' rather than 'time' and when you make that shift in emphasis the whole approach changes." I do not know if there is a key to Mr. Pirsig's book, but if there is, it is surely this simple word: good. And it is interesting as*

*well as entirely fitting that the etymology of good refers to the
Old English "god," from a prehistoric Germanic word
meaning "to unite."*

But perhaps the most serious of the pilgrims is Henry Gurr, a
retired physics professor from South Carolina who maintains a
Web site dedicated to Pirsig. He sent me the confirmed GPS way-
points so that there might be no deviation from the original journey. Gurr traveled the entire route himself two years ago in his red
Ford Escort.

"You must take the secondary and tertiary roads," he wrote.
"You must see the back-country, and get away from the well-
traveled routes. You need to go slow, stop, and talk to everyone,
no matter where you are. . . . I learned that 'not having the time'
defeats the very purpose of traveling. Every mile, every stopping
place, has its own rewards. To quote Pirsig in *Zen and the Art,*
'What's your hurry? . . . There is nothing up ahead that's any better than it is right here.' "

None of that, however, means I have to leave at dawn. Pirsig's
journey merely points the way so that others might find their own
paths, and mine does not begin so early in the morning.

I couldn't connect to the Internet at the E&I last night, but so
what? There was drinking and conversation to be had. But what
happens when there is no conversation, if I make it high into the
mountains, where the truckers fear to drive and silence rules the
night? Where the bike slogs along the highway with just her
engine and a feeble, wavering needle on her dim speedometer? Is
that then the time to fill the darkness with technology's babble, or
is it the moment to shut down and look for the stars?

By September 1954, Bob and Nancy had saved quite a bit of
money from their casino jobs and wanted to make a go of it writing in Mexico's warm and cheap south. They hitchhiked down to
the border, found their way to the very base of the Gulf of Mex-

ico, and settled for a while at the river port of Minatitlán. But the writing did not come easily to Bob. It never would.

Living together on the bank of the Coatzacoalcos River, they decided to build a sailboat they could sell for a profit and made many long bus trips to Mexico City to find English-language books on the subject. Bob hired a boat carpenter, and Nancy, who spoke Spanish, bought an expensive shipment of hardwood from a lumber operator far to the south. First, though, they built a dinghy from local wood, which they used to explore the river, learning the culture and experiencing the country together.

But despite many months of effort, the venture failed. The hardwood for the big sailboat was never delivered, and the carpenter would get drunk and disappear for days at a time. "Well, they warned me, *'El tome!'* He drinks! And so he did," wrote Pirsig years later in *Lila*.

One night a big *Norte,* a norther, blew in off the Gulf of Mexico and it blew so hard. . . . Oh, it was a big wind! Almost bent the palm trees to the ground. And it took the roof off his house and carried it away. But instead of fixing it he got drunk and he stayed drunk for more than a month. After a couple of weeks his wife had to come begging for money for food. That was so sad. I think partly he got drunk because he knew everything was going wrong and the boat would never get built. And that was true. I ran out of money and had to quit.

In the summer they returned to Minnesota; they both took on some freelance journalism, and Bob also began working as a technical and commercial writer. After a couple of years, Bob went back to school to finish his master's in journalism—he wanted to get out of the freelance grind and become a teacher. Chris was born in November 1956, and seventeen months after that, his brother, Ted.

"He fathered two children, bought a farm and a riding horse and two cars and was starting to put on middle-aged weight," Pirsig wrote in *Zen and the Art.* "His pursuit of what has been called the ghost of reason had been given up. That's extremely important to understand. He had given up."

But Bob Pirsig, child prodigy and certified genius, was not a regular guy. The "normality" of his life, combined with the reintroduction of the academic pursuit of his ideal, would torture his mind and drive him mad.

The next stop that's mentioned is for gas at Hague, an hour west of the stop for breakfast, but my bike's got plenty of gas. She can travel about two hundred miles on a tank, half the distance of a car but probably twice that of Pirsig's little motorcycle, and so I cruise through town confidently. Just as well, really, since there's no longer a gas station among the few buildings to either side of the road. At the west end of town there's an abandoned station that must be the old place, but it's very hot now, well into the 90s, and there's little point in sticking around to look at it. It's just one of the thousands of abandoned buildings in this state, boarded up and given up by their owners after too long on the market, with nobody moving in to invest and the young people moving out if they don't work on the family farm.

Back in the last town, Ashley, there'd been an Internet café right on the main street that really stood out. Jitters, it was called, with a funky sign of a shaking cup of coffee that would have looked at home back in Minneapolis. "When life isn't intense enough" was the slogan on the sign. It shared a front door with the local newspaper (the *Ashley Tribune,* "Telling it like it is— serving the Ashley area since 1901"), and I could imagine a reporter sitting in the coffee shop, fingers trembling from the caffeine, writing up the local council meeting. I used to do that, a long time ago.

I'd have stopped for a cappuccino and a chat, but the late start and potentially long day urged me on, just as they keep me going here, through Hague—until a mile from town the speedometer stops working. The needle falls motionless to the bottom of the dial. And more important, the odometer stops, too, making it difficult to know when the tank is low, since the bike has no gas gauge; the trip meter should be reset at every fill-up. Only one dial on the whole bike and it has to break.

It's got to be fixed, but there are no trees to offer shade from the relentless sun, except for the ones I just passed in Hague, so I turn back toward town and stop opposite the abandoned gas station, where the Pirsigs had stopped briefly thirty-six years before and where they had taken the time to change the oil and lube the chain. This is an easy repair with the multitool, for the cable is not broken but has just shaken itself loose, so I'm back on the road again quickly.

The heat of the engine bakes against my jeans as I cross the border into South Dakota and cruise into Herreid. The Zen riders had paused for a rest in a leafy park while Sutherland went off to find a drink in a bar, but again I press on. The road's heading south now, and there is no crossing at the river until Mobridge, more than thirty miles to the south. Here's the park on the right and a whole bunch of bars, but I keep going to the river, to make up for the late start.

There's construction on the road about a half mile ahead and heavy equipment going back and forth. A steamroller is driving slowly north toward me with a line of traffic behind. My thoughts are far away. A car is overtaking the roller, pulling into my lane. The driver will pull back when he sees the bike coming at him, but I move over to the right of the lane anyway, to make myself more visible.

But the car is still in my lane, accelerating from 30 miles per hour, a couple of hundred feet away and headed straight for the front of the bike.

It's a large Buick, just the driver inside, holding a phone and looking down. The roller's coming up on the left, and a ditch to the right, where the side of the road should be, is filled with construction barrels, and I'm riding right on the edge with nowhere to go.

And at the last moment, perhaps just a few dozen feet away, the driver sees me, jams on the brakes, and lurches back into his own lane behind the roller, a puff of smoke coming from the tires. *Whoa!* We pass without looking at each other. At the end of the line of traffic, the driver of a construction truck who has seen everything raises his arms in supplication—a giant shrug—and waves at me. I return the gesture. What else is there to do?

But I'm shaken by this close call, and I ride a little farther past the construction and then pull over at the next side road. A small sign shows that the road leads to a cemetery. The trees in a coppice to the left are all dead. A pile of junked cars lies off to the west.

I've got to get to Mobridge. I need a break.

The Pirsigs had a close call on their trip, too. A couple of days farther on, in Montana, a car towing a trailer had come right at them in a misjudged overtaking maneuver. That car, too, had swerved back into its lane at the last moment, shaking up the travelers considerably. They stopped soon after for a lunch of junk food and beer, so in Mobridge I pull in to the Yellow Sub restaurant and order a submarine and two bags of chips with a Coke. It's my equivalent. This used to be the A&W, where the travelers had stopped for burgers, and besides, I need to cool off before crossing the river into the Dakota Badlands.

Across the Missouri River and over the Standing Rock Sioux Reservation, towns will be farther apart, and the sun will be even hotter. There may be rattles in the bike, but as Pirsig proved, the rattles in the mind can be far more dangerous.

CHAPTER FOUR

South Dakota

THE AFTERNOON'S WEARING ON, and camping tonight doesn't seem such a bad idea. It's as hot as it's ever been, just over 100 degrees on the gas station thermometer here at McLaughlin. After I crossed the river and climbed the long rise through the reservation, the undulating hills were light green and gold with scrub grass and bare of trees or fences or any landmark. Inside the gas station, the conversation's about the heat.

"Yesterday was a hundred, too," says a woman to the clerk, lining up to buy lottery tickets. "Too hot for working. Make me lucky today!"

The air-conditioning is welcome, and the Gatorade is cooling me when another motorcyclist walks in. He's the only other person I've seen in days who's wearing a jacket. And thick gloves. And heavy black riding pants. His BMW is parked outside, and he wants an ice cream. He's an older guy, and we greet each other like old friends, together against the heat.

Leon says he's heading back to New York from Spokane, where the BMW Owners of America were holding their annual rally. Before long I tell him about the near miss at Herreid, and it feels good to share it with somebody who'll understand—like lying on a motorcyclist's couch right here in the gas station. Leon understands only too well. No shrugs from him.

"Heading out to Washington there was thick fog as I got close to the mountains," he says. "I couldn't see thirty feet and could barely see the road, so I was riding on the center line to feel my way along. Then a pickup truck came at me, and he was doing the same thing, right on the center line. I thought I'd bought it then. But I guess my time's not up just yet."

Leon eats some more ice cream. "This'll be my last big trip, though," he says. "I'll be home in a couple of days, and I'll park the bike. Still ride it, of course, but this'll be my last big trip."

Looking at him, I think he might be seventy years old. Or sixty, or eighty. Hard to say in the getup, and he's still wearing sunglasses. Thin hair and some missing teeth. Looks a bit like John Sutherland. Probably the other side of seventy after all.

"Well," I kick in, "it'll be your last big trip for a while perhaps. Heat like this will take it out of you."

"Yeah," he says, and he's not looking at me or at anything anymore. "For a while. For quite a while." He finishes the ice cream and throws the stick in the trash. "You have a good ride." And he nods and steps outside into the furnace. The thermometer is in the shade, but we're riding in the sunshine. He's gone in moments, back on the road I just came in on, heading home to hang up his spurs.

People look puzzled or sympathetic when they see a rider dressed heavily in extreme heat. I've been covering up pretty well so far because the wind will dry the skin faster than a hair dryer, and that causes sunburn and exhaustion, not to mention cancer. Leather jacket, jeans, high boots, mesh gloves, and a full-face helmet may not be comfortable to slip on, but they let a rider stay longer in the saddle, and out on this exposed dirt bike I need all the help I can get. And if the worst happens and I should slide down the road, there'd better be something between the asphalt and my flesh.

Then there's the basic danger of riding a motorcycle, as I just experienced. Murdercycles, some call them, or coroners' specials. Sure, they're more dangerous—less protected—than cars, but the risks can be minimized with training, education, and attitude. The key is attitude. A motorcyclist should always back down and ride defensively, a lesson that is easy to remember on an overloaded, underpowered dirt bike.

There are also times when a driver might be trapped after an accident, whereas a rider may be thrown clear, and often a bike is more maneuverable than a car, so a rider may avoid an accident in the first place. Whatever. Most probably when your number's up, it's up. Remember the eagle?

This is empty land now, flat-topped hills sloping above the grasslands on either side of the road, and it's not too welcoming. I just stopped at a gas station store for a cold drink, the same place where Pirsig's group also stopped in 1968 and got into an argument with a drunken woman. A group of teenage boys in the store stared at me until I left. They were sitting under a hand-carved wooden sign: "Kennedy's car killed more people than my guns." This is a very long way from that bridge in Massachusetts.

And back at McIntosh, a car followed me closely along the main drag, where there were no other signs of life and as many stores boarded up as open. It was clearly time to leave. I need to find that campground. It'll be cooler and breezy under the trees; the water of the reservoir will lap soothingly against the beach.

But as I approach Lemmon, the clouds build across the sun, and a strong wind picks up from the north. Just as I make the decision to buy some marshmallows in town to roast over tonight's campfire, a bolt of lightning shoots down from the darkened sky off to the right. The decision is immediately canceled. In fact, the whole camping plan is annulled.

In case any extra persuasion should be needed, a powerful gust slams into the right side of the bike, pushing me straight into the oncoming lane at fifty miles an hour with no warning whatsoever. There's no traffic in that lane—there's very little traffic period— but the bike is bulky enough and light enough to have a serious problem with wind like this one. Who knows how long this storm will last? Better look for a room in Lemmon, the nearest town to the campsite and already visible about ten miles away, across a shallow valley.

The rain is falling in sheets on the northwestern horizon, gray and foreboding, while the sunshine to the east reflects in the bike's mirrors. From here I can't tell whether the rain is already in the town, but it's probably not. The white water towers and roofs would be obscured if the storm were upon them, and although there's an enormous backdrop of ever-shifting darkness to the west, the low buildings of the town are still clear. A car coming from the west has a dry windshield; the next car, a minute later, has its wipers moving slowly. The road is dry, but a third car from the west, driving more quickly, has its wipers moving at double speed.

There's the town-limits sign, and just in time the Prairie Motel is on the left. I pull straight in while everything's still dry and the way into the motel parking lot is still clear.

It's an older motel, a little run-down, with rooms on three sides around a large forecourt, and a covered veranda that runs the length of the front of the rooms so the housekeeper doesn't have to get wet going from door to door. It's a safe bet there's a room available since the place looks empty. Standing on its own is a prefab family home and office, and I park the bike near the step and walk in.

The office seems empty, but there's a teenager half hidden behind the counter, sitting on a low chair and reading a book. I don't notice her at first, not until she looks up and the movement of her pink hair catches the eye. I ask the obvious question.

"Hi, do you have a room? Just for tonight? Just for me?"

She stands up and smiles a friendly smile. There's always a concern at the end of the day that someone will look up and down my bug-covered jacket and offer a sneer, but nobody's done so yet and she just keeps smiling gently. "Let me have a look," she says, and pulls a large reservation book over. It has days marked on it, and rooms, and it looks to be just about empty.

"Do you want smoking or nonsmoking?" I tell her nonsmoking, and she studies the book some more. "Here you go. Room twenty-eight. It's okay." She asks my name and writes it in the book. The place *was* just about empty.

Handing over the credit card and filling in the form, I ask if she's heard the thunder and add, "There's going to be a really big storm. You'd better batten down the hatches."

She shrugs. "Didn't notice. I was reading. You can park your bike under the veranda if you like, to keep it dry."

This girl's okay after all. She's average height and seems average everything in her baggy orange T-shirt and jeans, except for that short pink hair. Tomboyish, perhaps, with no makeup. Pale skin—maybe she's a blonde when she leaves the dye alone. Brown eyebrows and roots—maybe not. And she looks smart but doesn't really sound it. She hands over the key, and I go out to move the bike. It's spitting rain. It'll start hard soon.

By the time the bike's parked under the veranda and the bags are inside the room, it's raining steadily and the wind's blowing the trees every which way. The air's quickly cooled, and it's wild to sit outside on a plastic chair watching the water bounce high off the ground. The parking lot turns to a pool, and a few leaves sluice through suddenly formed rivulets, flash floods a couple of inches deep. It's a chance to feel pleased with the world, for I'm still clean and dry and safe and in for the night as the air howls and the whole sky seems to shake. Maybe this'll be a good evening for some television or catching up on e-mail. The wind blows harder and the tree limbs bend, but then it relents and the rain splashes less hard against the ground, and then, as quick as it started, it's over.

Ten minutes at the most.

And the sun emerges from the bank of clouds, and the pools in the motel lot begin to steam. Just six thirty and I've stopped for the day. More to the point, a rainstorm that could have been sat out with a cup of coffee in town just compromised the integrity of the journey. The Pirsigs and Sutherlands camped tonight, and I'm kicking back at a motel, wondering what's on TV. So much for the integrity of following as closely as possible—and it's only the second day.

The forty bucks for the room is already paid and the bike's unloaded, so I'm staying here tonight. But the evening's young, and the sun's now shining. I'll go take a look at that campground.

The bike fires to life, light without the luggage. This is the reason I ride this motorcycle. With nothing else on the seat and no jacket or gloves or even a helmet for this short trip, she's light and maneuverable and fun. No worries now about the clutch or the brakes. I cross town to the southward turnoff and head toward the campsite a dozen miles away at the Shadehill Reservoir, the throttle responsive to every twitch and the brakes strong. But the sky's dark to the south, and soon drops of rain are spitting in the wind. A little farther on and it's plain I'm heading back toward the storm.

Here, though, knowing I don't have to ride into it but can turn for the motel whenever it builds, the soft light, filtered and diffused through the moisture, seems beautiful rather than threatening. It outlines the few trees and the cattle in the fields against the huge darkness of the sky. A strip of sunshine falls on the rolling hayfields, moving slowly with the clouds; telephone poles mark a driveway that leads far off to the horizon, where a farm stands in solitude, defiant against the emptiness. When a light rain falls, evaporating against the road as soon as it hits, then soaking the pavement just a couple of hundred yards farther on, it's time to head back to town.

With no helmet and the wind different, the valves sound noisier, and the exhaust note is less mellow. If the valves can't be adjusted yet, at least I can use this time to change the oil.

Pirsig changed the oil on his little Honda frequently, and although he never comes right out and states it, he was surely just dropping the waste where it drained, perhaps digging a small hole for the thick pool and covering it like a shallow grave. That was 1968, don't forget, when the environment wasn't the concern it is now and oil was not of today's quality, so it would break down quickly and take the engine with it if the rider wasn't careful. On any vehicle the first secret to long life is to change the oil regularly, to rinse out any crud from the engine and make sure the lubricant is always lubricating.

It's been nearly two thousand miles since the oil was changed, so I stop at the gas station in Lemmon for three quarts of the best-quality stuff on the shelf for the bike and some cold Bud for me, then bring them back to the motel and park under the veranda again. This isn't the '60s, though, and the old oil needs something to drain into, so I head back to the office.

The girl is still there, half hidden again and still reading.

"Hi, do you have an old milk jug? One you won't want back?"

It's best not to give too much detail when you're about to start motorcycle maintenance on the front stoop. But she doesn't mind and heads into the back, emerging with a four-quart plastic jug. Perfect. I'll cut a large hole in one side and use it as a drain pan.

Back outside the room, I take the tools out—pliers and a 21-millimeter socket wrench—and lay the milk-jug pan under the bike. But it's wise to be prepared in case the oil splashes on the concrete, so it's back to the office for the final supply.

"Hi, do you have a newspaper or a bit of old paper, just to lay on the ground?"

This is surely giving the game away, but the girl still doesn't seem to mind. Nobody else has checked in, anyway—the book's still empty—and she seems bored, so I ask her name. Lacy, she says. Maybe she's older than a teenager after all. She's quite cute, with a round face, bright eyes, and fresh, clear skin, and I feel a little guilty for even noticing. She finds a newspaper, and I head out to do the job.

It's an easy thing to change the oil on Jackie New. First, make sure the engine's nice and hot so the oil will be thin and quick to drain; then remove the filler cap on the side of the engine to release any vacuum inside. This is where you need the pliers, because the cap will be very hot. Then, after laying the newspaper underneath everything to protect the ground from splashes and placing the drain pan under the drain bolt, take the socket wrench and pretend to undo a bolt from anywhere else on the engine. This ensures that you know which way the socket wrench must be set to turn, since the drain bolt's being underneath means it's not obvious whether you're turning it clockwise or counterclockwise—at least it's not obvious to me. I once stripped all the thread from the drain hole of a motorcycle when the bolt was overtightened, turning the socket wrench the wrong way and refusing to accept that it wasn't just very stiff. It cost $200 and a month's wait for a new pan.

Once the wrench is set to turn in the proper counterclockwise direction, crouch down and use it to remove the large drain bolt, trying in vain to catch the hot piece of metal before it comes loose and falls into the pan, where it will be covered by a stream of scalding oil. Try to remember to have some paper towels at hand for wiping your oily fingers so you don't have to go inside afterward to get the towels, smearing oil over every doorknob between the driveway and the kitchen, treading grease into the carpet.

Outside room 28 the thin oil falls like water into the pan, splashing a little on the newspaper. No need to replace the filter this time. The engine is void in less than a minute, so I replace the drain bolt (being *very* careful not to overtighten it) and pour in two quarts of the new oil. Replace the filler cap and turn over the engine with the kick-starter to work the oil into all the nooks and crannies, then pour the drained oil from the pan into the now-empty containers of oil, screw the tops back on, and put them to one side to dispose of properly.

Now comes the most important part: drink beer for ten minutes before rechecking the level.

It's during this last ten minutes of the maintenance that Lacy walks over from the office with the cordless phone in her hand. Mine's the only name in the book so far, and she really is bored. She really is cute, too, out in the sunshine, as she sits with me now on the veranda's stoop, stretching out her toes in her sandals and cocking her head to one side. No toenail polish. She doesn't need makeup, but the dye job looks homemade and her figure's indiscernible under the baggy clothing.

"You've come a long way. Why are you traveling?" she asks.

It's a different question from "Where are you headed?" but my mind's already racing with memories of road trip movies and sexy waitresses and cute motel clerks jumping on the hero's bike, to be whisked away from their boring lives in the desert or on the prairie. There's no easy answer to the question, so I ask if she's ever heard of *Zen and the Art.*

"Are you kidding? That's my favorite book. I haven't read *Lila* or anything, but I thought Pirsig was just so clued in. I read it two years ago. It's the best book I've ever read."

Well, that's totally unexpected, like Jeremy in Oakes. I tell her about retracing the route, and she looks at me like I'm a rock star. "Wow! I can't believe it! That's totally cool."

I'm taken aback. She knows all about the book's connection to Lemmon and to the Shadehill Reservoir as well, so I ask what the campground is like there. Then, impulsively, I say that I'm headed back down that way now that the oil's changed and ask if she'll come along as my guide. She's delighted. Smiles all around. When the owner gets back, she says, she can leave with me, and she heads back to the office.

I look at my oil-stained hands and go inside for a shower. I'll have to make sure I wear the dress shirt tonight, as well.

It was late when the Zen riders arrived in Lemmon. They were sore and tired from the long ride and the heat, but Chris wanted to camp and they did so to please the boy. They bought steaks at a supermarket and rode down to the campground and wrestled with the wind to build a fire as the sun dropped over the horizon; in the darkness, they ate by the light of their motorcycle headlamps. Chris wasn't happy and, with a fumble, dropped his plate of food. There was about to be an argument when Chris got up and wandered off, complaining of stomach cramps.

Pirsig explained this at first as Chris's being "a complete bastard," but as the Sutherlands pressed the issue, he admitted that Chris's stomach pains were not only mostly imaginary but also a sign of the start of mental illness.

This notion must have been terrifying to a man who'd fought schizophrenia and hadn't come out of the battle all that well. The image of Pirsig sitting in the light of his motorcycle lamp, cutting his pocketknife into the shadows of his steak and explaining all this while his son wanders in the darkness is both endearing and enduring, and it's one of the reasons I'm here.

Half an hour later, there's a knock on the door, and it's Lacy, with the motel owner standing behind her. The first thought is that he's going to slug me for chatting up his innocent young clerk, a girl young enough to be my daughter, but no, he's here to take our photo together.

His name's Mike, and he's Russian. Things are getting stranger and stranger.

Mike says he once spent six months riding a Honda Gold Wing all the way from Indiana to Prudhoe Bay, on Alaska's Arctic coast, then across to Newfoundland. He's pleased to take our photo, first with Lacy's little disposable camera and then with mine, as she and I stand by the motorcycle and clutch the pink-covered book.

Since the bike is as big a part of this journey as she is, I tell Lacy that Jackie New must be ridden to the campsite and offer the pillion seat. Lacy shrugs and says okay. She's ridden on a motorcycle only once before, and it was a frightening experience—the young rider had tried to impress with foolish stunts and reckless speed. I look to be far more responsible, so she trusts me, she says.

What she means is I look like her dad, I'm sure of it.

I fire up the bike, and she climbs on behind, both of us helmetless, Lacy holding on to my jacket pockets for security. Mike waves good-bye as we head back past town and turn south toward the campground.

The dark clouds are gone, and there's no threat of rain as we cruise south on the straight road, the sun reddening to the west as it prepares to set and the shadows lengthening on our left. The bike feels smooth for the new oil, rejuvenated and ready for adventure; Lacy's small body is pressed against my back, and I can feel her breathing.

We're riding slowly, and conversation is easy without the helmets. I call back, "Are those beehives over there?" and she tells me that the honey is best when the hives are next to clover, as it is on her family's farm. Where her dad is.

The road seems to take forever because it's so straight, but in fact it's just fifteen minutes south to the reservoir. There's still some light as we pull into the state recreation area. We ride first to the picnic ground, where the trees and shoreline match the book's description, then to the camping area, where the RVs and trailers are set up on paved drive-throughs, very different from the way it was in Pirsig's time.

The sun is stunning now as it sets over the water—red clouds across the entire western sky and a red orb sinking past the opposite shore. All is still. I park the bike and we walk down to the water and mosquitoes come up to greet us. Lacy swats one from my neck. And suddenly it's dark and time to get her home.

"What are you doing tonight?" I ask brashly. "Want to go for a drink?" After all, I'm not busy, and I kind of like this adulation. And then, as an afterthought, "Are you old enough to go for a drink?"

She likes this and takes it as a compliment, stating that she's twenty-one years old and she'll be going for a drink anyway because that's all there is to do in Lemmon, so she'll be pleased to bring me along to her favorite bar. "Meet the locals," I'm thinking. "That's what this journey's all about, isn't it?"

Thirty-six years before, outside the tents at the Shadehill campground, Robert Pirsig was sending shivers down the spines of the Sutherlands by quoting to them from Goethe's ballad-poem "Der

Erlkönig" ("The Erlking"). It's a recollection from a fragment of Phaedrus's memory in which a father tries to protect his son from a ghost in the fog, a goblinlike creature who eventually steals the son's life away as the father tries to escape with his son on a galloping horse.

At the beginning of the Zen journey it seems clear that the poem is describing the Pirsigs themselves, with Chris as the son, Pirsig's narrator as the father, and Phaedrus as the evil goblin trying to kill the child. As the journey reaches its conclusion, the reader may recognize that first impressions might have been wrong.

In fact, as Thomas J. Steele explains in the *Guidebook to "Zen and the Art of Motorcycle Maintenance,"* it would be more accurate to think of Chris as the father, Phaedrus as the son being carried, and the narrator as the evil one. Little is as it seems.

Lacy and I ride back toward town in the darkness, for the clouds that have been so beautifully red are now obscuring any light from the moon. I'm wearing sunglasses for the bugs and riding more slowly than before because the road's become as murky as it was in Leon's fog.

I can feel her breathing again as her young body pushes against my back on the short seat, the air colder now than before, and what I'm thinking is "Twenty-one. That's half of forty-two. Half my age. Exactly half." The way is dark, and who knows where we're going.

CHAPTER FIVE

Western North Dakota

THE ROOM IS DARK as dawn approaches. I brush in and out of sleep, listening to Lacy's labored breathing on the bed beside me. I can't stop thinking about last night.

What was the name of the bar? The Trail's End? Seems appropriate. The place was near empty and about to close, but Lacy knew the bartender, a young woman named Jenny, and she'd agreed to serve us for a while.

We talked a lot about Lacy's short life. She's had two jobs so far. There was a part-time job at a psychiatric care facility, which she took on to help pay for college. The stress of looking after the patients alone at night became too much, and one day she collapsed from the pressure. She was admitted to a clinic for ten days. It took another year to get off the medications, but she's clean now. Her family pulled her through.

Then, after leaving school, she started a minimum-wage job that included lifting heavy stuff, but she slipped a disk in her back and can no longer lift any great weight. She reads all the time and keeps a list of books that she's either finished or wants to find: the most recent additions are *Atlas Shrugged* and *Animal Farm.* The details are coming back now as I listen to her breathing beside me. I'd asked which book she'd been reading when I walked into the office, and she pulled it out of her bag to show me: *Powers of Mind* by Adam Smith. It's got Zen in it, she'd said. "Hey, come to think of it, I was reading about Zen when you walked in." I asked which chapter, and she found it and showed me the title: "The

Ballad of the Zen Cowboy." "I guess that's you," she said. "You're the Zen Cowboy."

We drank to that. The beer kept coming. I can still taste it in the dryness of my mouth.

Jenny brought out some dice, and we threw for the shake of the day. Only one throw per person was allowed on any day, and it cost a buck.

"This is how I'm going to get rich," said Lacy. "All the money at once. I'm going to win the lottery."

She rolled the dice from the cup and landed five twos, which won the entire pot. We were stunned. That's how Lacy ended up with $115 in cash. So she ordered more drinks, fancy ones, and they were the beginning of the end: a round of Jäger bombs (a shot of Jägermeister in a highball of Red Bull), a round of cotton candies (Southern Comfort, Peachtree schnapps, and cranberry juice), and because it seemed right, a couple of red-headed sluts for the two of us. God knows what was in them, but they tasted great. I think. And more beer.

Then she asked the question: "Are you married?" It came out of the blue. "Yes, I am," I told her. I couldn't lie, thanks to the wedding ring on my finger. But everything had shifted with the blur of alcohol. Lacy just shrugged. Home seemed so far away—slipped behind the pale frosted glass, into the fog. My marriage vows were so long ago, and my ten-year marriage seemed inconsequential—it was five days ago that they left, and we'd still not spoken. Who left whom, anyway? Who flew away with the kids?

I can remember the moment in the bar when I first touched Lacy. "You can't waste this brain lifting boxes," I'd said, and stroked her pink hair. It was softer than I expected.

Then the jukebox stopped, and we went up to it to feed it some quarters. I steered her by her waist, which felt slim and firm beneath the thin T-shirt. At the machine she chose some of the tracks and asked me to choose some others, but most of the familiar names were bands from the '80s, when she was in kindergarten. What the hell. The music kept getting louder and the drinks kept getting stronger. And there was more beer.

It was 2 a.m. when we left the bar, with the shake-of-the day pot spent and back in the till and "Hotel California" winding up on the jukebox—because "it's about a hotel, and you work at a motel." Lacy walked with me back to the room, our arms around each other. She'd gotten some off-sale beer, and we cracked it open outside the room, sitting in the warm night on the white plastic chairs. There were two cars in the lot besides Lacy's. A couple of air conditioners hummed. No mosquitoes. We talked and drank for a while, holding hands, touching. Then Lacy stood up and squeezed my hand. "I have to use the washroom," she said, and I thought, "This is it. She's going inside. This is it."

Twenty-one. That's exactly half of forty-two. Exactly half.

And five days ago I was saying good-bye to my wife and children. The devil on my shoulder was shouting, "Throw ten years away in five days—*go for it!*" There was no angel on my other shoulder.

After a while I called to Lacy through the door, but there was no reply. I went inside and found her passed out on the bed, fully clothed, curled up facedown. Her T-shirt had ridden up a little at the back, and I could see a small scar at the base of her spine. Lifting boxes. I covered her loosely with the spare blanket and lay down beside her, resting my hand on her waist as I had on the walk over. She lay oblivious and still as if made from wax while I lay on my side, looking over her shoulder and through the crack in the plastic window shade. The tear was large enough that I could see some stars and a tree with its leaves waving in the quiet breeze, lit softly by the light of a gibbous moon.

At Shadehill, Chris wandered back to the campground after the others had clambered into their sleeping bags. He wanted to chat with his dad. The stomach pains had gone, the complaints had gone—he was a regular little boy again. "What was it like when you were a kid?" he asked his dad, and in response got "Go to *sleep,* Chris!" He cried softly into his sleeping bag. The narrator lay there in the dark, imagining figures in the fog coming to call him to task.

Eventually light begins to filter through the tear in the window shade and for a long time its beam slips down the wall and the morning begins to establish itself. Lacy doesn't wake. I go into the bathroom to change clothes, running and splashing the water, flushing the toilet and coughing loudly, but when I walk back into the main room, she's still lying there in exactly the same fetal pose, exactly as she'd lain down in the night on her way back from the bathroom. I open the shade and the room fills with soft light; I can see the small scar on her back again, where her T-shirt and now the blanket have lifted.

I have no idea what to do.

Above all, she'll want to be gone before the motel owner begins his day. There's time yet, though—it's not even seven o'clock. When I step outside, the world is still fuzzy and the warm breeze rubs against my face like a towel. It'll be hot again today.

I read outside for a while, coughing like a smoker—we'd all smoked in the bar the night before, a sure sign for me that I'd been drinking too much—but Lacy's subconscious just won't take the hint. Eventually I go in and shake her shoulder gently. She opens her eyes, sees me, and sits bolt upright on the bed, looking around and searching for her bearings.

"I've got to go," she says. "I'm so sorry. I've got to go."

And she picks up her bag and the book notes that had fallen from it and her jacket and stumbles out to her car. As she opens the door, she looks back at me, no longer the Zen Cowboy, and relaxes a little.

"I'm sorry I made such a mess. I've got to go."

A mess? Yes, the room's a mess. Now she's gone, and I'm trying to tidy it.

She's left her sunglasses behind, and I place them on the little particleboard writing desk. I gather up the beer bottles lying around outside by the plastic chairs. One of them has a broken neck and I push my middle finger into it to hold it. It slices deeply into the flesh, and there's suddenly a lot of blood. The wound must be rinsed in the bathroom sink, and it needs a Band-Aid, but even once the bandage is in place, the blood continues to seep around its sides.

This really is a lot of blood—it's going all over my hand and pooling in the space beside my wedding ring on the other finger before dripping away into the sink.

The irony's not lost. For the first time since it was placed there ten years ago, I must ease the ring from my finger to clean away the blood underneath and stanch the wound. The gold band slides quite easily over the wet skin, and a fresh Band-Aid stops the blood at last.

Now it's time to pack the bike and get back on the road. It was a traveling day for the Pirsigs, a hot one again but good for making miles, and there are a couple of hundred to go, back up into North Dakota and over into Montana. Jackie New packs quickly and the room is soon empty of luggage, but it's important to go around one last time and make sure nothing's forgotten.

And sure enough there it is, on the sink. The ring. My bloody ring. Ten years it's stayed on that finger, and now I can't remember to put it back on.

I rinse it and sit back on the bed, the bed that Lacy slept on, and turn it over and over, studying it for the first time in a very long time. Nothing fancy, just a plain circle of gold. I've thought about it a few times in the last several years, especially since the boys have come along and changed everything, but have never before removed it. Its circle has no beginning and no end. A few scratches but still bright. Dry now, it's a little more difficult to squeeze back onto the finger, but with a bit of force it settles into the small white groove in the flesh, touching the Band-Aid on the finger alongside.

. . .

A big part of me wants to just go, get the hell out of Lemmon, but that would be too much like a one-night stand. So I walk over to the motel office across the forecourt to say good-bye to the owner. We were chatty yesterday when he was taking the photos, and it would be good to know that everything's okay this morning.

There he is, in the office. The little breakfast room next door is full of noise. Sounds like Russian being spoken, loud Russian. What's his name again? Mike—that's it. Mike.

"Hello, Mike. How are you?"

He looks up, and his face is inscrutable. A face for poker. If he saw his clerk slip out of room 28 this morning, he's not showing it. He purses his lips and gives an amiable nod. "Very good, thank you." And a shriek hoots out from the breakfast room.

"We're up early this morning," he says. It's a clipped accent, very precise, very correct. "My wife is talking to family in Israel. It's not so easy on the Internet—the delay's about twenty seconds, so we're always talking over each other. But it's not so different even when we're all in the same room."

Through the doorway, a beautiful woman and a young girl are making faces at the Webcam on a computer set up in the corner. "It's good for her to speak Russian with someone other than me," says Mike. "Even if it is through a computer."

There's more chat about the hot weather, and he's not giving anything away about maybe having seen Lacy. It's still early, so we're both happy to talk and the conversation is clearing my head a little. He asks what I do for a living and smiles broadly at the reply.

"A journalist! Is that so? So am I! Would you believe it, with me owning this place?"

We end up outside with cups of coffee, sitting at a rickety metal table as his wife and her daughter continue to laugh and shriek inside. Just as motorcyclists are drawn to each other, if only to argue, so are journalists, though he no longer works in the business and we're as disparate as any two journalists can be.

"I worked for Time Life as more of a researcher than a reporter," he says as we sip from foam cups of black coffee—which is helping my head a great deal.

"I speak Russian, and back in the eighties they wanted somebody who could keep them informed about the Soviet Union. I didn't do much writing—more fact gathering and checking for the others at Time Life, but I quit in the end. Too much back-stabbing."

Was journalism Mike's first career?

"Oh, no. I was in the army before. My family moved from Russia to Israel when I was eleven, and when I was old enough, like everyone, I joined the army. I was a tank commander, the guy who sits in the turret up top. I was in the army for ten years, until we went into Lebanon and a shell hit us broadside. Just exploded through the armor. Everyone in my tank was roasted alive, everyone except me. I was blown right out of the turret and broke my back on the ground. My friends in the tank were dying right there beside me, and I couldn't move. I was taken to the hospital and stayed in bed for six months. But when they released me and I went home to my parents, I kept thinking about my dead friends in that tank. It put me into a very deep depression. They'd been trapped inside, and so I trapped myself inside my parents' house. Didn't go outside for a year."

This is heavy-duty stuff, totally unexpected over morning coffee.

"A friend was studying music at Indiana State University, and he wrote to me with the details of how to apply for a scholarship. Journalism was available, so I applied and was accepted and took it, and then we both went to work for his dad at Time Life. Funny how the world works, isn't it?"

He tells me he's soon to turn fifty and that he has a son who still lives in Israel. His first wife died and the beautiful woman inside is his second wife, whom he'd met while traveling in Siberia and proposed to there, but she arrived here only six months ago, with her twelve-year-old daughter, after years of waiting for a visa from the American authorities.

Yet the big question is still unanswered: What's he doing owning a motel in Lemmon, South Dakota? It has to be asked directly, and he squints a little and smiles again. Everyone asks eventually.

"This is only my second week here, you know. I bought this place on the Internet. I think it's going to be okay, but I'm not really a businessman. Money never turned my crank, you know, except for a while.

"I left Time Life and joined Cantor Fitzgerald as a Russian consultant, working in the World Trade Center. That was the high life, all right! There was money everywhere! Lots of stress, but the brokers were better than the journalists—they didn't take their jobs away with them on weekends, and they played as hard as they worked. I had a good time there.

"Then, when I was on vacation one day, the plane flew right into my office and killed everyone."

The ripples of 9/11 are still being felt in every part of this country. Even over a coffee outside a quiet motel in South Dakota, where a mother and daughter are laughing into a computer camera at a joke being told six thousand miles away, and where an expatriate Russian Israeli is staring into the distance, thinking of the bodies of his friends in New York burning like those of his friends years before in Lebanon.

Once again he was clear of the flames and once again the impact broke him.

"I went to pieces. There was no job to go to, no more Cantor, no more World Trade Center. I drove a cab for a while. I would go to my dacha—you'd call it a cottage—north of the city, where I had no amenities, just the woods and a stream, and I loved the solitude. New York was over for me. That part of my life was over. I just wanted my wife and her daughter to come here so I could start again.

"When they finally arrived, ready for our new life, I went looking for a way out of New York. No bosses yelling at me. No commuting for an hour and a half just to get to work to be yelled at, then driving home again. No high buildings. I found this motel, and I love it. We can make a good life here."

The noises inside have stopped, and we both notice as we sip the coffee. The call to Israel is over, and Mike purses his lips again.

"She's not so sure. She was a teacher of art history at the university in Novosibirsk and she had a full life, the life of an intellectual, but here she doesn't speak English so well and it's hard for her to make friends. She has such conversation—such life— but not in English, not yet. We came here and I saw all this openness, all this air to breathe and space to live, but she said, 'Why did you bring me from one Siberia to another?' But this is not Siberia—this is South Dakota. There's a lot here if you want to look for it."

Not everybody loves the country over the city. In Minneapolis or Denver or Winnipeg, which are the closest large cities to Lemmon, Mike's wife would find others like her, but Minneapolis is five hundred miles back down the road. We're less than a two-hour drive here from the geographic center of the United States, but sometimes, when you're right in the middle of something, it means everything that matters is elsewhere.

The morning's pressing on, and although Mike invites me to stay another night and drink vodka with him and meet his family, I'm on a tight schedule and must leave. I'll come here on the way back, though, and tell him so. Guess that means I'll catch up with Lacy, too.

"That will be good," he says. "I do not think we'll be full. They told me when they sold me this motel that it would always be full, but it's not been so and I think they were not so honest. They just wanted to retire and leave. But we don't need much now. Perhaps in the winter we'll close up and go south for a while. My wife might like that."

We stand and say good-bye with a smile and a firm handshake, man to man. Turning to leave, I remember the beer bottles in the room and the sunglasses on the desk.

"Oh, Lacy left her sunglasses in my room last night when we got back from the campground. They're on the writing desk."

"I'll let her know," he replies, and, almost as an afterthought,

"I'd have thought she'd miss them this morning. The sun's very strong today."

The Zen riders left after breakfast and made this into a traveling day. In the book, Sylvia Sutherland was plainly impatient with the two Pirsigs, for she wanted to get out of the heat and didn't want to deal with a whining kid. Pirsig, on the other hand, was slowing everything down because of a concern for the condition of his rear tire, which was wearing more quickly than expected on the hot pavement. It's the little descriptions of Sylvia here that she probably disliked the most, not cruel or vindictive but certainly not complimentary.

Several years later, when Pirsig finished writing *Zen and the Art,* he showed drafts of the manuscript to the people mentioned in the book. "It really isn't me!" said Sylvia. As he described in a letter to the DeWeeses after they had read their copy:

> Sylvia was kind of thrown by the way I switched everything around, and Chris was really shook, so I guess you probably have some of the same feelings. I explained to them that the story isn't really about them, that they are like a Greek chorus there to "Oh" and "Ah" and give a semblance of reality to a tale that seems always to ride at the very edge of incredibility and needs all the help it can get.

But even so, many readers who accepted the tale as gospel couldn't see this, and to them Sylvia and John will forever be remembered as shallow, two-dimensional. Chris will always be that whining boy on the back of the bike. Nancy and Ted got off lightly—they're barely mentioned and never named.

The sun is not so ferocious as yesterday, but the wind is the strongest yet. I'm back up into North Dakota already and thinking of the lonely people in Lemmon, people who don't deserve to be lonely, people who will thrive if they can only find friends to understand them.

This was a hard slog for the Zen riders, and it's rough today, too. The wind from the northwest is incredibly strong, blowing rivers through the high grass in the fields alongside the road. It's all the bike can do to hold 60 miles an hour into the gusts. At one point I ride some distance past a historical marker beside the road before, curiosity winning the moment, I turn back east to read it. Now that the wind's behind me, the bike speeds to 80 miles an hour with ease. The muscles of my forearms, neck, and back, strained against the pressure, relax and stretch; like this I could ride all day.

The sign describes the buffalo hunt that took place here in 1882 in the valley of Hiddenwood Creek. It tells of fifty thousand buffalo blackening the hills and five thousand of them being slaughtered; two thousand Sioux butchering the animals and hanging the meat to dry. It was the last great hunt, the end of the buffalo, at least the end of those killed in a traditional way for food and not just slaughtered for their hides by the white hunters. The field is empty now, yet its grass is swaying and moving in the wind, still alive.

The sign goes on to describe the encampment in this place by General Custer one July eight years before the hunt, on his way to look for gold in the Black Hills with thousands of men and horses: "A smooth grassy plain covered with tents, hooded wagons and grazing horses, a band in the center playing familiar airs and an atmosphere cool, fresh and bracing."

I sit there with Jackie New's engine thumping gently and try to picture the scene 130 years before, but cannot. This would be the point in the movie where the scene fades to a flashback, but it just doesn't work; this field is alive with movement, but it's not the movement of people, not now. Today's travelers stay on the road and keep their windows closed, and they'll be in the Black Hills in three hours, four with a stop for lunch.

Not me, though. I'm going the other way, into the wind. I turn the bike around, and a gust nearly bowls us over. My back tenses, arms flex, and neck starts to ache. And I can't stop thinking of last night. I feel guilty, but it's not clear why: Because Lacy is so much younger and more vulnerable? That's a big part of it, but how about that I'm married and was ready to cheat on my wife? I wanted to last night, that's for sure. It could have been closure to the last few years of frustration at our partnership having been taken from us by the boys, but now I think it would just have been crappy. That's not the way to do it. Dodged a bullet there. I'm sober in the sunshine, and there are many miles still to go, into the wind.

The road is very bad now. A sign even warns of it, but it's redundant because the ruts and undulations are throwing the tires from side to side. The tarmac is bumpy, and there's no rhythm to be found, no soothing *clickety-clack* here. Within a few miles the speedometer cable shakes itself free again, and I pull over at a small park off the highway in Scranton for the fix.

It takes just a couple of minutes, and there's time to pause for a drink of water at a picnic table in the shade and look around. The street's wide and empty, but the air is full of the sounds of workers a couple of blocks away feeding wood into a mobile chipper, tidying the town. There's even a restaurant just down the way that looks like a good place to stop, but I should press on to Bowman and eat where the Pirsigs ate. I've not eaten since the submarine yesterday at Mobridge, across the Missouri. Drank a lot, but no food. My wife fusses about my meals, but she's far away now.

The bike looks just the same as Jackie Blue did nineteen years ago—on the way through Montana, after visiting the Sturgis Motorcycle Rally, I'd stopped for a cool drink and a rest from the wind at a place like this, near the Custer battlefield at Little Bighorn.

It had been a relief to leave Sturgis, for earlier in the week I'd gone out to some bars and, stopping to relieve myself afterward in a dark alley against a wall that turned out to be the police station, I'd been arrested and charged with "depositing filth in a public place." Spent the night in jail. On that Monday morning the campground was deserted and I had a date in court to reclaim my $50 bail, but since the cop didn't show, the case was thrown out and I'd practically leaped on the bike to leave town. Hours down the road I finally paused, as I'm pausing now, and pulled out paper and a pen.

It was the first thing I wrote about that trip, part of what would become a letter to my mother:

Billings, Mont.
12 August 1985

I understand now that the value of this Trip lies not in the places I visit but in the people that I meet. People like Jack Crowser of Sturgis, who came to try to bail me out of jail at 2:30 a.m., despite only meeting me briefly once before; John Hughes of Sturgis, who offered free legal help provided I send him a post-card sometime, merely because I ride a motorcycle; Billy, the roughneck from New Mexico, and his girlfriend, Pickle, who gave me coffee and dinner around the campfire after everyone else had gone home, despite being too broke to afford a packet of cigarettes.

Sitting at the picnic table, muscles tired from the road, looking at the bike ready and willing to take me west, I feel very comforted.

Is it a road forward or a road back? It doesn't matter.

As the Zen priest said, "Does one really have to fret about enlightenment? No matter what road I travel, I'm going home."

CHAPTER SIX

Miles City, Montana

I<small>T'S ABOUT NINE O'CLOCK</small> in the morning, and I'm sitting beside my motorcycle on a shady rock behind the Olive Hotel in Miles City, Montana.

It's one of the oldest hotels in town, with a big, airy lobby and wood paneling everywhere, and proud of its heritage. It's cheap, too, at less than $40 for a large room overlooking the main street. Now it's time to clean up the motorcycle a little because this is an important morning. I'm going to visit Bill, one of the most famous motorcycle mechanics in the literary world.

The Zen riders stayed at a hotel here, perhaps even this one, and took some time out in the morning to reorganize, doing laundry and the like. Pirsig wheeled his motorcycle around the back of the hotel and adjusted the tappets, later describing the exercise in his book as an analogy for cause and effect in everything that seeks to add quality to anything. Do *this*, and *that* will happen. If the fit is well adjusted, all will move smoothly, but if it's loose, the rods will pound away and can even damage the motor. He'd have been in his element as he fiddled and poked away, free from distraction and taking the time to think through the riddle of why his spark plugs were running a little rich, with too much soot collecting on the porcelain. Eventually he realized that Montana's higher altitude and thinner air were making the difference and set off for Bill's Cycle Shop to buy different jets for the carburetors.

I'd barely parked late yesterday afternoon when a large man

wandered across the street to say hello. His name was Miles Milligan, and he said he owned a number of motorcycles; he hardly stopped talking about bikes for the next twenty minutes as I stood there with the saddlebags over one shoulder. He talked about Harleys and Hondas and everything in between, and I listened politely as he voiced an amiable opinion on the entire two-wheeled world.

Finally, when he paused for breath, I dived in and asked if Bill's Cycle Shop might still be in business. After all, I needed some chain lubricant.

No, he said. Bill retired a few years ago, selling the store and moving to his house at the airport.

"He's still around?"

"Sure he's around," said Miles, "though not so sprightly now that Parkinson's disease is taking over. Give him a call: Bill and Bonnie Bergerson—they're in the book."

I took a long shower and rode over to a Wendy's for a hamburger, trying the Wal-Mart next door in case it sold chain lube. It didn't, so it was back to the room to stare at the phone. What was there to say to Bill? Really, all the man had done was sell Pirsig some carburetor jets and new rubbers for his foot pegs, and that was thirty-six years ago—what would we talk about?

But if I didn't call, I'd never know, so I found the listing and dialed the number. "Hello?" said a woman on the other end.

"Is this the right number for the Bill of Bill's Cycle Shop?" When she said it was, I told her about traveling the route of *Zen and the Art of Motorcycle Maintenance* and asked if I could speak with Bill. "Of course you can," she said, and added kindly, "Bill's voice isn't what it used to be. You'll have to listen up."

After a moment a man came on the line and said hello, speaking in a loud, hoarse whisper. I introduced myself and told him about this journey. I said that I would like to come by in the morning and tell him about it. Would he be at home?

Sure, he said—anytime. He'd seen Miles Milligan in town a little earlier and had already heard about me. "Be looking forward to it." He gave me directions—somewhere up near the airport—and that was that. Another connection made solely through riding the motorcycle.

I picked up the pink-covered book. Time to read again about Bill.

In Pirsig's story, Bill wasn't at the shop when he first called—someone said he was probably fishing—and the place was untidy, but when Bill returned, Pirsig recognized that it was actually well ordered; its owner was the kind of man who knows where everything is in the clutter and will search for days if it's moved by even a few inches. He was fair and knowledgeable, and he commented that the best way to learn about motorcycles is to work on them and rebuild them.

That's it. Less than a page. But enough to warrant a call thirty-six years later from a curious passerby.

In preparation for the visit later this morning, I'm on the shady rock behind the Olive Hotel, well rested and checking over Jackie New in case Bill's critical eye should find an obvious fault and I'm dismissed as a charlatan.

The spark plugs are clean—two of them in the one cylinder for improved combustion, which is about as technically advanced as this motorcycle gets—and the tires are safe, though their tread is wearing down on the straight, hot roads. The brakes are still soft, and the clutch still slips, but Bill will never see it. The drive chain is a little slack, though, and certainly needs oiling. Better tend to that.

This is an ideal spot for it. It's to the west of the four-story hotel, so the sun will be hidden for an hour or so yet, and in a dusty little area of rocks and dirt at the bottom of the side steps. It sounds bad, but it's perfect. The rocks are large but not so big they can't be moved, so I slide a couple into place and make one into a seat and another two into a support for the bike high enough to raise the rear wheel off the ground. The bike does not have a center stand, so the wheel cannot otherwise be safely raised, which makes all the difference when lubricating the links because you want to spin the wheel slowly to revolve the chain. The alternative is to push the bike, lube some chain, push it some more, lube some newly exposed chain, and push it and lube it a dozen more times, probably a hundred feet up the road. No—it's way easier to set it on a stand and take a seat yourself. The dirt is handy in case some lubricant drips, for the dry dust will quickly absorb it, and there'll be no telltale trail of oil. And it's great to be at the bottom of the steps because I can nip inside for free coffee from the pot in the lobby. Who needs a fancy workshop?

In *Zen and the Art,* Pirsig admits to stripping the thread on his chain adjuster by moving it without slackening it off first, which seems ludicrous for somebody otherwise so careful and well trained. I loosen the chain-adjuster screws, one on either side of the wheel, and then the rear axle bolt. The axle floats on the swing arm, and I push the adjusters in another notch. That'll do it.

The rear brake link must be loosened now for the slightly greater wheelbase, making taut again the longer chain that's stretched a fraction of an inch over the miles. It's just a couple of turns of the brake-adjuster nut. Then I lock another nut into place against it so that it doesn't move, and all is as it should be. Don't forget to retighten the axle bolt and the chain adjusters.

Now I sit back for a moment and take a sip of the coffee. A woman with big frizzy hair, wearing a tank top and jeans too tight for her middle age, walks past, and I ask her to take a photo of this mini event and she's pleased to do so. She's never seen a digital camera before and is amazed by the moving image on the screen. Still, she steps back and tells me to say "shit" for a smile and presses the button and hands the camera back with a laugh. Once she's gone, I check the display and see that she didn't press the button hard enough. There's no photo.

Another sip of the coffee and then I pull the spray can of lubricant from the grocery bag of tools.

This is a tiny little can that was supposed to be a great space saver, small enough to fit in a jacket pocket. In truth, it's only enough for a couple of lubrications at most and cost about the same as a can that holds twenty times as much oil, so I should get a proper-size replacement for it. I'll use this one all up on the chain now. I turn the rear wheel with one hand, looking for the chain's split link to act as a starting point.

How many times will this wheel turn before I get to California? I forget about it out on the road, as I forget about all the workings of the bike, aware only when something feels different or sounds improper, but sometimes that's too late. I find the link and begin to shoot sticky oil on the chain, directing it between the sliding metal of the links, happy to empty the entire can to make sure everything's lubricated.

Three years before, the chain on this same motorcycle broke at 70 miles an hour as I rode to work on a six-lane expressway. That is one of the most dangerous things a rider can experience. It just snapped and fell away on the road, but it could as easily have wrapped itself around the wheel and locked everything up, spilling me onto the asphalt to be struck by passing cars. One small link fails—a twenty-five-cent pin—and if I'd not been in the outside lane, able to coast without power onto the shoulder of the divided highway, the experience could have been catastrophic.

So much for the argument that sometimes bikes can be safer than cars—it works both ways, and this was after more than twenty years of riding and performing my own maintenance. Installing and lubricating a chain is so simple—why hadn't I done it right? I'm doing it right now, though. Taking all the time that's needed for a quality task.

A man walks past who looks like he should be the partner of the frizzy-haired woman, and I ask if he'll take my photo. Sure, he says, and then looks with astonishment at the flickering image on the camera's screen. He's never seen a digital camera before, either. But he steps back, points and shoots, and hands the camera back with a grin.

"You've gotta love technology!" he says. It's a pretty good picture, too.

.   .   .

I check out of the room but leave the luggage in the lobby so I can ride unencumbered the few miles up to Bill's place. The clerk's watching over it, and there's no question it will be safe.

The directions aren't too clear because, to tell the truth, I was confused about the airport: Bill seemed to be saying he lived *at* the airport, which made no sense.

It's a couple of miles north of Miles City and then the first right, but that takes me to some kind of private hunting club with a glorious view from the bluff. This is open land, no longer rounded hills but crags and cliffs with brown sage grass in the fields, green in the trees and by the ponds, cut through by the Yellowstone River below. There's another road opposite the entrance to the municipal airport, and I make a couple more wrong turns into small subdivisions of ranchland, each property with its own barn and horses and fields, but nothing that seems right.

Finally it's time to knock on a door and ask for directions. "Oh, he's up at the airport," the home owner says. But I rode past the airport already. "No, not the town airport—*his* airport." And the man tells me the roads to take.

He wasn't kidding. Bill lives at an airport. His long driveway is one of the runways, straight with smooth gravel, lined with white marker cones. Behind the bungalow is a hangar, and walking toward me from the front door is Bill, a huge grin on his face. He's a large man, but his gait is stilted, his steps short and bouncy, like a puppet's. His hands are gnarled and curled and almost useless, but that doesn't stop him from offering what grip he has in his handshake.

"You found the place, then," he says with that same hoarse whisper.

Bonnie comes outside as well, shorter and stouter and the very image of a perfect grandmother, with a friendly, smiling face. "Will you come inside?" she says. "Here, let's sit in the kitchen."

The house is neat and tidy. An easy chair in the living room is obviously Bill's, raised and set forward so he can get back into it and then lower it down with a lever, but this morning he seems to have little trouble sitting on a regular chair beside the kitchen table. They look at me expectantly, with interest, and it's time to talk about the journey.

"That damn book," says Bill. "I got a lot of interest at the time, when it came out, but it's died away some now. But still people sometimes call, people like yourself."

Bonnie chimes in. "Bill didn't think the book was very fair to him. He would never have left the shop open, and he didn't fish. That wasn't good business. We didn't stay in business by being bad at business, leaving the shop open to go fishing."

Fair enough, but otherwise Bill comes across pretty well in the book, way better than the Sutherlands, for instance. He nods appreciatively as Bonnie watches him.

But again there's one burning question that overshadows all the others, right up there with why a Russian journalist is running a prairie motel. Is this really an airport? And how come Bill and Bonnie live smack in the middle of it?

"I love to fly," says Bill. "I bought my first airplane in the sixties, and now I've got six of them." He names several—a Piper Cherokee 180, a 1947 Stinson 108-1, a couple of J3s. "But in the seventies," he continues, "I had an argument with the city airport when they told me I couldn't do something, so I said I'd start my own airport. They said I couldn't do that, so I said, 'You'd better sharpen your pencils!' If anyone tells me I can't do something, that just makes me want to do it all the more.

"I started this place in 1978 on four square miles of land. There are forty lots sold now and probably another ten left to be developed. I sell them to pilots who want to keep their plane near their home. Bush pilots mostly, who don't like to be told how to do stuff, people like me.

"I can't fly my planes anymore because of this Parkinson's, but when I get the urge, I call up a neighbor and they take me for a ride. They do the taking off and the landing, but I take over when it gets upstairs. Planes are like motorcycles: once they're in your blood, they're always in your blood."

. . .

If they'd known about each other's interests at the time, Bill Bergerson and Bob Pirsig could have talked about airplanes back in 1968, not just about motorcycles. Pirsig had taken flying lessons in the '50s, and while courting Nancy he'd sneaked her into his diminutive instructor's very small plane for a half-hour flight, even though he was not yet certified to fly solo. "Afterward, he confessed that for a few moments he was afraid that we wouldn't get off the ground because I weighed so much more than the instructor," she wrote to me. "We flew around looking down on the magical scene below and feeling special, different from everyone else."

Bill's hands are curled in front of him on the breakfast table, the fingers incapable of movement, but he's grinning the same large smile he offered when he greeted me. Bonnie watches him and nods.

Does he still have anything to do with motorcycles? Obviously he can't ride anymore. When did he sell the shop?

"Oh, I have a bike," he says. "I'll show it to you in a while."

Bill tells me that he sold fifteen thousand motorcycles during his career, moving seven times to larger stores as the business kept growing. Others saw his success and opened their own bike shops in competition. "They all said, 'We're going to put you out of business,' and I said, 'Go right ahead. Sharpen your pencils!' They never did. We outlived fourteen other dealers."

There was no secret to the store's success, just hard work and treating people fairly so they'd come back. "My father was one of the most honest men I know," says Bill, "but everyone took him for a ride, and he died with nothing. I swore I wouldn't let anyone take me for a ride. I've taken some god-awful chances in my time, but I'm one of those guys who don't quit easy."

Bonnie is smiling at him and agreeing. Then she adds, "He

said if ever there was a computer in the store, that would be when he'd quit, and that's what happened in 1994. I always did the books, and I stayed on at the shop for two more years to computerize it, but it wasn't easy. After thirty-seven years as the boss, to become an employee with the same employees—and you have to keep your mouth shut all the time. I had to leave, too."

Bill built this bungalow for Bonnie when he left the store, as well as a few of the houses on the airpark subdivision, and it's solid and warm. He learned the trade from his father. Five years ago the Parkinson's began to affect his muscles, but it's done nothing to his mind. Why did he become a mechanic and not a carpenter?

"I always loved motorcycles, but I didn't have any money to own one. Where I was born and raised, in Biddle, Montana, population seven, when I'd hear riders coming into town, I'd run down the street just as far as I could go to meet them and stand in the road and ask to ride back with them.

"There was a Harley dealer there named Krumpe. He was so short he couldn't put his feet on the ground when he sat on his Seventy-four, so he'd start it and we had to push him off while he kicked up the kickstand to get moving. I'd look at the bikes he had around, and he'd say, 'Bill, if you can make that bike run, you can ride it this weekend.' So I did. And when I finally got a bike, I couldn't afford for someone to work on it, so I had to keep it going myself. That's how I learned."

He started the shop in 1958 with two mechanics, selling boats and motors; three years later he began selling the new little Honda motorcycles as dealer number 289. He had also taken on the Harley-Davidson franchise, but that lasted only a year.

"William H. Davidson walked in the door in 1961 and said, 'You can't sell rice grinders!' He canceled me on the spot. Never did like the man. I met Mr. Honda later, at the tenth-anniversary convention, and he was very nice."

Mr. Honda was probably impressed with Bill, too. His shop had sold ninety-five of the Japanese bikes that first year, seventy more than expected, and over time Bill gained a formidable reputation as a Honda mechanic. He found some problems in Hondas that even the service managers couldn't cure and worked out a way to fix them. He'd work on any make of bike and sometimes used the Honda parts to fix them better. The business expanded when he started selling Kawasakis as well.

The bike shop's still in business, though with a different name and on the other side of town. Bill and Bonnie don't like the way it operates, either.

"They do everything by the book there, and that's not the way to be with motorcycles. When I had the shop, I hired a bunch of mechanics from the institutions and I fired them all. They could put it on paper, but they just couldn't apply it. I'll take a street kid any day. They can't afford new parts for their bikes so they have to fix the old ones. That was me—I was one of those street kids, and I'm still going."

He'll be seventy next month, he says, and though the degeneration of his nervous system has changed his life irrevocably, he refuses to let his body get the better of him.

We rise from the table and, as promised, walk back through the house to the garage to see his motorcycle. The enclosed breezeway is well designed, no steps and no drafts from outside, and the large garage is tidy and well ordered. Tools lie on a shelf at the back, and a large chest in the corner is a bit jumbled but certainly better arranged than most. On the other side of the family car is a blue-and-red Kawasaki 550 LTD with a sidecar attached, its chain rusty from lack of use. The sidecar was probably added when Bill's balance started to go.

Beyond that, in the center of the garage, parked on three broad wheels, is a polished yellow custom-built Harley-Davidson 45 trike. Bill grins that huge grin again.

"My kids gave me this on Father's Day this year," he says. "Goes pretty good, too."

It has a suicide hand shift for the three gears to make up for Bill's inability to move his boots on a regular foot shifter, a single seat in front of a large mesh luggage carrier, the rock-solid stability of a heavy trike, and all the cool of a Harley-Davidson. He turns the key and punches the starter, and with a *THUMP* it proves it has all the sound, too.

"Want to ride it?" he asks.

Of course, but then I notice a license plate lying loose in the carrier. "BILL 45," it says. "That just came yesterday," says Bonnie. "I haven't gotten around to putting it on yet."

It seems absurd that a man as capable as Bill is now incapable of even turning a screwdriver. I offer to put the plate on in return for the ride up and down the runway, and Bill is pleased to accept, shutting the engine off with a knock of the button. Now comes the proof of Pirsig's claim: Does he know exactly where in the garage to find the right screwdriver? "It should be on the tool chest," he says, and there it is on top, right where he says. The old plate comes off quickly, and the new one goes on, further proof that this is Bill's bike and nothing's going to stop him from damn well riding it if he wants to.

He climbs on, starts the bike again, and shuffles the shifter into reverse. The bike backs out of the garage, and he lines it up facing down the runway.

"There you go," he says as I settle onto the broad leather seat. "If you see a plane coming in, give it the right of way!"

And with a twist of the throttle on this old Harley-Davidson, restored by his son-in-law and presented with pride by his children, I head off down the gravel.

Bill's watching from behind, and I'm acutely conscious of being careful, but it's hard not to relax as the speed builds and the trike drops into second and even into third gear as the runway blurs past. The road approaches too soon, and I slow down to turn around, looking up to see Bill standing there in front of the garage, watching me as Bonnie has been watching him. I ride back toward the house and the speed builds again, and somewhere halfway, at around 40 miles an hour, I feel sure that if I lifted back on the handlebars, the trike would rise, leaving the gravel and heading up through the few wisps of cloud, breaking free from the ground and all that holds to it. There's no gravity, and I can fly, free of limits, free of pain, free of everything, free to be just me. It's going to get better now. And I look ahead and see Bill watching, and I know he knows this feeling and longs for it and craves it and refuses to ever let go of it. And I know that he never, ever will.

At the hotel the coffee's still in the pot and my bags are still in the lobby. Everything straps on, the bike sagging a little with each layer of luggage. Jacket on, helmet on, I head back down Main Street to the other end of town to find the new Bill's Cycle Shop and buy some chain lube.

It's here, past the McDonald's, on the other side of the interstate, a huge warehouse-size store with a different name and more than a hundred bikes and ATVs on display. At the back corner are the parts counter and accessories, with chrome aftermarket parts hanging on a pegboard display and some shelves lined with cans and bottles. I look around but can't find the chain lube, so I ask a guy behind the counter who's chatting with one of the mechanics.

"It's over there, bottom shelf," he says, and points, then carries on the conversation with his friend.

There are three kinds of chain lube, none of them familiar, so I take a while to read the labels and then pick one just because it's the most expensive. At the till the parts guy asks my name. "Mark," I say. "Hello."

No, he says back—he needs my full name, and points to a piece of paper stuck with tape to the till's computer monitor. "Sorry for any wait," it says. "We are using a *new more efficient* computer system. Thank you for your patience." It won't let him process the payment without his inputting a name and address.

I give him my name and home address, two thousand miles away, and he types it all in without any interest and hands over the change.

I take some time to wander through the store and look at the new motorcycles. There are no other customers and only two salespeople, absorbed at their desks with their computer screens. No one approaches me. This has the feel of the Wal-Mart last night, when I was searching for the chain lubricant. Come to think of it, it feels like the Wendy's, too, and even the Burger King, except there isn't an old farmer in the corner with a story to tell. There are no stories in here at all, just row upon row of shiny new metal and plastic machinery and posters on the walls promising excitement and satisfaction. Two-dimensional posters for a three-dimensional store. It's quiet, too, except for the soft sound of a radio somewhere in the service area at the back.

Outside, I buy a can of iced tea from a vending machine before settling back on the bike and the highway. The drink is cold and delicious, and I didn't have to speak to anybody to get it. What a way to travel.

CHAPTER SEVEN

Central Montana

THE EXIT SIGN READS "Hathaway," and this is where all travelers must sound their horn, according to the hotel clerk back at the Olive. "Everyone honks at Star's place," she said. "Everyone knew Star. She ran the best brothel in the state."

There's not much anymore at Hathaway, just a few minutes west of Miles City, but it's a good reason to get off the interstate, which is not the old meandering route of the Pirsigs and Sutherlands back in '68. There are some oil tanks and house trailers, and nothing looks lived-in.

A wooden house at the east end of the settlement is probably what's left of Star's place—it's the biggest building around, yet it's just a house, a clapped-out, clapboard, clap-infested two-story unpainted brown house with a small deck and a large overgrown yard, empty. So much for ill repute—it just looks ill. This was a brothel?

Even so, Jackie New's horn gives its feeble *toot-toot* as I putter by, not the deafening *HAHNK!* of the trucks that Star was used to hearing through the shutters as she bore down on her clients, and now I stay on Frontage Road, which hugs the main highway, heading west again. The side road out of Miles City wanders away north and south, and I would have doubled my distance just to avoid the thruway; besides, that stretch of interstate is pretty much a regular four-laner, so I'd hopped on to it. Here at Hathaway, though, I give the old road a try.

The final stop for today is Laurel, Montana, a couple of hundred miles that would take just three easy hours on the interstate, which runs directly through it; I'll add a couple more hours and try to find the older highway that the Zen riders probably took. Somewhere along this road will be the spot where they were almost forced into the ditch by the oncoming car and trailer, and I should figure out where that might have been.

As well, it'll be good to ride more slowly than I must on the four-laner—the clutch is slipping more at higher speeds, and its cork-covered plates shouldn't be too stressed before I reach the Beartooth Pass tomorrow. Darrell's warning about needing a strong clutch and brakes rings even more loudly now than it did in the bar at Oakes, nagging away as the miles pass and the mountains approach.

Right now, though, the road has no highway lines and is smoothly paved, dipping in and out of hollows; shallow ditches and verges to the side are covered with grass and wildflowers. The Yellowstone River keeps the fields more green now than brown. The sun is warm and the wind is mellow. Almost without warning, the road merges onto the interstate—there's no option without doubling back a dozen miles.

Everyone's on cruise control, and the bike's comfortable speed is ten miles an hour slower than the limit; everyone wants to overtake me, but can't if there's already a vehicle in the left lane, so drivers are riding my back end, trying to avoid the brakes. There's nothing to do but speed up; the engine races, but the bike doesn't go much quicker. I can almost feel the clutch plates scuffing away as their cork grips begin to shred.

"Let's just get over the Beartooth," I'm thinking, and then, "Please let the brakes slow everything down on the other side." I can rest up and make repairs in Bozeman—the Pirsigs did—and so what if I don't get to San Francisco on my birthday, on this magic day when I turn forty-two? I'll get there eventually.

There's an exit a few miles farther on, at Rosebud, and I take it gratefully. The ramp ends at Butte Creek Road. My boys would love that. "Butt Crack Road? Was it really smelly, Dad?"

We've still not spoken since the airport, but I'll call from Laurel. I should. It's good to have space, and there's plenty of space here in Montana, but it can get lonely, too. The greater the space, the greater the solitude.

It takes some thought to work out that today is Thursday, and the seven-hour time difference plays havoc with long-distance calling. The best time to find them at home is their early evening, when I'm always in the middle of nowhere, far from a reliable phone. Like now.

My cell phone doesn't work here, as usual, and there are no obvious phones in Rosebud. In fact, it's about the most miserable-looking community I've encountered so far: a town of a couple of hundred people, the houses unpainted, the trailers shabby, yards full of rusted cars and junk. It looks like a younger version of Hathaway and headed in the same direction. Which trailer's the whorehouse?

There's the Longhorn Bar and the post office, which seems to be the only place that's seen any maintenance in the last generation. I ride around trying to find something, anything, that's endearing. No mountains yet—they're still just over the horizon—only some planted trees. Every house has a cluttered yard, and every home needs paint, maintenance, TLC. There are no stores, no focal point, just houses and trailers and a school, the post office, and the bar.

A few people stare, so I get back on the side road, forking west away from the interstate, which dips a little to the south. But the road is pretty, and again the wildflowers grow in the grass at the verge. This road runs near the main highway almost as an after-thought, as if the engineers had forgotten to remove it when they came through here with the interstate soon after the Pirsigs traveled this way.

The bike is running comfortably now and I'm looking for places where the near accident might have occurred, but frankly, it could have been anywhere. The GPS on the handlebar has a number of places along here marked off on its small screen as waypoints: brief references in the book, a couple of potential near-crash sites. The map shows no other routes across the state here except this road and the four-laner; roads that branch away travel for miles to the north and south, ending at ranches or oil derricks. To tell the truth, I'm not really watching for the way-points or too bothered about finding the near-crash site. It really doesn't matter. It's not very Zen to follow a strict route. For all I know, Pirsig made the whole thing up to suit his narrative. "Much has been changed for rhetorical purposes," he wrote.

If there's one thing Pirsig knows about, it's rhetoric—the art of persuasive communication. Having resumed his "normal" life and earned his master's in journalism at Minnesota in 1958, he worked awhile as an advertising copywriter. Soon he moved with his family to take up a teaching position at Montana State College in Bozeman, where he specialized in rhetoric and advanced technical writing. This was a fairly basic school, much less prestigious than the University of Montana; students called it Moo-Yoo, the udder university. "You'd ask a student why his face was all bloodied up," Pirsig recalled years later, "and he'd reply, 'This guy said a Chevy's better than a Ford.' " But academia was a step up from the advertising business, where he'd hit a low point writing promotional blurbs about mortuary cosmetics for trade magazines.

It was here that he began to develop into an academic radical, withholding grades from his students to keep them focused on the *process* of education instead of just its results. It was here that he met a fellow English instructor who introduced him to Native American anthropology, prompting him to visit the Northern Cheyenne Reservation and try peyote. It was here that he started taking sleeping pills. And it was here that another teacher at the college casually commented to him one day, while watering her plants, "I hope you are teaching Quality to your students."

Most anyone else would just have nodded and said, "Sure," but Pirsig was not most anyone else. He was a hyperintellectual who agonized over the metaphysical. "Quality," he wrote in *Zen and the Art*, "you know what it is, yet you don't know what it is. . . .

Obviously some things are better than others . . . but what's the 'betterness'? . . . So round and round you go, spinning mental wheels and nowhere finding any place to get traction. What the hell is Quality? What *is* it?"

So began his spiral into madness.

As the road heads west and the fields stretch away to high, flat-topped buttes in the distance, wisps of soil pick up on either side and swirl into dust devils in the eddying wind. Yesterday's gusts would have blown them away, but today the air is still, circulating locally in concentrated blasts. One of these mini tornados, perhaps fifty feet high, picks up in a field to the right and follows me awhile before fading back into the ground.

My feet come off the pegs and drag along the road, and I stretch and once again have the feeling I enjoyed on the very first day. Not the flying I felt on Bill's trike—nothing will match that—but flying as the bike blends into the road and into me and the miles pass slowly but steadily. The tightened chain makes for less noise and a smoother ride.

Up ahead a heavy truck turns from a driveway onto the road, and I catch up to it quickly, swooping past; a week ago, I might have cursed when he pulled blindly into my path, but today I'm relaxed and on schedule and it just doesn't matter.

The town of Forsyth passes, and the road pulls away completely from the interstate to find its own route north of the Yellowstone. The horizon will show the mountains soon. The hills are growing, and the road is starting to wind, letting the bike bank and corner around the curves. The route straightens again, and here's a stretch where that treacherous car might have appeared, with enough distance to build speed and confidence in overtaking but providing no escape for the oncoming motorcyclists. The ditch is deep to the side—that would do it.

Some of Pirsig's events may be questionable, but as a tour guide he's dead-on. When he says there's a tree, there's a tree, even thirty-six years later.

A little farther on is a strange town named Hysham. Its buildings are large and cavernous, and in the center, right under the water tower, is the white stucco Yucca Theater, which might as well be in New Mexico for its Santa Fe style, except a life-size white concrete buffalo stands guard outside the door. Opposite is a huge bar and restaurant—perhaps this is the "enormous, high-ceilinged old place" where the shaken-up riders pigged out on junk food. I don't bother to stop. I'm in the rhythm now, with no phone, no radio, no distractions from my thoughts and the ride itself.

The road runs straight west through the ranchland until it reaches some hills and then twists south along their base. Now this is truly fun—swoopy, let-it-out-and-holler fun. At 60 miles an hour, the bike is leaning well into the curves, and Jackie New's horn toots at the cattle that watch from the fields on the left.

It's almost like bull riding, and just as I let out a ringing *yee-hah,* the road turns without warning to unpaved crap on a corner and an almighty pothole bottoms the suspension, almost throwing the bike into the fence alongside. I get back under control, but another pothole opens up under the front wheel, and the handlebars twist to the side as the bike is leaning, as if I'd just hit a giant rock, sending me into the oncoming lane, where once again the bike regains its composure only to smack into a series of ruts that bounce the luggage all over the rear of the seat.

I can't touch the brakes, I can't touch the throttle, and the bike's heading for the ditch.

Slow down. Let things calm down, and steer back gently into the lane. The bike kicks about but finally straightens out, and control returns with the lower speed—and a pickup truck appears from around the approaching bend, which I'd have hit head-on if I'd been just a few seconds later coming down the road.

Whoa! I pull over. My hands are shaking.

A hundred feet up the road, just before a sign that says "Rough Road—25 MPH," is a plastic pipe coming from the hill's undergrowth, with clear water splashing from it onto a tree stump. The stump's been placed there to rest containers on, so I ride slowly up to it and park. No other traffic passes for a long while; I squat beside the bike, beside the road, and think about the closeness of this escape.

Finally, no longer trembling but in need of a wake-up, I go to the pipe and take a long, cool drink. Off to the south there's a giant cloud of brown dirt rising from an irrigated field. Another dust devil?

It's too far away to see the cause, but there've been enough devils now. These things happen in threes—everything happens in threes. I wipe my wet hands on my jeans, put the helmet back on, and sit on the bike, then kick it into life and pull away slowly. The road stays bad for a few more miles, but I stay below the 25-mile-an-hour limit and it's no big deal.

What was it back in Wisconsin? Life's fragile and death's unexpected—the eagle showed that.

The road passes flat-topped rocks shaped like mushrooms. An abandoned settler's house nestled on a curve with a huge fallen tree in its yard tells a story for another day. Soon the road rejoins the interstate and heads straight west to Laurel, and I take it and hold the speed at 70, easy to do now that the wind's pushing from the east.

There's another stop to make first, though, and I pull off at the point near Billings where the highway from the northeast joins the highway from the southeast. Somewhere here is a coffee shop where I paused nineteen years ago coming up from the Little Bighorn site.

None of it's familiar—just large truck stops with pumps and trucks and RVs, each with a gift shop and restaurant—so I head to the Flying J for a coffee. The weather to the west has begun to look ominous, and the waitress asks which direction I'm headed. When she hears that it's west to Laurel, she breaks the news: "There's rain over to the west, and hail, too. You might want to make it just one cup or stay here for a while. I never like riding in the rain."

She doesn't look like a bike rider, but I guess you can't tell anymore: doctors and waitresses ride Harleys. Hell—Krumpe couldn't even reach the ground from his saddle, and that didn't stop him from riding.

It was different nineteen years ago, when the waitress sat me at the back of the coffee shop, poured me a coffee, gave me the bill, and suggested I drink and pay and leave. Must have been the dirty leathers, because I'd shaved that morning for the judge. I forced four cups of coffee out of her before I left, riding north for the Canadian border.

Climax, Sask.
13 August 1985

It was time to change the oil on the motorcycle. This was my second day alone with the bike after leaving Sturgis and it had to be ready for the empty road.

At the shop, somebody sold me two pints of oil and gave me a pan and told me to stay outside. Insurance restrictions, they said. I loosened the big bolt from underneath the engine and watched the oil pour out. The wind caught the stream of hot, thin fluid and whipped it around, splashing it onto the ground, making a pattern on the pavement and spitting at my hand as I tried to move the pan to catch it. The wind always takes me by surprise.

So much for their insurance restrictions. Because of them, the shop now has an oil stain on its pavement.

After, I headed north, back across the Missouri. Somewhere near the Canada border, I ran out of gas and had to push the bike for half an hour to a gas station, the first in more than eighty miles.

Fresh oil, a strong and well-adjusted engine, determination and youth—all of it hobbled by misjudging the distance to the next gas station. As I pushed the lifeless bike along the road in the heat, flies and mosquitoes humming all around, blinking from sweat, I made a promise: never again. For the sake of a spoonful of gas, it's come to this.

That was the first and last time I've ever run out of gas. Usually it's a lesson that needs to be learned only once.

The rain stayed away, and now here's a Super 8 at Laurel. The Zen riders are believed to have stayed at the Hurzler Hotel, which has long since closed down and now lies empty, awaiting renovation. They slept well and enjoyed the cool air from the mountains, but now there's nothing to be seen because of the low cloud, and it really doesn't matter. That pickup truck was an almighty shock, much more so than the Buick, and now the weather's closing in for the ride tomorrow over the Beartooth.

The TV forecast at the Flying J shows rain in the mountains, which won't help at all, especially if the rain will be snow at the summit. Photos on the Internet show the road closed by many feet of snow just last July, and the dark clouds of doubt are hanging now as surely as those over the mountain.

At the best of times, riding in the rain is a miserable experience. On the way to Minneapolis, there was a whole day of rain and wind and cold, with the spray from the trucks knocking visibility down to a minimum.

For much of the time I'd been stuck behind a window-frame delivery truck and unable to pass—the truck would speed up whenever the road widened and slow right down when traffic appeared. There was a picture on its back door of a window, painted to look like you were peering through the panes at the pretty landscape on the other side, with sunshine and flowers and green leafy trees. "Kolbe and Kolbe," it said. "You'll like how we do the curves." But its slipstream was bashing me from side to side like a beaten boxer, catching the broad sides of the luggage and pushing around the bike's tall front wheel. It was a cruel irony to be stared down by the scenic countryside on the truck's door. I didn't like how it did the curves at all.

My boots, supposed to be waterproof, were soaked through, and my feet were wet; my jacket, supposed to be waterproof, was soaked through, and my leather jacket underneath was close to saturation. My gloves—well, the dye stained my hands such a dark black that when I finally stopped at a restaurant, the waitress did a double take as she handed over the menu.

Outside, the rain bounced high off the pavement. A couple of young women in camisoles and shorts sprinted out to the SUV that a friend had just started up in the parking lot, only to find themselves waiting as the friend scrambled to unlock the passenger doors. They were soaked through in seconds. I'd spent three hours in that deluge.

I drank coffee until the rain let up a little (which was a lot of coffee), then filled the bike's tank before riding west into the heaviest downpour yet. Cars were pulled over on the side of the road, and sheets of water spread everywhere on the asphalt. There was no underpass and trees were not a safe shelter, so I pressed on. And after ten minutes the storm passed and the sun came out; within an hour I was dry and the rain was just a memory.

A memory that's come back to haunt me now. It could be the same again tomorrow—or worse, with snow and switchbacks. Better think this through in a place that's warm and dry.

The Super 8 is bright and the sheets are clean and there's lots of hot water and the TV works well, the first time all these amenities have come together since I left Minneapolis. Families are checking in, carrying their suitcases from the car, and later taking a swim in the pool. There's even a truck parked outside with a pair of immaculate Harley-Davidsons strapped onto its bed, all shiny chrome and polished paint, staying clean on the way to Sturgis while the owners stop to launder their clothes.

In the room there's finally an Internet connection, also the first since Minneapolis. My in-box is clogged with spam, in the middle of which is an e-mail from my wife. It's a short message—she's concerned for my safety and missing my company—written a couple of days ago as I was checking into the room in Lemmon.

The message doesn't cheer me, alone in the sterile room. It's a reminder that I'm very far away from those who love me. I wanted to be here, to get away completely for a while and think things through, but at the end of the day, alone and distant and coming to rest, perspective changes. A week's not long, but it's a lifetime on the road. No need to write a reply—I'll call in the morning.

There's a steak house around the corner, and it's a comfortable place to sit and read the descriptions in the pink book of what I may encounter tomorrow: "the dark ominous mass" of the mountain, "snowfields in June," "places where you could throw a stone and it would drop thousands of feet before coming to rest." The weather was chilly but sunny and dry for the Zen riders; it's going to be cold, wet, and slippery for me.

Why am I doing this, again? Not so sure now. To discover something? To relate more directly to the book that inspired me? To see some of the beautiful sights that Pirsig describes so eloquently in his spare narrative? To get away from the wife and kids? Or is it to get back in touch with the person who rode this way nineteen years ago? Great—that guy ran out of gas a mile from a service station. Has anything really changed? It's all well and fine while it's fun and teaches something useful, but it's ridiculous if all it's teaching is that I'm an idiot who's rapidly riding up to potential serious accident number 3.

Look at the warnings, which have been fairly clear so far: Darrell in Oakes pretty much stating flat out that Jackie New isn't safe for the Beartooth Pass; a Buick coming straight at me just when there is nowhere to go; a pickup truck, one of a handful of vehicles to drive on a stretch of crappy road in an hour, nearly wiping me out when I lose control at full speed. Above all is the eagle staring with its glassy eyes, lifeless proof that the very strongest can be killed in an instant.

The steak comes. It's good. I put the book away and unfold the map, studying the twisting contours of the Beartooth while chewing the tender meat. Hairpin after hairpin as it rises in a tight squiggle five thousand feet above the mountain's base. The flavor of the steak—better than the Miles City burger, better than the Mobridge submarine—helps calm my thoughts, and the beer that washes it down helps me sort things through.

There've been so many restaurants over the years and so many maps studied. I'm always looking for squiggly lines like this, and I've never avoided a challenging road. The fact is I didn't hit the Buick, nor did I hit the pickup, and who knows if Darrell's ever been west of the Missouri. The bike is running well, and Bill showed clearly this morning that if you want to do something badly enough, you can do it. All that today showed was that I should slow down a little more and not be cocky on unfamiliar roads. So the clutch is slipping and the brakes fade easily—slow down and they'll be fine.

Exist in the moment—that's one of the great lessons of Zen itself. And when the second beer comes, I remember a haiku that sums up a great chunk of Eastern thought—the notion that intuitive insight comes from direct experience, which can be neither taught nor told:

> *When walking, just walk.*
> *When sitting, just sit.*
> *Above all, don't wobble.*

If the Pirsigs could do it on that overloaded little Honda and the Sutherlands could do it on that stiff old Beemer, surely I can make it on Jackie New. And if not, it won't be for lack of trying. Time to raise the beer mug and tap it on the map. "Here's to you, Bill. This is for you."

The condensation from the mug leaves a smudge on the map, blurring the ink of the mountains and puckering the paper.

. . .

At the motel, sleep comes long after midnight.

The eyes are moving from the corner, floating, flying over the bed. Wings are beating the air, whipping up devils in the room. Feathers brush my face; talons scrape my head. The eagle is flying around the room, diving and rising, clutching and knocking. It doesn't want to be here. It's caged, and it wants to break the window. It flies into the glass hard and wheels around to fly at the window again and again.

In the morning the TV shows black rain symbols all over the route south to the Beartooth. Everything's wet outside, although it's no longer raining. The Harley-Davidsons have gone, and my dirt bike looks very alone, chained to a lamppost in the middle of the empty parking lot. I reach for the phone and make the overseas call. The machine kicks in and I hang up. I want conversation, to speak with my boys and my wife.

The saddlebags are not yet repacked; still holding the phone, I reach in and take out the mysterious birthday box, wrapped in tissue paper and sealed in its plastic bag, awaiting the end of this journey. I turn it over and over, then replace it.

What was there to say on the phone, anyway? Maybe I know how to maintain my motorcycle, but it's way more difficult to find the right words to maintain a relationship.

I'll ride slowly today, and carefully. I'm going over that mountain.

CHAPTER EIGHT

Wyoming

THE CLEAR WATER in the shallow stream beside the road flows swiftly, tumbling over pebbles and rocks in its hurry to get to lower ground. The road is long and straight and belies its steep ascent—I've risen a thousand feet in the last few miles as the route heads toward the stream's source in the dark mountain ahead.

The peak has been winking through the cloud for a while now, higher and closer than expected. The road goes from wet to dry to wet again as the dark skies swirl and separate, never clearing but mixing together in different shades of moving gray.

Pirsig wrote that this route was not planned beforehand but a detour to take advantage of the scenery, decided upon just that morning. Memories came back to Pirsig of his visits to the high country when he lived as Phaedrus, and he was intrigued by what he could remember and curious to have a look.

They were probably running ahead of schedule, too. After all, straight through on the interstate it's just 130 miles to Bozeman, a couple of hours tops, but cutting south this way and over the roof of America, then through Yellowstone Park, it's at least twice that distance and much slower going. If all goes as it's supposed to, I'll stay tonight at the cottages north of the park, where the motor-cycle manual should be waiting.

I'm an automaton now, barely thinking. "When riding, just ride." I stopped a little while ago to put on my waterproof over-trousers and rubber boot covers, for the water on the road was spraying up from the front tire and splashing below the knees; that's okay for a short while, but if the road stays wet and it keeps on splashing, I'll be damp and cold down there in half an hour.

I got a late start this morning, not pulling away until checkout time, eleven o'clock, reluctant to leave the motel's warmth. There was a spread of cereals and juice and coffee in the breakfast room, and I ate while listening to a pair of mothers and daughters get to know each other at the table opposite. One was returning from Washington to Michigan, the other driving just as far as North Dakota. The little girls watched a cartoon on the corner TV as their mothers spooned food into them and talked about how far they'd get today. The woman from Michigan hoped to be home late tomorrow; the woman going to North Dakota said she'd arrive tonight but had no idea what to expect—she was moving there to live with a man she barely knew in a house she'd never seen. "It's not very big," she said, "but it's supposed to be comfortable. I hope it's comfortable. It's difficult starting all over again."

The bike's running well and plodding along the straight, climbing road with a full tank of gas. The clouds are thick over the mountain ahead. So much for *Zen and the Art of Motorcycle Maintenance;* this is more like *Lord of the Rings.*

Pirsig had enjoyed the mountains, finding a peace and solitude there that allowed him to think with a clarity impossible at home. Life was getting tough down in Bozeman. The college had plans to turn itself into a university, and Pirsig was opposed, arguing that titles and qualifications should be secondary to the principle of pure learning—a bit rich coming from somebody who'd already earned two degrees. The governor noticed his opposition and apparently placed him on a list of fifty radicals to be monitored, but then, Eleanor Roosevelt had once been banned from speaking on the campus. Montana in the late 1950s was not known for liberal views.

Life was also tough at home. Pirsig—Phaedrus—would spend

the night thinking, distracted from his family and his teaching and all else that mattered. "We used to ride in the car to look for you," said Chris in *Zen and the Art*.

"Whoever saw you first would get a nickel. And then we'd stop and let you in the back of the car and you wouldn't even talk to us."

"I was thinking hard then."

"That's what Mom said."

If that really happened, Chris would have been about four, peering through the windows, jockeying with his younger brother for the first glimpse of the self-absorbed professor they were supposed to love.

Nobody in Bozeman could have imagined that Pirsig would thread these experiences together a dozen years later to create one of the enduring works of twentieth-century American literature. At the time he believed he was thinking about "Quality": subject, object, or whatever. But what he was actually thinking about was the very beginning—and the very core—of *Zen and the Art of Motorcycle Maintenance*.

The rain starts properly just after Red Lodge, the gateway to the Beartooth Pass and really the last chance to turn around before encountering the looming wall of the Absaroka Range.

The Zen riders stopped here to eat, but I stop only to take more waterproof clothing from the sailor's bag. I'm already wearing the electric vest on top of a T-shirt and underneath a sweater, though it's not yet switched on—with the leather jacket as well as the Gore-Tex jacket, I'm not yet cold. I'll unplug the GPS unit, too. If water hits the exposed socket that provides its power, it could blow the bike's single fuse.

This is just a light rain, enough to keep the road damp and soak through any clothing that's unprotected but not enough to be much of a hazard. The greater danger is the poor visibility from the fog that's starting to build as the road continues to rise. Full-face helmets are notorious for their visors misting over easily as the warmer air that's trapped from the rider's breath condenses on the inside. Normally it's best to ride with the visor open a crack to allow better air circulation, but this can't be done in fog if my glasses aren't to mist over. I exhale downward now, pulling in the lower lip and pointing out the top lip so the warm breath leaves the helmet as quickly as possible. The visor mists over on the outside, too, and I wipe it clear with a wet glove as often as is practical, streaking droplets everywhere in a fine smear of water.

There are expensive sprays and creams to apply to visors to prevent all this, some of which sometimes actually work, but when the fog's coming in as thick as this mountain soup, you're better off just lifting the visor and squinting into the wind. If I didn't wear glasses for driving, it might be better to blink back the water, but then there's nothing to prevent a speck of crud from flitting directly onto the eyeball and making matters far worse.

I keep pushing on at the mountain's base, slowly and steadily. The road turns hard to the right and starts to climb all the more.

Traffic is light, with cars few and far between. Commercial vehicles are forbidden past the wooden gate that closes the road, but sometimes RVs make their way up the slope, usually with a line of cars behind them. In the past, riding a motorcycle on a road like this, I found it frustrating to come up behind slower-moving traffic, but this time I'll go carefully, pulling over whenever cars come from behind to let them pass. Should have done this behind that window-frame delivery truck. I'll not catch up to anybody here, that's for sure.

Hairpin turns twist the road back and forth as it ascends the side of the mountain. The speed limit is posted at 15 miles an hour, and that's just fine. I stay in second gear and push steadily on, wiping the visor, exhaling rhythmically downward and out the helmet, climbing and climbing.

There's no proper sound inside the helmet except for the muffled chug of the bike's engine—no wind, no birds, no machinery off in the distance. I can hear my breathing, regular but beginning to labor from the unfamiliar altitude, and after a while I hear the sound of blood pumping through my ears.

It's so hard to concentrate on just riding and not thinking. It's no good.

A memory comes of being on a silent plane far away, flying through the night over the Sahara, looking out the window from high above onto the black sand that melds seamlessly into the dark sky, filled with stars and lit by a brilliant moon. The aircraft's engines were humming in the background, and the only other sound was the soft hiss of the air vents—and blood pumping in my ears. I was scared, flying alone into Nigeria to spend an uncertain couple of weeks working in Lagos, having been primed with stories of corruption and robbery and violence.

Eventually the plane began to descend, and after another hour, just before midnight, the pilot announced that we were ready to land. The lights stayed off, but outside the night was still unclear as the plane hummed lower and lower. Small specks of light below became more focused and showed themselves to be fires, lit in garbage cans on the street. Nobody spoke, and few passengers looked outside, but I kept staring through the window, searching for any familiar sight, my heart racing.

Climbing the mountain now, switching back and forth from east to west and north to south, I stare straight ahead and try not to think of what's outside, on the edge of the pavement: a drop into the fog to the road I just traveled on, a hundred feet or more down. When a gap clears in the mist, a glance shows the narrow ribbon farther down than I expected. Keep looking ahead! Straight now to the next hairpin turn, staying in second gear, not once touching the brakes, climbing and climbing.

The silence of the mist is toying with my mind, and I try to blank myself away inside the clothing and the helmet, but an image comes of the airport at Lagos, one of the most corrupt and dangerous cities in Africa.

Pale and nervous, I was set aside by the immigration officer for a shakedown but released when a richer-looking family came through. At the luggage carousel, calloused hands grabbed at my rucksack. The porter, deaf and mute, scurried the bags through customs, then produced written notes to hustle the payment he'd arranged with the customs agent. I refused to pay, not understanding the deal. A friend's friend on the sidewalk waved him away and drove me through the dark, rutted streets to a cheap hotel. My room was on the sixth floor. The elevator didn't work, and my companion passed on some local wisdom as we climbed the stairs.

"Never leave money in your room. Never leave your room carrying money. And don't trust anyone you don't know. Life's fragile here and everything's unexpected."

I've reached the Rock Creek Vista. I pull in to stretch and shake away these old memories. The elevation is above nine thousand feet here, and the mist is thicker and colder, leaving nothing to see at all. A minivan pulls in behind me, and a family in shorts and rain jackets spews out to use the washrooms. They don't bother with the "Welcome to Montana" map on the display board, which is mostly obscured behind streaks of water. As an afterthought, I ask the oldest man, the father, to take a photo as proof of my having been here, and he does so from inside his van, returning the camera with a thumbs-up.

The bike's still running. I keep going, climbing and climbing.

Straightaway I'm back in Lagos. It's been locked away so long, this memory, that it won't be easily shut back up.

Safe in the room, I used my camera's timer to take a photo of myself, wide-eyed and culture shocked. The phone that cost extra didn't work, and the TV picked up only one station, which had gone off the air for the day. I swallowed a malaria pill and slept fitfully. In the morning a fruitless taxi ride into the congested city cost five times the going rate, but as the days progressed and people emerged who could be trusted, the shock faded and the savvy began; leaving two weeks later, never to return, I had a clearer sense of the way things worked.

Nothing seemed to operate at all at the airport; by any logic the entire city should have shut down and folded in on itself. But there's always a way and the spirit always prevails, and Lagos is still there, still struggling, living well and living rough, making the best of what it has.

Each day came slowly and steadily back then, as I climbed those stairs every evening to the safety of the room and its protected space to recall the lessons of the city—direct experience, neither taught nor told.

This road still climbs, but it's straighter and less precipitous. High sticks, twelve feet tall at least, mark the side of the pavement at intervals for the snowplows, which are ready year-round. There's no longer a plummet to the road below, and now there are no guardrails, just foggy meadows with pale, short flowers. Lagos fades and a haiku comes forward, another famous piece of Zen wisdom:

> *No sky at all;*
> *No earth at all, and still*
> *the snowflakes fall.*

There's snow in the air!

The rain is snow, not sticking to the road but melting as it falls. Smudges of white appear in the field alongside, and there's an overlook ahead with a sign that's coming through the mist and—

Yes! The very top at last!

There's a wooden sign beside the meadow: "Elevation 10,947 Ft." Wyoming now. There's little to see up here in the mist. The fields drop away on all sides into grayness; water is everywhere in the air, and flakes of snow flutter gently through it, disappearing before they hit the ground.

Can this really be the very top? Is this as high as it gets? And was that really all it took, just a slow and steady hand on the throttle?

Of course not—there are other mountains yet to climb. Zen itself teaches that there is no final mountain peak, that there isn't even a mountain—the only thing that matters is the *act* of climbing, and the greater the ordeal, the better it is. It's not the result that's important but the immediate here and now.

And here and now I'm on the top of this mountain, and it's cold and wet and bleak and feels wonderful.

It was Zen that brought me here and Zen that helped get me to the top. Just as readers who like motorcycles are attracted to Pirsig's book, so are readers who appreciate Zen. And both sides are often disappointed that *Zen and the Art* isn't really about either motorcycles or Zen. But then, Pirsig states this clearly right up front.

The title came a year or so before the journey even began. Pirsig knew what he wanted to tell an audience about "Quality" and had prepared an essay for Sutherland that touched on their differing views on motorcycle maintenance. As students of Eastern philosophy, they were familiar with Eugen Herrigel's seminal *Zen in the Art of Archery,* published in English in the '50s, which argues that even ordinary tasks can have a spiritual dimension— tasks like shooting arrows or fixing bikes. "The 'art' of archery" wrote Herrigel, "does not mean the ability of the sportsman, which can be controlled, more or less, by bodily exercises, but an ability whose origin is to be sought in spiritual exercises and whose aim consists in hitting a spiritual goal, so that fundamentally the marksman aims at himself and may even succeed in hitting himself." The title of Pirsig's essay, and the larger book that he knew he wanted to write, came from this text.

But if there was to be a book, Pirsig needed a story to hang it on. The motorcycle journey with Sutherland had already been planned; Chris was to come along for the father-son bonding experience. Before the bikes' wheels even turned, Pirsig had pitched his proposal to as many publishers as he could track down.

"I am working on a book with the somewhat unusual title *Zen and the Art of Motorcycle Maintenance* and am now looking for a publisher," he wrote on June 6, 1968.

"The book is, as the title says, about Zen and about motorcycle maintenance, but it is also about a unification of spiritual feeling and technological thought. Part of its thesis is that the division between these is a deep root of the discontent of our age, and it offers some heterodox solutions. Two sample pages are enclosed. If you are interested in seeing more, please let me know."

There's a famous story of perseverance, according to which the proposal was pitched to 122 publishers, with only one accepting it. In fact, that is not quite the case. For a start, Pirsig sent identical copies of the body of his letter to all 122 publishers; it could as easily have been 1,000—the '60s equivalent of spam. As well, 22 expressed an interest, but only one person, Jim Landis, a twentysomething editor at William Morrow who'd been hired just a year earlier, would stick around through the full four years of writing to accept the final manuscript. The pitch had been addressed to Morrow's editor in chief, John Willey, and consigned to what publishers call the slush pile with other unsolicited proposals.

"What I guess was unusual about Bob's letter was that he'd gone to the trouble of getting John Willey's name, so this was a slush-pile letter with a difference," recalled Landis when I wrote to him. "Had Bob not gotten Willey's name, it's possible the letter might not ever have made its way to me."

Landis wrote back on June 10 with encouragement. Pirsig had his response before the journey began. At the top of the Beartooth he knew the ascent of the pass would be part of the book.

"He told us at the time that 'I've been looking over your shoulder,' " Sutherland had said back in Minneapolis. "I never saw him making any notes, but then the man's a genius. A tortured genius and far from perfect, but you can't overestimate his brilliance."

Beside the mountain-pass sign is a Harley-Davidson cruiser, its rider standing alongside rubbing his hands together, dressed in a leather jacket and chaps and an open helmet. Florida plates. Bet he's cold.

He's traveling home from Seattle, he says, but took this day trip without realizing how cold it could be up here. We chat a little, and I offer him my spare dry gloves, which he can return a few thousand feet below in Cooke City, but he turns down the offer. He's looking forward to a coffee there, he says, maybe with some rum in it.

On the other side of this mountain, the road drops a little, turns to the left, and the fog begins to clear. After just a minute the road can be seen switchbacking down through the meadows; no steep drops but plenty of snow in the dips and creases of the land. The fog's thinning quickly, and it's not long before patches of blue sky can be seen through deep holes in the cloud above. The road is dry here, except for streams of water melting from the scattered banks of snow.

I ride past a snowbank where tourists are tossing snowballs at one another; farther along to the left, horses are galloping their riders along a trail; to the right, boaters are fishing on a small lake.

A thousand feet below the summit at a gift shop, a couple with a big Honda Gold Wing give a nod and a smile as I pull in to park. I buy postcards and a bumper sticker and go outside to clean some of the grime off Jackie New's front fender to make a space for the sticker. "Beartooth Highway, WY," it says. From now on that sticker will be a reminder that both of us made it to the top and over to the other side.

It's downright sunny in Cooke City. There are rows and rows of motorcycles lined up in front of the restaurants and bars on Main Street, nearly all of them clean and glinting chrome, unlike the vehicles coming down from the summit, where a dark cloud still hangs. These riders have come from the west, through Yellowstone, and most are going to turn right back around again to avoid the weather I've just ridden through.

The guy at the summit with the Harley is here, too, but he's ignoring me now. We passed back and forth on the way down, riding separately but each assuming the lead when the other pulled over to take in a view of meadows, woods, lakes, or streams. We waved at each other a couple of times but gave it up after a while, and now, surrounded by other Harley riders in town and no doubt enthralling them with his tale of survival, he doesn't even acknowledge my nod as I park at the end of a long row of Hogs.

The best coffee I could find comes in a foam cup from a young girl with a French accent, but it tastes weak and disgusting and ends up in the trash, still almost full. Rum wouldn't have made any difference. Everything's overpriced, so I get back on the bike and head west again along the narrow highway that cuts a path through an evergreen forest.

Just a few minutes later and I'm at Yellowstone, America's first great park.

Pirsig hated places like this. His route west skirts the famous attractions, avoiding Mount Rushmore and the Devils Tower. He visited Yellowstone only because the approach intrigued him and then spent the least possible amount of time there. He was happiest high above the tree line, far beyond the encroachments of towns and cities, building fires against the cold and damp, free in the thin air to just sit and think and explore what he called "the high country of the mind," where thoughts have fewer boundaries and new trails of philosophy are waiting to be blazed. A place where, Albert Einstein wrote—and is quoted in *Zen and the Art*— "a finely tempered nature longs to escape from his noisy cramped surroundings into the silence of the high mountains where the eye ranges freely through the still pure air and fondly traces out the restful contours apparently built for eternity."

That's not for me, though. I'll take a snug Super 8 any day, or an attentive server at a decent steak house. By all means, wander the trails of natural beauty all day long, but it helps to know there's someplace warm and cozy waiting as the night draws in, as there will be today at the cottages at Gardiner.

It's a smooth ride through the meadows of Yellowstone, passing the vistas or pausing whenever the cars all park to look at a lone elk or bison far away. It's still a revelation that the bike just stayed in second gear all the way up this pass that Darrell had touted as such a killer and now is coasting down the gentle slopes in fourth gear after the first mile or so of mild switchbacks. No fancy GPS. Just a single piston pumping up and down, driving a wheel. A seat in the middle and a world inside my helmet. I never even turned on the electric vest.

The clouds are dark off to the northeast, but I'm still headed west and there'll be no more rain today. The road is dry and smooth. The traffic's busy in the park, but at least the air is warm now. The weight of the mountain has been lifted from my shoulders, and this bike and I are capable of anything.

I pause at a overlook to gaze over stunning miles of river valley that drop away far below. The bike's parked right on the edge. The light is fabulous, with striking shadows from the rain off to the side. A little car with New York plates drives in, and a man and three teenage girls, probably his daughters, climb out. They're relaxed and laughing, and he tells the girls he'll be a while as he sets up a camera, so they giggle and chat some more at the edge of this gorgeous view. When I ask, he's happy to take a photo of me with Jackie New, pictured from behind, me gazing wistfully across the valley, but the picture on the digital screen is not what I expect: instead of a conquering hero I see a shabby motorcyclist with creased clothing and scraggly hair.

I ride over the river into Mammoth Hot Springs and pause for a cool drink in the town square. Then I'm out the North Entrance and headed to the Hillcrest Cottages at Gardiner. The river runs alongside the road, and this time I'm headed in the same direction, going with the flow on the downhill slope.

When I reach the town, I see the cottages on the right, just as Pirsig described them. The travelers rested here for the night, relaxed and content in the warmth, sitting on a bench and listening to the water bumbling over the boulders in the river below. It was a big night for Pirsig, for the next day he'd ride into Bozeman and meet his friends, who'd last seen him as Phaedrus.

He was crossing the river from one life to another, sliding into the skin of the distracted academic who'd been there all the way from Minnesota, pressing for space on the little bike as Chris hung on behind.

There's a sign on the office door that says the owner is off cleaning a cabin, but he's not so far away, puttering around in a hat that says "I'd Rather Be Fishing." He opens up the office, and there on the counter is a large FedEx package with my name on it. *Thank you!* Three hundred foolscap pages containing everything anyone ever needed to know about a 1985 Suzuki DR600.

"I guess that's for you," says the owner, Art. "I figured I'd see you soon enough."

He hands over the key to cabin 9—there's no clue to which was the Pirsigs' cabin, though it doesn't really matter—and I mention that I'm following the Zen route.

"Ah, yes," Art says. "We get people like you from time to time. There was a professor from Rochester here just a few weeks ago, said he was doing the same thing."

He says the cabins haven't changed much at all from the way they were thirty-six years ago. This is heartening. Pirsig makes a point of praising their solid construction and even compliments the original owner, who built the place. For Pirsig this was a time to pause and reflect on greater matters, and shabby accommodations would have been a terrible distraction.

I ask Art if the town has changed much.

"Sure, the weather's something bad," he says. "It's been so dry the last ten years that all around is changing. Last year the grass was all killed by the sun, burning it away with no moisture to protect it. And the rivers are running more shallow, which heats them up and stresses the fish. They had to close three of the biggest rivers around for fishing last year because of the drought. They might not be the same again."

Cabin 9, at the near end of the row, is clean and basic, a little kitchenette at one side and a tiny fiberglass shower stall behind a door at the back. As usual, the luggage starts taking over the floor and the bed.

I set up the laptop on a small table and turn it on to download the day's photos, but it doesn't want to boot properly; it's searching for some missing file. Who knows what's going on? There's nothing mechanical in a computer—no obvious cause and effect—so I set the drive to defragment and walk away as the little colored boxes on the screen start flipping by. Besides, the important thing now is the bike's manual, to see the secrets behind the clutch and be reminded of the elusive thing that needs adjusting if the bike is not to drop a valve into the piston, as Jackie Blue did all those years ago.

It's only five o'clock, and there are still a few more hours of daylight—this must be my earliest arrival so far. Time to get something to eat.

The main road is a strip mall of rafting companies, business after seasonal business sitting high on the cliff above the Yellowstone. Whatever commerce has been lost to the struggling tourist fishing industry is being chased by the white-water rafters: the Yellowstone Raft Company, Wild West Rafting, Montana Whitewater, even the Flying Pig, all of them lined up along the river. Battered school buses are coming and going, packed with teenagers and towing flat trailers with huge rubber rafts strapped to them.

At a rafting company where some very fit, very tanned people are coiling rope, a bare-chested guy suggests the Park Street Grill as a decent place to eat. "I like it there," he says. "Good food and not too expensive." But across the bridge the Park Street Grill seems pretty new and fancy inside, and entrées are going for $20, more for the steaks.

I keep walking. The Pirsigs ate in town, so perhaps there's still a place that was in business then. Sure enough, on the other side of the main street is the Town Café, with a sign out front that says "Family Owned and Operated since 1967." It's packed, too.

That'll do. In through the gift shop, past the tables, I take a seat at the counter, order a steak, and spread out the manual.

"I had to phone home today and ask Dad for another five hundred dollars," says a girl on the chair alongside me, picking over a salad and talking to a friend beside her.

"He gave it to you?"

"Sure he did. He always does."

"You know, Kelly, you're such an all-American spoiled brat."

"Yeah. It's great, isn't it?"

The steak was good and I've bought a couple of cans of cold Budweiser from the gas station and now the tools are spread out in front of the cottage, ready to go at those valves. The manual states the correct clearances, and they're not the figures I'd recalled.

It also describes the cam chain tensioner, hidden behind the left engine cover, the chain that grew so slack it destroyed the top end of Jackie Blue's engine. It won't need adjusting today because the distinctive warning rattle hasn't sounded yet, but it probably will before this trip's done if it's left untouched. The oil must be drained for access to that adjustment, though, so I'll wait on it for now. The level's fine—that's good.

This is another comfortable spot for maintenance, with a little bench to sit on and check the manual. It will be more involved than changing the oil or lubing the chain, so I take some time to prepare, pulling the right tools from the grocery bag and lining them up as a doctor might arrange scalpels. No hurry now. Remember what it says in *Zen and the Art:* "Peace of mind produces right values, right values produce right thoughts. Right thoughts produce right actions."

The gas tank has to come off to provide access to the top of the engine, and for that the seat must come off first, for it helps to lock the tank into place. And before even that, the plastic side panels must come off so that the bolts that hold down the seat can be loosened. Sounds involved, but it's not and takes only a few minutes; I once spent an hour and a half struggling with a Kawasaki sport bike just to get at the battery, which was concealed within the frame.

When the side panels come off, I carry them into the cabin to keep them out of sight—nobody needs to see the keys and the credit card taped to their insides.

The cottages are filling up now. There's a pair of bikes parked opposite, an unlikely combination of Harley-Davidson Heritage Softail and BMW K1200 GT, a laid-back American cruiser and a German tourer that's comfortable all day at 100 miles an hour. Their owners aren't around. Maybe they're at the Park Street Grill.

And just as the tank's coming off, a pickup truck drives over from the office, and a large man with a goatee steps out from behind the wheel. A woman gets out the other side and carries a suitcase into their cabin while he walks over to say hello and to see what's happening. He never says his name, but it comes out quickly that he has a Kawasaki Drifter at home, in California, and has no time for Harleys.

"I had one once, but I sold it to a guy who wanted it more than I did," he says as his wife comes out for another suitcase. "Damn, it was uncomfortable. Rode it all the way from Sturgis to California, and when I got home, I just parked it in the garage and that was the end of that. I didn't even unpack it for a week."

He wishes me well and wanders into the cottage empty-handed while his wife comes out for a third suitcase. The TV comes on inside, and when the woman walks out for the fourth time, I say hello and ask if she'll take a photo of me fixing the bike. She's happy to help and takes a couple of pretty good pictures as the valve covers come off.

I wipe away the oil from the metal covers and lay them on the ground as she makes two more trips to the truck for the final pieces of luggage.

The guys with the bikes walk back and nod hello, going inside their cabin briefly before coming out to sit on their bench, just as the Zen riders would have done in the peace of their summer evening back in '68.

There's a problem, though: for me to adjust the valve clearances properly, the piston must be right at the top of its stroke so that the valves are in the correct position, and I can't place it precisely without removing the cover on the side of the engine that allows the piston to be turned manually. And the only way to unscrew the three-inch rotor cover, sealed by a screwdriver notch at least an inch across, is to turn it with an extra-wide flat-head screwdriver. There's such a screwdriver at home in the garage, but not here. I didn't think to bring it, so I prod and chip away with the largest flat-head screwdriver in the grocery bag, but it doesn't have enough width to turn the cover.

Now would be a good time for an introduction across the way.

The guy with the Beemer is Jim, and the guy on the Harley is called Nick. Jim can't help me: BMWs have fancy tool kits for their gearhead owners, the best in the business, but there's nothing large enough to do the trick. Nick can't help, either: he's been letting Jim provide the tools. These Harleys aren't sold with tool kits, supposedly because their owners already have all the tools they need but really to cut production cost. Most modern Harley owners wouldn't know what to do with the tools, anyway.

The three of us stare at the cover awhile. So much for peace of mind and right values—this is just frustrating. I get the hatchet to use like a hammer and bash away on a regular screwdriver, hoping to apply the force that might make the difference; I joke that I should take the hatchet to the whole bloody engine, but Jim sees the large curve of the hatchet blade and puts the two together. Sure enough, pushing the blade into the large notch, then twisting the handle turns the cover loose. There's always a way.

The two guys wander back to their bench, and I carry on with the task at hand.

With everything laid bare and the piston moved around to its appropriate position, it's simple to feed the feeler gauges into the spaces between the tappets and the valve stems and adjust the distances so that the thin metal testing strips fit snugly into the gaps.

Pure mechanics, straightforward metal pushing on metal, no mystery, everything cause and effect.

The light's fading now, and it's time to lock the adjuster nuts into place and tighten the covers. I place the tank carefully back in its cradle and fix the seat and the side panels. It looks no different from before, but the engine will run better now, more fluid, less clatter.

With all the tools stowed away, the moment's right to wander over, can of beer in hand, to Nick and Jim, still chatting softly on their bench.

"Aren't you going to start it to check it?" asks Nick, but I don't want to make the noise now that the guests are settling in for the night. Really, though, it's grown too dark to fix any problem, so it might as well wait for tomorrow. The motor, with all its truth, can run in the morning.

"Fair enough," says Jim. "Want a cigar?"

Sure. And some of their Cheetos, too. They ask where I'm headed and Pirsig's book gets mentioned and Jim remembers it: "Hey, that's the one about the guy and his kid, right?" He didn't finish it but says he might try again now that he knows he might have slept in Pirsig's cabin.

They're both machinists on their way home to Pennsylvania after riding out to California. They made it all the way to the coast to see the Pacific.

"We've got to get out, man," says Jim. "Both of us saw our dads stay at home all their lives, and we said we don't want to do that. We arranged our vacations together and just told the boss we were going. Our families didn't mind, either—we spend plenty of time with them and just want some time to ourselves now. We have to hustle back 'cause we're due at work on Monday, but I think we'll be calling the boss and telling him we'll be a couple more days."

"Jim's good at hustling along on that German bike," says Nick, "but I don't go so quick on the Softail. That's okay—he waits up."

I tell them I'm headed to the Pacific, too, and hope to be there within the week.

"It's beautiful, man," says Jim. "If you've made it this far, you'll make it there okay. Maybe not tomorrow, but you'll get there."

We chat a little more, quietly under the stars, the water falling softly and constantly over the boulders in the river below. At last it's time to say good night and go into cabin 9 and head to bed.

Lying under the blanket, I hear a gentle hum from the laptop on the other side of the room. That's right—it was left running, readjusting and defragmenting its hard drive. I get up and tap the keyboard to light the screen. All done, says the message. The computer's fixed now and working fine again.

CHAPTER NINE

Western Montana

NICK AND JIM ARE GONE by the time I draw open the cabin's curtains in the morning. Their bikes fired up around seven thirty. It was too early to start the day and too warm under the covers. This is a short but big day and there's not far to go, so I'm in no hurry.

By the time I leave the cabin, a couple of hours later, the sun is already hot in the blue sky. When Jackie New's engine fires up, she sounds lovely. No rattles, no chain lash. She looks good, too, stripped down the way she should be, not overloaded with bags and cases to weigh down the balance.

There are plenty of parts now on Jackie New that made that '85 trip on Jackie Blue: the seat (though repadded) and the speedometer; the carburetor and clutch cover; the side panels, covered in stickers from places she's visited. The best of all is the luggage bracket, welded on the right side over the muffler: created from the tubing of an old lawn chair, it keeps the saddlebag away from the hot pipe. The original bike came with no such bracket and on her very first trip with a pair of saddlebags the plastic panel over the muffler was not strong enough to support the weight of the bag resting against it and the plastic began to melt from the heat.

I found an old hockey stick lying in a ditch and wedged it behind the panel, up against the exhaust tubing. The wood of the stick was already cured, so the muffler's heat did not affect it and it kept the panel and the bag away from the hot metal. But when I headed west across the prairie, the stick finally caught fire and melted half the panel, sending flames shooting against my jeans and burning through the saddlebag, toasting half the underwear inside. In Saskatchewan a welder formed a bracket from the discarded chair to sit over the muffler, making it into a resting place for the bag just an inch from the pipe but far enough away to avoid another mishap.

It would be good to have a similar bracket on the left because the saddlebag there is less well supported and swings in close to the chain guard. It's not dangerous, but it looks asymmetrical, and why not make the bike look as good as it can? One day I'll find a welder and get it done. But for now all is well, and it's time for breakfast.

The menu at the Town Café seemed promising, so I head back there now. Looking at the bike parked in front of the restaurant between two pickup trucks, knowing I'm almost at the halfway point on the journey to California, I couldn't feel better. She's stripped down, unencumbered, running sweetly and well. It's a good start to the day.

The same seat is open at the counter, but this time, in Kelly's place, there's an older woman with big hair who is talking to her silent husband with her mouth full. After ordering, I scan the paintings and other items on the wall to pass the time: wolves in the snow and a strange skull on the overhead beam. The woman spreads jam on her toast, pokes the bread into her mouth, and points her fork at her husband. "Well, if it's the second-deepest lake in the Western Hemisphere, which is the deepest?" she drawls through the muffling bread. "It can't be Lake Superior, because Superior's in the States, and they said it was the deepest in the States. So which is it?"

"Well," he answers, "perhaps it's—"

"And it can't be Titicaca, because that's the highest. Maybe it's the highest *and* the deepest."

"It could be up in—"

"What's that lake in Switzerland? Maybe that's the deepest."

You know, I think I know the answer to this, and if somebody else speaks for a moment, perhaps this woman will use the time to finish her mouthful of toast. I lean across and chip in. "I think it's Crater Lake, in Oregon."

This trip is taking me there; I'm supposed to arrive next Wednesday. The woman turns and smiles, not interrupted in the least and seemingly pleased by the attention.

"No," she corrects me. "That's where we're talking about now. We're just coming from Crater Lake, and they told us it was the deepest lake in the States and the second deepest in the Western Hemisphere."

"Yes," says her husband. Is that an English accent?

We chat because there's nothing else to do. They're a lovely couple, if only she could stop talking for a moment. I decide I like them a great deal. They're witty and well traveled, an unlikely pair who seem to work well together, the man resigned to his conversational fate.

There's a rare moment of silence. "Have you ever heard the expression 'Can't get a word in edgewise'?" he asks. "That was coined for Claire. She just has to—"

"Nonsense, Jeremy," she says. "But when I have something to say, I'm not afraid to say it."

They're on their way home to Dallas from their son's wedding in Oregon, which is why they stopped at Crater Lake a couple of days ago. They say the water is so clear that if a newspaper were held six feet below the surface, it could still be read from above. "Well, before it starts turning to mush," points out Claire. And they add that it has no streams or rivers to feed the water in or drain it off. "It's all rainwater," Claire states.

Pirsig stopped at the volcanic lake as a side trip the day before reaching California, mostly in an attempt to bring Chris out of the shell he could not penetrate. Claire asks why I'm headed there, and I begin to tell them about my trip. They know *all* about it.

"That's a great trip and a great book," says Jeremy. "I read it years ago. Didn't he used to be a journalist?" Yes, he did. It comes out that Jeremy was also a journalist, and Claire stays quiet so he and I can talk about a subject we both hold dear. He's worked as a writing coach, but his specialty is French translation. I ask if he's translated any famous books.

Only one, he says. "If I'd played my cards right, that could have been the only one I'd ever have needed to translate, too. They give me the option of a percentage of the royalties or a flat fee, and I've always taken the flat fee. Right to do so usually, too. But a few years ago I translated a book called *The Diving Bell and the Butterfly*. It was a best seller in France and sold well here, too. Now it's being made into a movie and Johnny Depp was considering it, so it'll sell even more copies. I took the flat fee and they gave me twenty-three hundred dollars. If I'd taken the percentage of royalties I'd be a rich man now.

"You know, even Johnny Depp's bloody manicurist will make more money off that book than me. But that's the American way, I suppose."

Johnny Depp never did make the movie, but a lot of people will earn a lot of money from Jean-Dominique Bauby's story—except Bauby himself. An energetic and vital Parisian journalist, editor in chief of the French *Elle* and father of two young children, he was incapacitated at age forty-three by an extremely rare form of stroke.

It rendered him completely paralyzed, able only to blink his left eye, but by means of that single movement he dictated his beautiful and inspiring memoir. As someone would intone the alphabet to him over and over, he'd blink at the letter he wanted, day after day for two months, until his remarkable story was complete.

It was published in France to critical acclaim and commercial success. Two days later, he died.

After their night's respite, my congested bronchial tubes once more begin their noisy rattle. My hands, lying curled on the yellow sheets, are hurting, although I can't tell if they are burning hot or ice cold. To fight off stiffness, I instinctively stretch, my arms and legs moving only a fraction of an inch. It is often enough to bring relief to a painful limb.

My diving bell becomes less oppressive, and my mind takes flight like a butterfly. There is so much to do. You can wander off in space or in time, set out for Tierra del Fuego or for King Midas's court. You can visit the woman you love, slide down beside her and stroke her still-sleeping face. You can build castles in Spain, steal the Golden Fleece, discover Atlantis, realize your childhood dreams and adult ambitions.

The view back south is picture-postcard perfect. A break in the trees leads to a gap in the mountains, revealing even higher mountains crested with snow. A few white clouds float high in the blue sky, and as the road drops down beside the river to the plain, yesterday's oppressive slab of rock gives way to another world.

At Bozeman the bells ring two o'clock as I ride up to Montana Hall. Arrival here in the summer of 1968 was undeniably the closure of a huge circle for Robert Pirsig.

He'd taught here, in Montana Hall, in the center of what's now Montana State University. Depending on how you look at it, he was either a lousy teacher or a great one. Lousy because he was so anxious and high-strung that he'd sometimes get physically sick before teaching a class, and then when his students would hand in work, he might refuse to reveal their grades. He once shouted out, in the middle of a speech by the school president, "This school has no quality!" But great because he forced his underachieving, uninspired students to rethink what they were doing and why they were doing it; he considered the *search* for knowledge more important than the *attainment* of knowledge. The dumb students carried on with their flunking grades, but the ones he reached pulled their Cs up to Bs and As.

Why was he so anxious? Many years later he told an interviewer that "there was fear. All these ideas were coming in to me too fast. There are crackpots with crazy ideas all over the world, and what evidence was I giving that I was not one of them?"

Most of the campus is off-limits to vehicles, so I ride around awhile, probing the access roads to find a safe place to park where the luggage won't be touched. It's high summer, and the place is almost deserted; there are just a few caretakers and an occasional student walking or cycling the broad lanes.

The parking lots are too wide open to offer security, and their asphalt is too hot and soft, liable to give way beneath the weight of the side stand. I find some shady fir trees and lean the motorcycle against one of them. It's a short walk to the four-story building.

Montana Hall is an imposing redbrick structure, peaked roofs and a bell tower pointing sharply at the sky as if to stress the importance of seeking higher things. The west-side door is locked. Attempts at the back and the east are also fruitless. The corridors look dark through the glass.

In front the eight wide steps to the large wooden double doors beckon students and faculty, but not this afternoon; the entrance may swing open easily during the semester, but it does not invite visitors on a Saturday in July. The doors here, too, are locked.

When Pirsig returned here thirty-six years ago, the heavy doors swung open and the wooden stairs inside creaked beneath his feet as he walked up to his old classroom, but the building was just as quiet and foreboding then as now. It reeked of Phaedrus. Today, as I stand outside the doors and peer through their glass to the ornate wood paneling and red brickwork within, it's easy to imagine that a ghost might live there, entombed within its structure, within its soul.

Just as in '68, it takes a phone call to find Gennie DeWeese at home at the end of the canyon road, miles out of town, on the way up into the mountains. She answers with a clear voice, giving directions and saying she's looking forward to our meeting.

On the way, I stop at a liquor store for a bottle of wine and choose a California chardonnay, the only decent one in the store. The clerk, chatting on a cell phone, takes the twenty and rings up the sale for a fraction of the marked price, handing back way more change than he ought to.

I begin to point out the mistake, but he's already turned his head and is preoccupied with the call. "Is this the right price?" I ask, but he ignores me. Fair enough. Maybe Gennie can raise a toast later to the old-fashioned way of doing things. For now, though, I'll raise a quiet toast to the modern world. It just saved me fourteen bucks.

CHAPTER TEN

Bozeman, Saturday

THE PIRSIGS STAYED SIX DAYS at Bozeman, visiting Robert and Gennie DeWeese at their small ranch. The Sutherlands stayed a couple of days and then ended their two-week vacation by riding home reluctantly to a houseful of children in Minneapolis.

Pirsig was taking off most of the summer. His time was his own: Nancy was traveling with friends in Europe, and Ted was staying with his great-aunt Floss, Harriet's beloved sister, in Mankato, Minnesota. Pirsig revisited his college haunts, loafed around, fixed up the bike, drank beer and cheap wine, debated late into the night with his hosts, and most important for the narration of the story, took a couple of days to hike high into the overshadowing mountains with Chris. As it is described in the book, this attempt at father-son bonding is probably more illustrative of the mountainous challenge that faced their relationship than of the event itself.

The DeWeese ranch is an ideal starting point for a hike on the South Cottonwood Trail, which passes by just at the end of the road. As Pirsig's host says in the book, "You can start from right here and head back up the canyon. There's no road for seventy-five miles." Today, though, as I ride up the gravel approach, there are houses all the way and beyond. Big ones. Fancy ones. Million-dollar homes set back in the trees at the end of meandering driveways. And between them, amid a few acres of long grass and overrun wildflowers, the home of Gennie DeWeese.

I park at her studio next to the main house, outside an open garage-door entrance that's covered with plastic sheeting to let in the light and keep out the road dust and bugs. Gennie comes out when she hears the bike. "You found it," she says, the living image of her character in the book. "It's good to meet you."

Robert DeWeese died eleven years ago, but Gennie is still fit and active at eighty-three. She's long been the matriarch of the household. Her daughter, Tina, moved back to the family home after living as a hippie in Washington State, and the two women, both highly accomplished artists and lovers of the land, are content to live simply. When Tina's boyfriend, Tom, moved in a year or so ago, Gennie moved into an apartment in the large, high-ceilinged studio; she leads the way inside now, underneath scrolled canvases hanging from rolling hooks on the ceiling, past broad tables covered with paints and glues and brushes. Her paintings are mostly landscapes and observations of life, cunningly simplified with broad brushstrokes in oil. She laughs a lot.

She's also used to visitors. Three or four times a year, strangers following Pirsig's route come to her door. She's pleased to take the time with them, as she does now with me.

Today she's walking with a limp. "You'll have to excuse me—I cut myself yesterday," she explains. "A sheet of glass fell on my ankle." A white bandage lies beneath the straps of a sandal, with smudges of fresh blood showing through at the wound.

We enter a small lounge at the back corner, where she lives. There's a bed occupied by a sleeping cat, a table, a galley kitchen to one side, and a bathroom behind. On the walls all around are paintings and bronzes and plates, and shelves holding sculptures and pots, and hanging from above are the large scrolls. Everything exudes creativity.

"Want a drink?" she asks, motioning me to sit at the round table. "Would you like a coffee or some tea? Or something stronger?"

I ask for a cold drink, and she looks happy. "I've got some beer if you'd like a beer," she says, and then it's my turn to look happy because a beer would be great. She refuses my offer to fetch it. "You've traveled farther than I have today," she says. "You can get the next one."

An ashtray on the table is full of butts. A hardback copy of *Zen and the Art* lies beside it, no doubt brought out to show her visitor. She comes back with the beer, two bottles on a tray, and I'm reminded of the welcome accorded the Pirsigs and Sutherlands all those years ago, when Gennie stepped onto the balcony to greet her guests holding a tray loaded with cans of beer. "Bob gave us that book right after it came out," she says, lighting a cigarette. "It's signed at the front."

I look at it now—a first edition, well-read and a bit bashed up. On the first page, in neat handwriting, Pirsig's note to his friends, dated March 4, 1974, says: "There's something Escher-like about this. How can characters in a book receive autographed copies of it?"

The DeWeeses taught with Pirsig at the college, and the families have stayed in touch. Pirsig just bought a painting from Gennie, for his guesthouse, and she's quick to mention that she can't divulge his address. I tell her I'm not especially concerned with tracking him down, and she looks a little relieved.

"To be honest, he's quite intimidating," I say. "Is he really as intense as he comes across in the book?"

In *Zen and the Art,* Pirsig recounts in detail the evening conversations with the DeWeeses, about the role of technology and learning in the "topsy-turvy" late '60s. When I suggest that there's surely no way the author could recall all that was said so accurately, Gennie disagrees. Pirsig has a good memory, she says, and it all happened pretty much as it's written. She's read the book a few times, as well as *Lila,* and has enjoyed them both. He deserves his success, she says.

"You know, other staff at the college didn't really like him very much, and when the book started to sell well, most people here refused to have anything to do with it. The library stocked it because it had to but shelved it with the mechanical manuals for being about motorcycle maintenance."

The book's success was a surprise to many people. Pirsig was an unknown author, but respected critics from *The New Republic* and *The New York Times,* among other publications, proclaimed *Zen and the Art* a modern masterpiece. It still sells about sixty thousand copies a year, some through university philosophy departments, others to curious bookstore browsers. Pirsig certainly enjoyed the recognition of his views, which had been summarily dismissed by most of his Bozeman colleagues, but he soon tired of the attention. In *Lila* he laments the reputation he earned: "Once you become a celebrity, it satisfies some people to try to tear you down, and there's not much you can do about it." He seems never to have accepted the lesser success of the sequel, preferring to retreat into himself and let his writing stand on its own.

Gennie sifts through a sheaf of papers and hands over a letter that Pirsig wrote in 1991, shortly before *Lila*'s publication. "Crazy how these casual thoughts I've accumulated over the years have now turned into a <u>commodity</u>, to be sold all summer long by more than 100 salesmen to thousands of bookstores for millions of dollars," he typed. "It's kind of scary to watch it happen. I feel like the man at the circus who is about to be shot out of a cannon."

He was shot out of the cannon—and landed with a thud. *Lila* was to be his masterpiece, so important to him that he fought the physical pain of an infected gallbladder while completing it, delaying the surgery that could kill him but never the book. It laid bare his thoughts on moral values with a structure as intricate as that of *Zen and the Art* but was never accepted with the same enthusiasm, perhaps because it's more involved, even deeper and more intense, or maybe just because it has nothing to do with motorcycles.

Or perhaps it's because Chris wasn't around anymore. Sutherland told me of a time he spoke to a university class in Minneapolis about his experience with the Pirsigs on the Zen ride, and at the end of the talk there was only one question. A young woman who was blind stood up and asked for something that a close reading of the book's 130,000 words, translated into braille, never delivered: "What did Chris look like?"

. . .

Tina DeWeese arrives, a ruddy woman with a pretty face whose greeting is as warm as her mother's. There's been a crisis. Freckles, the family cocker spaniel, was found wandering a few miles away, and Tom and his daughter, Candice, have gone to collect the dog. "We're silly over animals in this family," she says.

Tina asks if I'd like to stay overnight, and it's the invitation I've been hoping for. Gennie had offered a place in an e-mail, but I wasn't sure if she was serious—where I come from, we don't invite strangers to sleep in our homes. Now, though, I'm a long way from home. The property has a creek running through it, and a mountain rises behind. The grass grows uncut, and wildflowers are everywhere.

"You're welcome to stay in the house," says Tina. "Or you can sleep in the yurt."

A yurt? I nod politely.

"People like it in the yurt," she goes on. "I lived in it myself for two years before I moved back to Montana, and I still sleep in it sometimes. That was a good life then. I cried the day I moved back into a house with a flushing toilet."

The yurt's out back apparently, down by the creek, and I tell her it would be a pleasure to sleep in it. Just as well—we're onto the second round of beer already, and it's a long ride back to Bozeman.

Tom walks in, Candice and Freckles close behind. He's tall and thin and good-looking, with smiling eyes and long white hair brushed back. He's a rancher and an artist, good with his hands. He says he holds a pair of reins as comfortably as a wax-sculpting blade, deriving as much pleasure from constructing a solid length of wooden fence as from casting a delicate cowboy bronze.

We talk awhile about the real estate development that's going on all around. At the end of the road is a ranch with more than a dozen luxury homes on it, even bigger than the houses I passed on the way here, all of them multimillion-dollar properties rising up the slopes, and Candice has been in some of them—she cleans houses to help pay her tuition. Those houses don't belong here, she says, and everyone agrees.

They nod when it's suggested that all the out-of-staters are the same, imposing their values on the land. Then Tom remembers the notable exception.

"Ted Turner's different," he says. "His ranch is over in the next valley, and he's opened it all up as he's bought each property, making it the way it used to be. I put up forty-seven miles of fencing on that land before he bought it and knocked it all down. Good fence, too. Hell, though—I got paid, and the land's better off without it.

"One time, Tina and me were driving through there and we saw a buffalo in the field and I thought, 'She's going to drop,' and we pulled over and waited and sure enough she calved right there in front of us. No help from nobody—didn't need it. Nature's a beautiful thing."

The day's wearing on, and Gennie notices. "We've got a lot still to talk about," she says. "Why don't you go move your stuff in, and I'll get started on supper."

Tom and Tina and Candice rise, and we thread our way back past the studio tables and underneath the hanging canvases into the late-afternoon light, now shaded by the range to the west. I pause before we start walking up the road and prepare to ask my question at last.

"Tina, if I ask you something, do you promise never to tell Gennie that I asked?"

She nods.

"What's a yurt?"

There are actually two yurts in the meadow below the main house. They're solid canvas tents, each about twenty feet across, that have been raised on wooden platforms in which wood and tools are stored. Mongolians carry their yurts from grazing place to grazing place across the plain, but this pair hasn't gone anywhere for a while.

The first yurt belongs to Nolan and Jessie, "tenants" of the DeWeeses who live there for free in return for help on the property and their good company. Nolan is an art student at the university, thirty-four years old; Jessie is a botanist with the forestry department, away upstate mapping vulnerable areas of flora and fauna. She's the one who makes the bucks.

The guest yurt is a little farther along the overgrown path, supported on a wooden base six feet above the long grass and wildflowers and wandering chickens; its deck is also the entrance, on the other side, to a short raised pathway through the woods that leads back up the hill to the main house.

Tina and Tom lead the way up the ladder and through the wooden door. There's a woodstove in the center that won't be needed tonight, some shelves and a few books and clay pots, a flashlight beside a large bed that takes up all of one side, an easy chair covered with furs, and looking over everything, a life-size bronze of a featureless man, arms spread slightly in supplication.

"I love this guy—I find him so comforting," says Tina.

I find him a bit creepy but am too polite to say so.

Oh, and there's a stuffed turkey in flight hovering from wires over a side table. Not stuffed like a Thanksgiving turkey but stuffed by a taxidermist, resplendent with feathers and a bright red wattle.

"This is great," I say. "It would be wonderful to sleep here tonight."

Tom and Tina look pleased. They'll see me at Gennie's in an hour, they say.

There's silence when they leave, except for the sound of a shallow stream nearby that's splashing its way down into the valley. I unpack a change of clothing and toiletries, roll the sleeping bag out on the bed, and sit in the fur-covered chair awhile, just listening to the quiet. After hours upon hours of hearing the muffled *chug-chug* of the engine through the motorcycle helmet, it's a pleasure to listen to the gentle splash of the stream.

I close my eyes and doze, pleased to do nothing.

Soon it's time to change. I put on the dress shirt and jeans, freshly laundered at the motel at Laurel. With a nod to the bronze guy and a glance at the turkey, I head out of the yurt and venture along the wood-planked walkway, more of a boardwalk over the mud than a path through the trees. Entering the basement of the split-level main house, I hear a new voice in the main room.

The new voice turns out to be Nolan, tapping away on a laptop on the floor while Tom and Tina busy themselves in the kitchen. He looks every inch the clean-cut American graduate student, a wiry Matt Damon in shorts and T-shirt. "Hey!" he says, looking up with a grin and offering his hand. "Good to meet you! Glad you're a guy who likes yurts!"

"Well, I know the yurt I'm in is a great yurt. I dozed off for a while down there. It's so peaceful."

"That's Cottonwood Creek," says Tom, entering the room. "Pure, cold water fresh from the top of the Gallatins."

"Good water, too," says Nolan. "Delicious for drinking."

"Well, after you've boiled it," says Tina, coming up behind Tom.

"Nah—you don't even need to do that," says Nolan. "I love to start the day by walking down there and scooping up a cupful and taking a drink."

"Well, I love to start the day by walking down there and taking a piss," says Tom. "And that'd be upstream of you."

Nolan shrugs and grins again. This could be a long evening.

As the four of us walk along the gravel to Gennie's just next door, a car speeds by on the road, spewing dust and stones as it passes. Tom shakes his fist.

"Goddamn speeders!" he shouts, shielding his eyes. "If I had my way, I'd park a dozer on the other side of the next hill and make them all smash into it. That'd keep their speed down. This ain't the interstate."

We wander into the studio and make our way between the worktables to the living area, to settle down again in the same chairs we vacated just an hour or so ago. Candice is here already.

The bottle of chardonnay is waiting in the center of the table, and Gennie is bustling around in the galley kitchen as best she can with her injured ankle. She's changed the bandage, but fresh bloodstains have appeared.

We're having a dish they call Oriental chicken, which Tina prepared. The ashtray's been removed from the table and the hot pots of food are placed in the center. It's tasty and filling, far better than a restaurant meal.

I begin with a question: "How long have you lived here, Gennie?"

"We bought the land in 'sixty-five," she answers, "moving out here from the town. We just loved it. The Indians had a name for this canyon. They called it the Valley of the Flowers."

"And those weren't potted plants," adds Tina. "This whole valley was full of wildflowers, like in our meadow and down by the stream. I'm so proud of those flowers. I'll never understand why people have to cut their grass. The true beauty is what grows naturally, not in fancy manicured lawns and clipped hedges like those places at the end of the road."

I quite like lawns and planted flower gardens but nod anyway. To each his own.

"I don't know who those people are up there at the end of the road," says Gennie. "When we came out here, we were the first intruders, but we had schoolkids, so as other people came in, everyone was always so nice. Those people are all gone now. Couldn't afford to stay, I guess.

"In 1965, the nine acres we have now cost us four hundred fifty dollars an acre. We put the house on it for another twenty thousand. Couldn't do that these days.

"It would have cost us a lot more to build the house, but a friend of ours was an architect and he designed it for free as an experiment and in exchange for some of my artwork. We like to trade things when we can—why not?"

"Nobody's going to be designing these new houses for free," says Nolan. "There's one up the road that's ten thousand square feet, and it's just a summer home for out-of-staters. It's not right. I'm not saying it's a piece of crap or anything—it looks like an architect's marvel—but it doesn't belong here."

Everyone's eating now, and Gennie's poured the wine.

"This is such a beautiful place that I can understand why people want to live here, but they bring all their city values with them," says Tom. "They have to have hydro and satellite TV and fresh water to sprinkle on their lawns every day, and it doesn't improve the land one bit."

Nolan doubts it's improving the lives of the interlopers, either. "They're not happy in the city because their needs aren't being met, so they move out here for the country life, but then they just move to the same kind of place they had before, some monster home, and they're not happy here, either. They think bigger's better, but it isn't always. I think the land is in deep trouble."

We talk for a long time about the encroachment of development in the area. Nobody likes it, but as long as prices are high and someone's prepared to pay, there's nothing that can be done. High prices for everything—now there's another hot button.

"I've never paid more than a hundred dollars in rent," Tina says, "but if I had to live away from this house in the world today—you know, where people are paying five hundred dollars, even a thousand dollars in rent—I don't think I could do it. I've never made that kind of money, and I'm happier for it."

"You turn on the TV, and it's all ads trying to get you to spend, spend, spend, and people do," says Nolan.

"Damn media," says Tina with a grin, and everyone looks at me and chuckles.

"More wine?" asks Gennie.

Now it's my turn. "I make no apologies for the American news media," I tell them. "The secret is to watch it smartly or don't watch it at all. You've got to figure out whom to trust and you've got to form your own opinions, not follow others. I think you guys are doing that okay."

"Well, you can't trust everything you see on CNN," says Tom, fixing his eyes on me mischievously.

"Hey, if it weren't for CNN making a profit, you wouldn't have Ted Turner able to come in here and rip down fences."

Everybody pauses from eating and smiles. Tom raises his palms in pretend defeat.

"I hope to hear a wolf howl before I die," says Gennie.

"Not in this canyon," says Tom. "They'd eat all the cows. People like me would have to shoot them, and then we'd get into deep trouble."

It's a quandary for him, he says. There's been talk of reintroducing wolves to the area and as an artist he respects them and appreciates them, but as a rancher he doesn't want them near his animals.

Tina and Nolan disagree. "We need wolves if we're to restore the land," says Nolan. "You remove the predators from the food chain, and the rest will start to fall. The environment isn't a simple thing; it's complex, and the more we mess with it, the more we screw it up."

Tom shakes his head. He's an advocate of wilderness but asks how ranchers will be able to defend their stock against wolves. "In five years' time they'll be selling hunting licenses for wolves in Montana," he declares. "But what can a rancher do if he doesn't have a license and there's a wolf in his field? People will be going to jail over a damn wolf."

This is a sore point for Tom. A few years ago he found a starving mountain lion and carried it home on his horse. He kept it in his barn for six months in as wild a state as possible, nursing it back to health and taking it into the woods to encourage it to hunt. Tom was about to return it to the forest, but government inspectors found it first.

He was arrested for possessing an endangered animal without a license. Eventually he paid the fine—hundreds of dollars—but he never saw the animal again.

What happened to it?

"Well, they'd have kept it in a cage while they figured out what to do with it and what to do with me," he says. "They could never show me any proof of releasing it, no paperwork at all. They would have held on to it too long; I'm sure they killed it. No doubt in my mind at all. Damn government."

Dinner's finished, but the evening is far from over. We take away the plates but leave the glasses; Tina puts the ashtray back in the center of the table, and I lean over and pick up Pirsig's first edition and hold it up for all to see. I ask who has read it and what they think of it.

Everyone but Candice, the youngest, has read it. Tina and Tom say they enjoyed it.

"But what's the big deal?" asks Candice. "Why's it so special?"

Everyone looks at me—after all, I think it's important enough that I'm riding an old motorcycle thousands of miles, following the route it describes. It's time to swallow hard and try to explain Pirsig's relevance in the new millennium.

A big part of the message of *Zen and the Art of Motorcycle Maintenance* can be boiled down to a truism: if a job's worth doing, it's worth doing well. Pirsig would spend hours considering a problem and its solution—how to fix a motorcycle, how to build a workbench drawer—and I so wish I had the time in my own life to devote to such satisfying pursuits. But I don't. At any given moment a dozen things are competing for my attention, and they usually get short shrift as the priorities get worked through.

All my friends are the same, especially the ones with kids. There's just not enough time to get to everything in this modern overstuffed, overtaxed, overindulgent world. Why spend an hour fixing your bike when you can do it in ten minutes and move on to the next thing? And why spend ten minutes doing it when you can give the work to someone else, even though it will take you half a day to earn the money that the service provider will charge?

The big problem, as Pirsig sees it, is that the service provider won't always do a better job, and your life may be a little bit worse off on account of his or her lower standards. After all, why should the service provider do a good job? He or she will probably never see you or meet you. Nowadays service providers may not even live in your country. Overseas laborers will be paid more if they can double the production rate of somebody like Pirsig— probably they can churn out a dozen motorcycles while he's still tinkering over his valves or his drive chain. Third world laborers can make a hundred cheap workbench drawers in the hour it would take Pirsig to think through the roller mechanism and disassemble his son's skates and construct a drawer that will still slide smoothly thirty years later.

Nobody aspires to be a third world laborer on a mind-numbing assembly line; we all aspire to create something that gives us true satisfaction. And as technology takes over our lives, we are increasingly losing the route to that satisfaction.

The key to finding it again is to recognize that it isn't the technology that's at fault but our ability to understand it and use it effectively. Most computers work just fine, but how many hours do we spend cursing them when we input the wrong instructions because we have absolutely no idea what they need in order to operate properly? Similarly, most people are decent, but how many arguments have been caused—even wars begun—because we didn't know how best to communicate something?

Pirsig recognized years ago that the world comes down to the scientific (which he calls Classical) and the artistic (which he calls Romantic). They're polar opposites, but the one cannot live without the other, the light and the dark, the yin and the yang, and too often we ignore the one at the expense of the other. If we can only discover the proper balance, which has been lost in the onslaught of the pressure of time and mass-produced everything, we can find what's missing in our lives.

He demonstrated this here when Robert DeWeese brought out the instructions for assembling a rotisserie. Baffled, DeWeese saw pieces of metal that needed to be put together in a certain way, but Pirsig saw endless possibilities, perhaps even the construction of something better than the rotisserie's designer had intended. Don't follow the instructions to the letter, he says, because they were probably explained by the factory worker with the most time to spare—the most expendable employee. Instead, consider what you have, consider what you want, and figure out for yourself how to make it happen.

It's the same thing in life, says Pirsig. Take the time to decide what you want; then take the *extra* time to make it happen according to your own terms. Slow down. Always remember that the real motorcycle that you're actually working on is the cycle called Yourself. Attain peace of mind. And he's right, even more so in our stressed-out new millennium, with its cell phones and Black-Berrys, than back in the three-network world of the 1970s. We're all so busy catching up that we've forgotten what we're chasing.

Those are the barest bones of the message. It becomes more complicated in *Lila*, where Pirsig introduces what he considers to be the pure philosophical answer to the question "What is Quality?" He calls it the Metaphysics of Quality and describes how it can be divided into Dynamic and Static, which can itself be broken down into the specific divisions of its evolution: inorganic, biological, social, and intellectual. Most people's eyes glaze over long before this point, including my own. I've just wanted the opportunity for so long now to devote time and effort to something without the phone ringing or rushing to get the boys to soccer practice. To do something for the pleasure of it without having to justify it first to my equally stressed-out wife. To sit and think, as Gennie does when she paints a picture, or Tina, when she sculpts a horse, or Tom, when he casts a cowboy bronze. And as I've been doing for the last week during all those long, quiet miles on the road to get here and will do again tomorrow on the road to California.

On a motorcycle in the countryside on your own, peace of mind is never far away. Pirsig understands that, and so do his readers.

. . .

Later that evening, long after the wine is drunk and the liquor is served and the ashtray is full again, we pause so that Gennie can turn on the TV for the opening skit of *Saturday Night Live*. It's a parody of the president and very funny. As soon as the show itself is introduced, she turns the television off.

We start talking about Zen and its influence on their lives. They've all read widely and understand it quite well. Gennie tells her favorite Zen story.

"It's the guy who's being chased by a tiger—" she says.

Nolan interrupts. "Are you sure it wasn't a wolf?"

"No, it was a tiger, and a very big one. He gets to a cliff and climbs down to what he thinks will be safety, but halfway down he sees another tiger that's just as big and waiting for him below.

"So then he sees some strawberries growing on a ledge, and he enjoys them for their sweetness."

The message of living life for the moment is not making it past the wine and liquor. "If it were me," I say, "I think I'd pick the strawberries and throw them at the tigers. Maybe they'd be distracted, and I could get away."

Gennie smiles at her young student. "That's very Western of you. Quite practical, but it's not very Zen."

And when the lesson sinks in, I imagine there is a wolf away in the distance, howling at the moon for Gennie.

At the end of the night it's a short walk back to the house and down to the yurt. All is very dark, and we need flashlights to guide the way.

From down the road, a light approaches and soon a car is over the rise and driving fast. We shine the flashlights at the driver to make ourselves seen, but the vehicle doesn't slow at all and passes in a cloud of dust and flying stones.

CHAPTER ELEVEN

Bozeman, Sunday

Despite the suspended turkey in the corner and the looming bronze statue, I sleep a dreamless sleep and wake early, the sound of the creek splashing with the same comforting rhythm as the day before. It's easy to lie there in the soft light of the morning, listening to the sounds of the meadow and the mountain. Under the canvas it's almost like being near the top of the ridge, the smell of pine needles thick in the damp air, and it would be good to share this with my family. I wish they were here now.

But the boys are still too young, just seven and four. They'd have gone to sleep long before us last night, then woken a couple of hours ago, ready to start the day while their mother and I lay in bed as the last of the alcohol settled in the blood of our tired bodies. The light would have roused them and my wife and I would have tried to wait each other out, hoping for just a little longer under the warm blankets, before hearing the door open and close and the young voices walking away, toward the river.

Then we'd have been out of the tent in our underwear, yelling at the children to stay away from the water. And another day with the family would have started a little too early and a little too quick.

So I'll just lie here awhile longer, weighing the pros and cons as the featureless bronze man stands guard. Eventually I see it's nearly nine o'clock. Nine o'clock! These people are back-to-the-landers. What must they think of a guest still in bed halfway through the day?

I dress quickly and am out of the tent in jeans and T-shirt, ready for the second half of the journey, though right now all I want is a decent cup of coffee. All's quiet inside the house—they must be out on the trail or feeding horses or something. I hurry over to the studio.

Gennie's washing last night's dishes and filling the ashtray again. She greets me with a husky voice and a warm smile. "I thought you'd be first up," she says. "That lot can never get out of bed in the morning."

She's still limping, but today's challenge is waiting outside—her Toyota picked up a nail and has a flat tire. She'll get Tom to fix it, she says, but I want to help—to barter my skills for lodging, a tire change for some coffee. She grins and shuffles off to the coffeepot.

It's an older wagon, messy inside in the way of a driver who doesn't care about cars—dust from the road over the fabric upholstery, and tools and strips of leather and bits of paper everywhere. It probably drives well enough, but parked on the grass driveway, it looks like a vehicle abandoned at the junkyard, especially with its rear tire totally flat.

It'll need a jack and a socket wrench and the spare. The door's not locked, and there's a doughnut tire under the wagon's warped floor, properly inflated, and a scissor jack in a cubbyhole to one side. No wrench, though, so it's back inside, where Gennie is measuring out the ground coffee, to ask where the tools are. She looks baffled and suggests that I check Tina's car, another Toyota, which is parked at the main house.

Sure enough, there's a socket wrench there on the backseat, so I take it down to the studio and start jacking up Gennie's wagon. It needs to be raised pretty high, and each time the axle comes close to the needed height to clear the tire from the ground, the jack starts to tip, and even though the hand brake's engaged, there's a danger the car will roll off the support. It could land on me and crush my arm, or it could just crash to the ground, maybe bending the axle. Then what kind of Samaritan would I be?

I drop the car back down and reposition the jack and start

again, then drop it again and reposition the jack a third time. Zen thoughts aren't helping here: "It's the effort of climbing the mountain that counts, not reaching the peak"; "this is all part of the journey"; "pleasure and pain are not so different."

I think about going inside for a while to enjoy the coffee for its richness, and I drop the car down again, but then remember the one thought that is the most comforting: right now, at this moment, I don't have any problems. I'm alive and I'm healthy and my family is well and my journey is under way, so there's no point in worrying about problems that haven't yet occurred. Make the most of what I have right now, which is a jack and a wrench and a doughnut tire that's properly inflated and a cup of coffee and a happy Gennie awaiting the triumphant mechanic.

The jack is repositioned, the scissors are pumped up, the flat tire clears the ground, and the nuts come off and the doughnut slides on. Easy, really. Tighten the nuts, drop the car, and throw the flat in the back. Inside, Gennie's pleased to hear she has ready transportation and one less thing to worry about, and the coffee is ready and I sit down and enjoy it, for its richness.

There's no small irony here. Pirsig changed his worn-out motorcycle tire at Bozeman and ran into problems, though the account doesn't appear in *Zen and the Art*. It was one of the chapters that didn't make the final edit, but it's in the *Guidebook*.

The story goes that Pirsig and Chris went to a garage in town to use its air hose and the father took a while to show his son how this basic job should be done properly: soaping down the rims for lubrication, leapfrogging the irons for better purchase, inflating and deflating the tube to let out any kinks. As he liked to do, Pirsig turned a rudimentary and mechanical job into an artistic one. In fact, he did the job so well that—to drive the lesson home—the garage attendant even remarked that "you don't see many of them changed like that anymore."

That was all very well, except that Pirsig couldn't get the wheel back on the bike's axle. It had to be forced. That just wasn't right, and so the father and son went for a walk around the block to clear their heads and figure out what might be the problem. They didn't figure it out and came back to stare at the wheel some more. Soon, though, it was Chris who noticed that the drive chain was caught underneath a bracket, preventing the wheel's smooth movement; when the chain was properly routed, all was well, and the pair fixed the bike.

The moral here is that it doesn't matter how much physical care you apply to something—if your mind gets stuck along the way or your heart's not in it, the work will be substandard. Quality will be lost. Substance needs art. Yin and yang.

There's no explanation in the *Guidebook* of why this anecdote was cut from the text. Certainly the publishers were looking to trim its many pages; the estimate is that Pirsig's finished manuscript was as much as 60,000 words longer than the published work. Perhaps the lesson was considered redundant: Pirsig had made a similar point earlier in the story, when he told of running out of gas on the ride up to Canada and failing to check the tank. Most likely, though, it was removed because it shows Chris in too positive a light too early in the story; so far, Chris has been behind his father both physically and metaphorically and unable to contribute, even during the just-completed hike over the mountain, when they *nearly* reached the summit. At the garage in Bozeman, Chris is beside his father and even carrying him along to the job's solution.

I wrote to Jim Landis and asked if he could remember why the section was removed; he had no recollection of it at all. Pirsig probably made the deletion himself, without prompting. The passage was cut because the narrator wanted to keep Chris in his place.

At Gennie's kitchen table we talk awhile about my route today. When Tina and Tom walk in, still exuding the same comfortable happiness of the night before, the conversation starts up again as if it has never ended, with coffee this time, and before long somebody mentions the *Saturday Night Live* skit. The talk turns to politics. Gennie and Tina and Tom don't like the government and they don't like bureaucracy and they sure as hell don't like the president. "If I met that man, I swear I don't know what I'd do," says Tina. Gennie asks me if I've ever met the president and I tell her I haven't. They nod and say that none of them has ever met *any* president.

I'm on my second cup of coffee now and don't want to leave just yet. So with a slight gulp, as if I'm about to dive into a deep pool, I volunteer that I did meet a former president once, long ago and far away. Really? they say, and their eyes turn my way.

In 1997, I worked in Africa as a media liaison officer for Care International, one of the biggest humanitarian aid agencies in the world. Fighting raged in Sudan, essentially dividing it into separate countries, the Islamic north and the animist south, and Jimmy Carter decided that he ought to come over and talk peace with the government.

To keep everyone happy, the former president would spend equal amounts of time in the north and the south, although most of his diplomatic efforts would take place in the north. So arrangements were made for him to visit a small and isolated town in the extreme southwest, Tambura, and view the aid projects there.

Close to Carter's heart was the cause of eradicating both river blindness and guinea worm disease, and a small American aid agency operated a hospital in Tambura that specialized in treating both diseases. Care was the only other agency in town, and it helped with everything else: providing clean water, good governance, and assistance to the farmers.

So I got a call one day suggesting I go to Tambura to make sure the media accompanying the former president were properly taken care of, which meant I should schmooze the journalists and try to get Care's good work aired on the evening news in a positive light. Looking up Tambura on a map, I found it nestled close to the border with the Congo and the Central African Republic.

This should have been easy—not only was Jimmy Carter a director of Care USA, devoting lots of time to the agency, but one of the biggest projects under way was the promotion of peanut farming in Tambura's arid soil. I could see the photo on the front pages now: the peanut farmer who became president of the United States shaking hands with a starry-eyed Sudanese farmer.

I flew up from Nairobi a couple of days before Carter's arrival. He'd be coming in for a brief morning on the ground with his wife, Rosalynn, and son Chip. There'd also be half a dozen journalists on the little government plane, big-time media from Ted Turner's CNN, *Time* magazine, AP, and *The New York Times*. I went in with Care's country director for Sudan and some other staffers to make sure all was well for this photo op.

But all was not well. The other agency, a small and dedicated medical organization based in Los Angeles, was concerned that its work would be overshadowed by the giant Care circus coming to town. This was its biggest opportunity of the year—maybe ever—to publicize its work, and it knew as well as I did that there'd be only one photo in the papers, one sound bite on the news.

Since I was the Care media guy, its representatives thought of me as the embodiment of the enemy. Yet all I wanted was to have a fair shake at the media and share the available space. The other agency wanted to freeze Care out completely.

In Tambura, I had time for a look around while high-level meetings were being arranged. Each agency was based in its compound on the edge of town, one on either side of the football field. The aid workers were all friendly enough with one another, but the other agency's PR person treated me with frosty disdain. At an evening meeting she told me flatly that if the president was to tour the hospital—the main reason for his visit to Tambura, after all—there'd be no time for anything else, period. And especially no time for a meeting with any peanut farmers.

Everyone looked a little uncomfortable with this demand, but the Secret Service guy, who'd also flown in early and was giving the final word on logistics for the visit, just shrugged. He was a huge African American in a stylish suit, and the Sudanese revered him. "You know, she's got a point," he said.

But I'd taken the time to wander around and now held an ace. "Well, thinking of the logistics," I said, "am I right that there's only one toilet here in Tambura that flushes? That all the others are squat-and-drops?" I turned to my nemesis. "In your compound, do you have to squat and drop?"

She turned a little purple but nodded.

"I think the president's going to need to use the can," I said to the agent. "He ought to be scheduled to come here to the flushing john, if only for a short time." The agent agreed, and the visit to the Care compund and peanut display was arranged with another shrug. Victory.

At the kitchen table, Tina thinks that part is especially funny. "What is it with people and flushing toilets?" she says. "They should move into the yurt for a few days."

The next day four people were assigned to clean up the toilet, Care's irresistible cinder-block hut, which sat in splendor inside the compound.

It was painted lovingly, two coats, white inside and out. A dozen rolls of the best paper were placed inside. Another worker was given responsibility for the country director's private stash—two rolls of supersoft, brought in his luggage from Nairobi—to be mounted on the holder just as the president was making his final approach through the compound. Care's annual report was left conveniently in a locally made wicker basket beside the bowl. Freshly laundered towels were ready to be placed on the rail beside the sink outside. Everything was swept clean, and the flushing mechanism was tested repeatedly.

The huge Secret Service guy was asked to use it, since we figured that would be the ultimate test, and he did so both gratefully and frequently, thanks to the local fruit he'd been enjoying.

I was curious to see if the other agency's PR woman would come over to make peace so that she also might use it, or maybe sabotage it, running off with the cistern valve, but she kept her distance. Oh, and we set up displays of peanuts and stuff, too.

On the morning of the visit, all was ready.

The towels were still clean and the toilet still flushed, despite its having worked overtime the previous day. I put on my best Care hat and carefully grubby Care T-shirt and carried a bunch of hats with me to place on the heads of anybody who might happen to be cornered by a camera. Right on schedule, the little plane landed, and the great man stepped out onto the gravel to greet the chiefs.

The first planned stop was the hospital, a short walk away, and I stood back while the other agency had its time in the limelight. The PR woman had made it clear I was not welcome in the hospital, where Care had no responsibility, despite providing its clean water, so I stood outside on a little bridge over a stream and rehearsed some sound bites I'd thought up the day before.

After a while the journalists had seen enough of the former president talking kindly with the patients and had taken all the video and notes they needed of the medical supplies that had been donated by generous Americans.

They left Carter inside with his entourage and came out to speak with the PR woman. She told them all about the horrific percentages of Sudanese afflicted by river blindness and guinea worm disease and about the statistical forecasts for their impact in the region. Nobody filmed her, though reporters took a few notes. And everyone looked really bored.

The CNN crew wandered over to the little bridge and talked about the flight home, then paused awhile, watching the stream flow quietly below. I looked up and nodded a greeting—this was the moment to strike.

"Hi," I said.

"Hi," said the journalist, and then, "You live here or are you just along for the ride?"

"Oh, I got in only a couple of days ago. I've been helping set up for the visit."

"Sure."

A pause for effect . . . "You know," I said, looking down at the stream, as if the thought had only just occurred, "it's too bad you guys couldn't have gotten here yesterday and seen this town then. The excitement was truly something to witness."

"Yeah, it's too bad, but that's the business."

Now here it comes, looking up slowly from the water to make eye contact . . . "You know, I don't know if the president can cure river blindness or get rid of guinea worm, but at least for just one day he can bring some hope to a little town in Africa that thinks it's been forgotten."

POW! Twelve seconds. Perfect. The CNN guy looked startled and then looked at his cameraman, who'd bucked up and nodded and was already reaching for his equipment. Then he looked back at me. "Do you think so? Would you mind saying that on camera?" The lens was in my face.

"Who, me? Oh . . . Well, if you think it's important, if it might help. I guess I could do that."

And in my Care T-shirt, I told a billion people around the world about the town. When they finished filming and hurried away, I wandered over to the bored-looking woman from *The New York Times*. "Hi," I said. "It's too bad you couldn't have been here yesterday . . ."

My rival happened along a few minutes later, saw the journalist scribbling my scripted comments into a notebook, and almost threw herself between us. "The president's leaving now," she said breathlessly.

Time for stage 2.

We had to drive over to the Care compound, where the schedule allowed the former president to use the facilities before getting back on his plane. There was plenty of time. At the entranceway a group of local farmers had prepared a display of peanuts, and Carter was keen to take a look.

He paused and chatted casually with the farmers, as easily as he had with everyone else, and it was clear he was truly a great man. Certainly here in Sudan he was loved, and his visit brought happiness to the town. I found the worker with the special stash of supersoft toilet paper, and he nodded at me happily to confirm that he'd put it inside on the holder.

All was humming along according to plan. Terrific.

After a short while the president looked around and spoke some words to the country director, who nodded and pointed toward the freshly painted white hut just inside the compound. For me, glancing across at the little building, it was as if a beam of light was shining down upon it from on high. The crisp towels were arranged on the rail outside, the sink spotless.

Carter smiled and strode over and tried the door.

It was locked. He tugged again.

"Hang on," said a woman's voice from inside.

Carter looked back at the country director, who was now standing at his side, wide-eyed and bewildered. "I just need to take a leak," he said. "Got a decent tree around here?"

And so former president Carter walked with the country director to the wall behind the little hut and relieved himself of the bottled water he'd been taking on to combat the heat. The country director did the same, probably more from good manners than anything else. The toilet flushed, and the AP reporter emerged. Before the door closed, I saw that the annual report was on the floor, not in the basket; maybe some good came of that, then.

The reporter washed her hands in the spotless sink and wiped them on the immaculate towels just as Carter wandered back, so he rubbed his hands on his trousers and, with a few minutes to kill, looked at me for the first time and smiled that toothy, beatific grin. I smiled back and stuttered out my other well-rehearsed line.

"Hello, Mr. President. May I shake your hand, please? I've never shaken the hand of a president before."

"Of course, young man, it would be my honor," he said, and I loved him all the more. He took my proffered hand with a firm if slightly moist grip and shook it warmly. I had absolutely no idea what else to say. Where do you begin?

"Do you work for Care?" he asked, no doubt noticing the hat and T-shirt.

"Yes," I said.

He looked at me expectantly as I blinked back, my head swirling with thought but vacant of response.

He smiled again and looked away. "Hey, has anyone seen Chip?" he called to the Secret Service guy.

I have the photo still, snapped by the country director as I shook hands with the former president. It was one of my greatest moments, the only time I've ever been speechless.

There's laughter all around the table. But the story has taken a while, and now it really is time to go.

Gennie and Tina stay in the studio as I leave with Tom. He says he wants to show me something. Pulling up the door to the garage of the main house and walking into its clutter, he goes to a sheet that's covering something large, and then, lifting off the cloth, he reveals an intricate bronze sculpture of small winged fairies, a dozen of them head to toe in a vertical ring a couple of feet across, rising and falling with the endlessness of its circle.

"Those are Montana fairies," he says. "I made each one separately. Could have made them all the same in the same mold and it would still have looked good, but it just didn't seem right to do that. There's a magic in this land that's being forgotten as the developers move in. They only see dollars and square feet, and nobody sees the fairies. I wanted you to see them."

Each one is different, with its own shape and face and wings, like the people who live in this house and along this road, and in this state and in this country. The bronze is solid and cool, fragile in its detail but strong in its material. "It took a long time to make this," says Tom. "Don't know why I did it—it just seemed the right thing to do." He puts the sheet back over the sculpture, hiding it again.

Out on the driveway I'm looking at my motorcycle when a thought comes to mind.

"Tom, you know how to weld, don't you?"

"Of course," he says.

"Could you weld a piece of metal onto my bike to help support the saddlebag?"

He shrugs. "Show me what you mean, and I'll see what I can do."

He takes a look at the back of the motorcycle and the empty space on its left side that needs filling in. I show him the bar on the right side that protects the right saddlebag from the heat of the exhaust and tell the story of using the hockey stick and setting my pants on fire up in Canada. And I explain how the bar had come from an old lawn chair and how well it's lasted. One like it on the left would do the trick. He nods and goes back into the garage, coming out a moment later with a long length of metal about as thick as his thumb.

"How about this?" he asks. "It's from an old chair, too. Follow me over to the neighbor's—he's got the welder I'll need in his shed."

He gets into the car and drives up the road in a cloud of dust, and I follow on the bike a long distance behind. The neighbor's farm is about a mile up the way and the place seems empty, but Tom's not bothered. He has an open invitation to use what he needs. He parks outside a drive shed and motions me to put the bike inside. We kick some cables and paint cans out of the way to clear space for Jackie New.

Tom's hooking up wires and hoses now and pulling a large electric arc welder and a gas welder into place. Then he squats and takes a long look at the back of the bike, at the luggage carrier and the seat and the rear tire, and he's thinking about the support bar he's about to create with the same care—the same *art*—he put into the Montana fairies.

"Okay," he mutters, rising from his haunches, and takes the

length of metal outside and cuts off a piece with a grinder. It's already curved into a U, and Tom grinds the ends flat and hammers off the edges.

He goes back inside and puts on a welding mask, squatting down beside the bike with the short piece of metal, ready to get to work. At the last moment he lifts the mask and looks at me. "Don't look at the light," he says. "It'll make you blind."

And Tom fires up the arc welder and dances his spark lightly across the metal of the luggage rack, adding a tack weld here and there, watching through the dark protective glass as the sparks flick along the edges of the bar. He fires up the torch and makes a small cut with the flame, no more or less than necessary, then resumes the job with the welder until there are no more edges. Soon there's just a smooth continuation of the metal in a downward U that will prevent the saddlebag from swinging in toward the tire.

He's concentrating on nothing else as he forms and shapes the hot metal, no longer part of a discarded chair frame but now a solid part of the motorcycle, as useful and functional as any other part on the bike. It's not an addition or an option but an intrinsic piece of the whole, and Tom knows this better than anyone as the white fire flashes and the metal joins, bonds, and transforms.

Then the light and the fire go out, and Tom lifts the mask. "It won't take long to cool," he says. "Let's see if there's some paint about."

He finds a can of black spray paint and coats the bare metal until it's the same color as the rest of the luggage rack. It's a much smoother job than the lawn-chair piece on the other side; it looks as if it's part of the original bike.

And to think that half an hour ago it was just a bit of old chair and my saddlebag would swing perilously close to the tire.

Even Tom looks pleased with the job. "That should hold up for a while," he says. And then, "Thinking of things that hold up for a while, let me show you something else," and he leads me to the side door of a neighboring shed.

Inside, we clamber over lumber and old fence posts and into a separate area, where two old cars are parked dustily and quietly behind a chained garage door—Packard 110 sedans from the early '40s. They've been stored here for years and untouched for about as long.

"It wouldn't take much to get these running again," says Tom. "This whole county—this whole state—is full of surprises. You see this farm and it's just a farm, but when you take the time for a closer look and see inside it a little, you'll find gems like this."

We clamber out of the shed again, and Tom looks up at the ridge on the edge of the farm.

"There's always something hidden," he says. "There's always more to everything than the eye can see. Sometimes it's good, but sometimes it's bad. Up there, for instance, I put up a mile of fencing for my neighbor and that's how come I keep my horses here and I can just come in and use his tools. This is the way Montana should be. When I put up that fence, I'd look down into this little Valley of the Flowers and think of how beautiful it all is.

"But if you go up there and look down the other side of the ridge, what do you see? A subdivision with seventy-two houses on it: seventy-two families mowing their lawns and sucking up the water. None of them are from Montana. It's criminal—there should be a buffer between the subdivisions and the land.

"I don't know what you call it, progress, I guess. I guess it's progress."

Tom won't take any money for the welding work. We drive back to the house, and I load up the motorcycle, the left saddlebag resting securely against the new support bar, forming a firm base for the cases and bags that are lashed down on top. Nolan comes outside, and he and Tom watch as all the bungee cords get fastened in place.

"I've got a system for doing this now," I say, and they nod.

"I've packed a lot of horses in my time," says Tom, "and I don't know that I'd do it any differently. Although I might wrap that cable through that handle to lock that case down."

He's right. The steel cable that locks the computer case to the bike while I'm riding and locks up the bike when it's unloaded and parked is looped uselessly in and out of the case's handle, not through it and around it. I joke that it was just a test, and we all laugh, then shake hands, and Jackie New and I ride away in a cloud of dust from the Valley of the Flowers. Let's hope it will still be there if I return.

CHAPTER TWELVE

Into Idaho

I'M MORE THAN HALFWAY NOW. Six days on the road with Jackie New got me from Minneapolis to Bozeman, and if all goes well, six more days will get me to San Francisco.

The traveling will be different from here on. There's nobody from the book to meet and no one I'm scheduled to chat with along the way. With the Sutherlands gone, the Pirsigs slept rough for three nights in a row: on a logging road, at a rustic campsite, and beside the road in a half-constructed subdivision. They became more introspective and self-doubting the farther they traveled from home.

A few miles east of Butte, they slogged up the Continental Divide on the little Superhawk, crossing its ridge into the strange new land of rivers that run to the Pacific Ocean. It's an anticlimax when I reach it, for it's not very high at all and certainly no challenge, some five thousand feet lower than the Beartooth Pass. The road winds through gentle hills, with cattle grazing in the fields alongside. But the weather's closing in. The hot sun of Bozeman is hidden behind the gray clouds skirting the Pioneer Mountains to the southwest.

It's well into the afternoon. My late start and Tom's welding have cut deep into the day's schedule and I'm at least three hours behind, but even so I'm off the interstate again, taking a little longer to follow the original route. The faster option slices right through Montana in a four-lane swathe.

Pirsig's description of the road became sparer as he felt the loneliness of the Sutherlands' absence; there was no buffer now between him and Chris. And after the visit to Bozeman and the welcome by the DeWeeses, who accepted him as the only person they knew to have his face, as Phaedrus, the pressure on the narrator to somehow come to terms with the father-son relationship could grow only more intense.

Pirsig had been lonely, too, when he left Bozeman in 1961. He'd recognized that at Montana State College he could never find the answers to his question "What is Quality?" and he sought out an education that might help him better understand the ancient philosophers who had also wrestled with the question. As well, and more practically, Pirsig knew he needed a doctorate to progress as a teacher. He'd found an interdisciplinary course at the University of Chicago called Analysis of Ideas and Study of Methods and enrolled with enthusiasm; he was accepted on the strength of his teaching experience. However, when he applied for a scholarship and sat down for an interview, the committee chairman was less impressed and fairly dismissive. The fanatically intense Pirsig could not leave well enough alone and went back to the mountains for the summer to research the chairman and the course, then wrote a stinging letter to the university that basically said that much of what the chairman believed in—the teachings of Aristotle—was wrong. Furthermore, it was he, Pirsig, who should be welcomed to Chicago to show the university the better way. As Pirsig explained it, "No one was really accepted in Chicago until he'd rubbed someone out. It was time Aristotle got his. Just outrageous."

It's hard to imagine a clumsier and more insulting communication, and it's not surprising that the chairman, who is never named in *Zen and the Art* but is based on the notorious Chicago academic Richard McKeon, was unimpressed. This was a professor of ancient Greek, after all, who has been called "legendary for inspiring cold sweat and raw fear."

According to Pirsig's account, he loaded his family into the car and their belongings into a trailer for the move to Chicago and locked his faculty-house door for the last time. Then the mailman arrived with a curt letter from the university saying he would not be admitted to the program. But with a new job waiting in Chicago and no reason to stay in Bozeman, Pirsig borrowed some notepaper from a neighbor and wrote back to say he was coming anyway and they couldn't stop him.

I'll bet *that* was a fun family drive.

The clouds are black west of Butte, and I pull in behind a pizza restaurant to dress properly for the inevitable storm. It's late—5 p.m. already—and if I'm to make it to Missoula, I'd better be dry and quick, so maybe it's time now for the first major break from the Pirsigs' back-roads route. I get on the interstate heading north.

But on the interstate the west wind is so strong I have to fight to stay in the right-hand lane. It's gusting and slamming me from the side and buffeting the bike. There's a high ridge off to the northwest and it looks as if the rain is over it and ready to blow onto the interstate, so after just twenty miles I leave this exhausting highway to resume the Pirsigs' route west through the mining town of Anaconda. Even rain is better than this broadsiding wind.

Now, of course, I'm headed directly into the wind, which keeps my speed down below 50 miles per hour, but at least it doesn't push me all over the road. All is gloom and dull light as the rain begins on the approach to Anaconda, with lightning ahead off to the west.

A faded tourist sign advertises the road as the Pintler Scenic Route, which reaches the same point near Missoula as the interstate but travels through the Southern Flint Creek Valley instead of around it. It also says the town is home to the world's tallest freestanding masonry structure (the 585-foot smokestack), which is "all that remains of what was once the largest nonferrous metallurgical plant in the world"—now a golf course. That seems like way too many provisos to hold any interest.

There's nobody on the sidewalks of Anaconda, although the buildings provide a little protection from the wind. As I ride slowly through on the wet pavement, dry in my rain gear but hunched like an old man, this whole quest seems foolish. The road is soaked, and perhaps the answer's just to pause and wait out the storm, as I should have done in Lemmon. But it's too late to pause now. It's 6 p.m. and time to think of stopping for the night.

As if on cue, I see a comfortable-looking hotel and then, just a stroll away, a pub called the Harp and Thistle. Pirsig would have stopped now, no doubt about it. But the road I'm on is one-way; I've already passed the hotel, and it's not so simple to turn around.

I push on to the edge of town and see what else there might be. If I do stay here tonight, I'll be more than a hundred miles short of my planned stopping point, a distance that will have to be made up each day if I'm to arrive in San Francisco in five more days, on my birthday. That's the goal, and there are no short riding days ahead.

And the rain starts to let up as Anaconda rolls by, and I pull farther away from the comfy hotel and the welcoming pub. The one-way road becomes two-way, and just as it does, a touring motorcycle motors in from the west. The rider gives a cheery shirtsleeved wave from behind his windshield, and it's such a surprise there's no time to wave back. No rain gear!

Forget Anaconda's seductive provisos—I'm not finished with this road yet.

Within a couple of miles the rain has all but stopped, and the light is soft and lustrous. The road drops slowly from the hills toward the valley, following a river that finally topples in a narrow waterfall off the rock and into a lake that feeds the fertile fields. The sun's grown warm; the road is dry. It's the same rapid change as last week at Lemmon, and I wonder if the clerk at the comfy hotel is named Stacey and the Harp and Thistle server is Deb, but there's no turning back now because the road is just too pleasant and the bike is running well.

Half an hour later I pull up in the late sunshine to the small town of Hall, where the Pirsigs rested away the afternoon in a shady churchyard. At last I'm catching up.

There's no shady churchyard anymore, though there are some shady areas in the gardens of a few houses now built in its place beside the old church. I press on, riding awhile with a little red vintage Corvette, top down for the older couple to better enjoy their Sunday drive. Soon after, the road crosses the interstate and the rain returns, and I ride through a torrential downpour into Missoula, where I find an older motel right next to the Holiday Inn Express—no high-speed hookup for the laptop but half the price.

It's just thirty miles short of the logging road where the Pirsigs slept rough, but it's a place to do some laundry and maybe watch a little TV and rest up for the ride tomorrow.

I've had enough of this rain, but something tells me it's over now. I've come through it and I'm still healthy and there's still money in the bank and the bike's still strong.

Outside the window, where Missoula's giant painted M rests on the hill, the oranges and reds of the last of the sunlight are spectacular.

> With a rush of wings the eagle flies a circle around the room and then straight for the open window, lifting the bedcovers and even the luggage into the air with the force of its suction. It flies out toward the hill and circles the summit, swooping and rising, calling and shrieking, as I watch through flickering eyelids, not closed, not open, not knowing.

The next morning, hot and sunny—a beautiful day for riding— there are flashing lights on the road up ahead to warn of an accident. It's a red sedan that's sideways in the shallow ditch, its front end crushed from the impact and windshield shattered, air bags filling the inside. No one there except a cop in a cruiser.

There's no obvious reason for it on such a pleasant day, a single-car accident on a dry, safe highway. Maybe the driver was drunk or had fallen asleep after one too many night shifts or was speeding when a tire blew. I'd learned my lesson about driving too casually on that bumpy road back before the Beartooth. Or maybe the sedan had been forced off to the side by an animal or someone else who was drunk or had fallen asleep or was distracted by a cell phone conversation. Like the guy in the Buick when I was crossing into North Dakota.

I've come a long way west since then. The road I'm on branches soon after leaving Missoula, my route climbing a couple of thousand feet to cross into Idaho at the Lolo Pass. It's smooth and wide and perfectly cambered, curving gently this way and that. The sky is completely blue, a contrast to the pine trees and small green grazing fields to either side of the road.

I can't go too fast because it's uphill, so I lock in comfortably at the speed limit and sway casually with the highway's turns as it climbs toward the next state. This is relaxing, almost meditative. The temperature's perfect when the breeze slides through the sleeves of the leather jacket and wraps around the back of the neck. The road is dry, and soon there's the pass and the "Welcome to Idaho!" sign. The GPS shows that the Pirsigs pulled over at the rest area here, where there used to be a restaurant and store, so I pull over, too, not so much to copy them anymore but because they've led me to some pretty good places so far.

The lot is large and I park in a quiet, shady area, but soon a car pulls in nearby. The driver, an older man, gets out to find a washroom and leaves his passenger, an older woman, in the vehicle. There are two small dogs, schnauzers that jump around on top of her, poking their heads out of the half-open window and yipping with excitement, but she doesn't move, just stares straight ahead. Why doesn't she get out?

Here the Pirsigs met a couple from Missouri on a Harley-Davidson, a real "high-miler," headed the same way but not inclined to share a campsite down the road. Pirsig wanted company at this point, and I guess I do, too, but not with the schnauzers, thank you. The riders talked about bucking the strong wind heading up to Missoula; it must have been the same wind that was blowing the bike around so badly yesterday. Must be July weather.

Pirsig didn't look for company often, but public places like this depressed him. He found that out on his own, with just the landscape and the earth's natural presence, there was no need to be lonely, but throw some people into the mix and it was a reminder that he didn't quite fit in. Technology, a bugbear in the book, is even more to blame, for it's constantly reminding people that there's a whole other world out there that excludes them. The problem is not the televisions and radios and computers themselves but the messages they relate—the subject over the object—and that's part of the reason Pirsig moved to Chicago, to better understand the messages' underlying purpose.

He'd found a job teaching rhetoric at the University of Illinois, which meant he was free to enroll in a different philosophy program across town at the University of Chicago; his students were average and undemanding, giving him free rein to pursue his own studies. He buried himself in the great books of the Greeks, including Plato, Socrates, and the chairman's own inspiration, Aristotle. He found an obscure reference to *arete*—a Greek word that means "virtue," or refers to the quest for excellence in everything in life—that predated them all. Digging even deeper, he found that its original morpheme, *rt*, was the root of words like *art*, *rite*, and *right*, and even the Sanskrit word *rta*, which means "the cosmic order of things." He remembered learning about *rta* in India and recognized its fundamental connection to the Greek belief in *arete;* it proved to him that he was not alone in his belief that quality should be the root of all philosophical inquiry.

He agonized over the relationship between *mythos* and *logos*—creative myth and current reality—and came to despise Aristotle's logical systems of order. These ideas did not go over well in discussions with the chairman. In perhaps the climactic moment of the book's philosophical sections, Pirsig, as Phaedrus, embarrasses the chairman in his own classroom in a debate over dialectic—

the art of examining the truth of something through question and answer, and the very heart of Pirsig's search for meaning. "Phaedrus the wolf," recalls the narrator, "down from the mountains to prey upon the poor innocent citizens of this intellectual community."

This is where Pirsig got his name for his former personality: from Plato's dialogue *Phaedrus,* in which a character is likened to a wolf. It all seemed to fit. But this is one of the flaws of *Zen and the Art*: Pirsig mistakenly thought it was the title character who was compared to the wolf when in fact it was another character in the dialogue, one named Lycias. If Pirsig had gotten his facts straight before the book's publication, he would probably have called himself Lycias, but instead he became Phaedrus, which in Greek means "brilliant" or "radiant." As he freely admits, that's a pretty good alternative.

The old man comes back and opens the car door for his passenger, presumably his wife. She is limping—that's why she was waiting for him. The dogs are on leashes, and the couple take them to the dog run.

Jackie New starts with the first kick, and I head southwest now, past the "Winding Road Next 77 Miles" sign, downhill all the way.

It was all downhill for Pirsig, too, after his classroom victory over the chairman. The questions that he'd come to Chicago to answer proved only more elusive. He was still popping sleeping pills, and he began wandering again, seeing warped quality in everything: the city gardens whose beauty fell so far short of the alpine meadows he loved, the brick homes so much less permanent than the mountains, the horizontal dimension of the city, spreading out and out and out. His mind spun with the ramifications of inferiority in everything and the inability of the civilized world to recognize the aberration he believed it had become.

A few days before Thanksgiving he returned to his apartment and lay on the bed with his eyes darting around the ceiling, corner to corner to corner, not stopping for hours at a time. Instead of going to the bathroom, he urinated on the floor, time and again, using the toilet only when Nancy finally yelled, "Fine! Piss on the floor for all I care!" For three days and nights he just stared at the wall. Nancy begged him and cajoled him to explain himself, but he would not speak to her. In his head he repeatedly heard a Christian hymn: *"You got to cross a lonesome valley, you got to cross it by yourself."* He sat in a puddle of waste, his fingers blistered from cigarettes left to burn to their very ends. When Nancy saw the blisters and the pools of urine, she called for help.

First she called her sister, who lived in Chicago, and had her pick up the boys and take them to her parents' house for Thanksgiving. Then, through the brother of a friend at the University of Chicago, arrangements were made for Pirsig's hospitalization. Finally, she called the police. Nancy described the scene to me in a letter:

> *When they were coming up the front stairs (we lived on the third floor) Bob suddenly became active and angry, and tried to get out the back door. I was truly afraid that he might jump off the small balcony outside our back door and kill himself. I barricaded the door as best I could and he, for the first and only time in his life, struck me. But then he gave up on getting away (which he probably could have done) and was taken away in either a strait jacket or handcuffs by two policemen.*

In *Lila,* Robert Pirsig remembers "bouncing through South Chicago in that hard-sprung police truck on the way to the insane asylum . . . that cop who grinned at him all the way, meaning 'We're going to fix you *good,* boy'—as if the cop really enjoyed it." He spent Thanksgiving of 1961 in a Chicago mental hospital.

"A kind of chaos set in," he told a reporter many years later. "Suddenly I realized that this person who had come this far was about to expire. I was terrified, and curious as to what was coming. I felt so sorry for this guy I was leaving behind. . . . It was a separation. This is described in the psychiatric canon as catatonic schizophrenia. It is cited in the Zen Buddhist canon as hard enlightenment."

Nancy sees it differently:

Whether it was enlightenment or mental illness is a question in his mind only. And in fact, it is not even a question there. In his heart he believes he is enlightened. The reason he insisted on that with me soon became clear. If he was enlightened and I was not, then every time he made a decision or spoke an opinion, it trumped anything I could say or do. We never argued. If I said anything questioning one of his declarations, he gave me a hard look and walked away. He would not dispute me, he simply refused to discuss anything. He stopped talking to me about anything real.

It was the beginning of more than two years of depression and clinical insanity. He was released from the hospital to resume teaching, only to quit his job and be readmitted to a psychiatric ward, then be released again to live in a house back in Minneapolis across from his parents on Clarence Avenue. Later, in *Lila,* he questioned the idea of insanity as a reflection on reality, asking, "Who is crazy here, and who is sane?" and "If there were only one person in the world, is there any way he could be insane?" He was sure he could beat this schizophrenic curse on his own but became more and more dangerous as he descended into confusion.

Then one day, in an argument with Nancy, he chased her around and around the house, yelling so loudly that his boys cowered upstairs, terrified. He grabbed his pistol, always loaded, and chased her some more before cornering her and pointing it at her head.

I must have said something that he didn't like and he intended to put a stop to that kind of talk forever. I believe I

*was kneeling in our bedroom and Bob was standing over me.
He spoke to me very quietly and coldly and I doubt I said
anything except perhaps to promise never to do anything like
that again, whatever it was I had done or said. It probably
lasted only a few minutes—it just seemed like an hour that
the gun was pointed and cocked, and I did believe it was the
end of my life.*

Finally he backed down, leaving her shaken and wrecked. She told his parents about it, and enough was enough. The cops were called and they came to the front door, covering the back exit, and he was taken into custody without a struggle. Maynard Pirsig, Bob's father, finally agreed to co-sign the papers that permitted doctors to administer electroshock therapy.

"They put a little rubber thing in your mouth," Robert Pirsig told the reporter, "and then they gave a drug like curare, used by South American Indians in their darts. It stops your lungs before it stops your mind. Before you go under you had a feeling like you were drowning."

Phaedrus, with all his questions, his searches, and his inability to find resolution except at the very end of his dream, was eliminated. Chris's father was gone.

A half hour farther along, there's a waypoint on the GPS and a sign into the trees that marks the Lochsa Lodge, a restaurant, souvenir shop, and gas station that's been rebuilt after having been razed by a fire a few years before. It must be the next stopping point in the book, the place where the Pirsigs ate breakfast and Chris began writing a letter home to his mom.

There in the parking lot are two motorcycles with license plates like mine and plate brackets from my local bike shop. One of them is even a Suzuki dirt bike, smaller and cleaner than Jackie New and much newer; beside it is a BMW cruiser, large and cumbersome, loaded down with bags.

Their riders must be nearby, so I park alongside and head into the restaurant. Sure enough, out back on the balcony are two suited-up motorcyclists, probably father and son, finishing breakfast. I greet them as if they were relatives.

They, in turn, greet me like an annoying brother-in-law.

"You rode all the way here?" says the man. "That's too much. We trailered the bikes to the Montana border. Much more comfortable. There's nothing on the prairies, anyway."

The boy looks at him and nods. I ask if the dirt bike is his, and he nods again. "I got it for him this year," the father says. "It's okay, but I wish it had a bigger gas tank—it'll only go eighty miles, and we've run out a couple of times already."

The man, whose name is Karl, says he and his son, Ken, are traveling through the area for a few weeks "just to see the mountains." They live ten miles from my home back east. Ken turned sixteen this year, finally old enough for a license and a motorcycle, and the two of them are taking each day as it comes.

"I've never planned a motorcycle trip in my life," says Karl. "I just go somewhere, and then when I get there, I figure out where to go next. We like to go up roads just to see where they end and we sleep out on the tops of the mountains, though I think last night was a bit high for you, eh, Ken? He doesn't like it when it gets too cold." Ken nods.

"We found a logging road near here and rode up it for an hour before pitching our tent. I'm not bothered about animals up there—not four legged or two legged—but we are bothered about running out of gas. Carry a spare can on the dirt bike, but it's not always enough." Ken shakes his head.

I tell them about following the Zen route, and Karl says he's heard of the book but has never read it.

Funny that, because they're following it more closely than I am. A take-charge father and his young son making their first motorcycle trip together and living rough, the way they like it, washing out their socks each night and chowing down on granola bars, waking up to cold mornings, riding wherever the fancy takes them.

They pay their tab and go out front, walking a little clumsily in their riding trousers and jackets, carrying full-face helmets. I go along with them. Karl looks at my GPS and asks a few questions, comparing it to his own, while young Ken gets on the dirt bike to go for gas and fill the can. I take a photo, we shake hands, and they're off.

I pull the pink book out of the left bag and walk back to the restaurant for a late breakfast. Somewhere near here is the logging road where the Pirsigs slept, and when the coffee comes, I read the passage that describes their camp and see Chris's question, which he asks his father as they walk back to their sleeping bags that evening after washing at a stream.

"Dad?"
"What?" A small bird rises from a tree in front of us.
"What should I be when I grow up?"
The bird disappears over a far ridge. I don't know what to say. "Honest," I finally say.
"I mean what kind of a job?"
"Any kind."
"Why do you get mad when I ask that?"
"I'm not mad . . . I just think . . . I don't know . . . I'm just too tired to think. . . . It doesn't matter what you do."
Roads like this one get smaller and smaller and then quit.
Later I notice he's not keeping up.

Pirsig didn't know it when he wrote his book, of course, but Chris would never grow up. He'd live only another eleven years and then be stabbed in San Francisco, at age twenty-two, staggering across the road before dying beneath a streetlamp from a severed pulmonary artery and a lung full of blood.

I have a couple of photographs from 1968, printed from the Internet, which I use to mark my place in the book. One shows Chris hoisted on the shoulders of his dad and John Sutherland somewhere at the Beartooth Pass, where they're all grinning for themselves as much as for the camera, and the other shows Chris with the two Sutherlands at the same place. The adults look a little more serious, but Chris is smiling happily, hands in his pockets with confidence.

Chris never liked the book that made him immortal. In truth, he'd enjoyed the trip and had happy memories of it. "For him, it was a fun summer trip with his dad," remembers his boyhood friend Jim Hayes, now a Chicago lawyer.

"He was not a complainer. He was not a protected, whiny kid. He was pretty much up for an adventure. But I always sensed, as much as a kid can, that he was intense and tightly wound and that he had anxieties that I just didn't have."

Chris attended the book launch but argued with his father over his portrayal as a confused and whining kid. Now, thanks to the success of the book and his untimely death, Chris will always be that eleven-year-old boy in the photos.

Had he not been murdered, perhaps he'd be like his younger brother, Ted, who refers to his dad as an "ex-father." They fell out after Chris's death, and the narrator's tired response on that logging road to his older son's question is a clue to the reason. His son wants a simple response—doctor, astronaut, plumber, teacher—but the father cannot give it.

After his release from the hospital, and by the time of the Zen journey, Pirsig had had a variety of jobs and had never been satisfied. When the stigma of mental illness prevented him from teaching again, he used his writing skills to produce scientific and technical articles on excruciating subjects like agricultural and electromechanical machinery. When his pilot's license was taken away because he'd been diagnosed as schizophrenic, he discovered simple little motorcycles, which he enjoyed for the freedom of travel they provided—not to mention the opportunities for solitude, even when Nancy was riding along on the pillion seat, as she loved to do. She had started a job on the copy desk of the *St. Paul Dispatch* that had helped them save money for the larger house on Otis Avenue. Pirsig was now working as a technical writer for a small firm making computer memory devices, earning an okay living but hardly appeasing the philosophical questions that still tormented him.

So perhaps it's not surprising that his narrator should have been unconcerned with his son's career; he couldn't even be sure of his own. But as he sat in this restaurant thirty-six years ago, helping his son write a letter to his mother, he knew that he would write a book and get some of his thoughts on paper, much as I know I will make the most of this trip, so that it will last long after my arrival in San Francisco.

Breakfast comes, and I close the book and then open it again, looking at the Peter Pan pictures of the boy who sat here with his father all those years ago. A boy who was unsure of his future but wanted to make the most of it and had no idea how short that future would be. Who could not know that *this* was it—to spark the imagination of a blind woman in Minneapolis and forever grin cheerfully from a photograph.

The toast is eaten and the coffee drunk. I walk back to the bike and place the book back in the saddlebag and rummage around. Those plastic bags make it difficult to find anything. Here it is, kept flat and safe inside another book: a picture of my own two boys, taken earlier in the month at my cousin's wedding. I want to see it now. I *need* to see it now.

They're wearing suits—their very first suits, a little too large, in matching gray, smart with blue neckties—standing down on the dock of the little river that runs beside my aunt's house. I love this photo because my older boy, Andrew, is smiling and standing with his arms clasped in front and his younger brother, Tristan, is standing beside him, a little shorter and goofier and a little toothier in the grin. They're pleased to be wearing smart adult clothes and anticipating the joy of the wedding that's about to take place.

In their eyes is a light of innocence and happiness and excitement for the future. But now I look at the picture and wonder if it might also be a Peter Pan photo. As I've seen so many times, even just an hour ago in that ditch, anything can happen.

But that's not the lesson of Zen, which tells of living for the moment and having no problems right now, enjoying the strawberries for their sweetness. So far as I know, both boys still have that light in their eyes. Now, though, it's a reminder of one of the greatest lessons of all: live as if you'll live forever, but live each day as if it were your last.

Maybe Pirsig's advice to Chris—just be honest—wasn't so bad at all.

I pull out onto the highway and carry on into Idaho, still headed downhill.

This road just gets better and better. Curves marked for 40 miles per hour can be taken easily at 60, and those that advise 35 need just a rolling off of the throttle and a steady hand at 55. No brakes, no gears, just an engine pushing the wheels along for turn after turn after turn.

I'm descending, but very gradually. The Lochsa River here is shallow and wide, not swift like the streams coming off the Beartooth, but fast enough for little whitecaps to form over the shoals. Small wooded islands break the water's flow, and the opposite bank is just a high slope of pine forest leading into the Clearwater Mountains. The sunlight blinks over the ridge and through the trees.

The road begins to level as I approach Grangeville, where the Pirsigs stopped for chocolate malteds. The sun is in my eyes and the trees are fewer, so I pull into a rest stop beside the river and dig out the water bottle from its place beside the sleeping bag.

The camping really can't be put off any longer, and today's thoughts have persuaded me not to give up on the Pirsigs so quickly. They stayed at a well-marked campground near the Oregon border. If I don't pitch the tent tonight, unafraid of animals both four legged and two legged, then I'll never do it.

I'm taking a drink of water, hot from the sun, and eyeing the sleeping bag and tent and thinking of tonight when a Harley-Davidson pulls in alongside me from the other direction. This is a real high-miler, all right: an Electra Glide with a rolled-up tent and poles strapped low to each saddlebag and spare tire tubes lashed low to the back. Everything else is packed away in the hard cases, but as the rider parks the bike and dismounts, he turns to his rear seat, where there's a small cooler tied in place. He opens it and slops around the packed ice before pulling out a wet and frosted bottle of water.

He grins. "It's a hot one, huh?"

Kent, who looks every inch a Harley rider, with long, grizzled beard and black T-shirt, is much less reticent about his road trip than Ken and Karl were about theirs. He's well organized, too, and having a ball because of it.

"This is the sixth week now, and I've got to be back by the weekend or my girlfriend will give me what for." He laughs. "Thirteen thousand miles so far. Hell of a ride."

He's coming back from Alaska and the high Canadian Arctic, where the highway shredded his tires and it took three days of riding at no more than 40 miles per hour on the gravel to reach Inuvik, in the Northwest Territories, up toward the Arctic coast, and return to Dawson City in the Yukon. He says he's making the trip because he finally has the time after serving a year in Iraq. He had ninety days before he had to get back to his job in Iowa grading roads, so he made the most of it.

"Hell, I don't know when I'll have another chance," he says. "I told my girlfriend that I've got to make up for the bike sitting still for the last year, and she didn't mind. She even flew up to Alaska for a week to join me and ride around. I've got to get back soon, though—last week I ground a hole in the tent going around Mount Saint Helens a little too quick."

He says he didn't like Washington State—too many tourists—and then asks about my ride. When I'm done telling him, he makes a kind comment about the bike, how it would be much better in Alaska than his heavy Hog, puts his bottle of water back in the ice cooler, and shakes my hand good-bye.

"Say hello to California for me!" he says. "I'll get there next time." And he's gone.

I didn't tell him, but I'd ridden Jackie Blue up to Alaska nineteen years ago—and shredded her tires in the Yukon. After heading north from Billings, I crossed the border and kept going north just as far as I could, through Edmonton and into the Northwest Territories, around the Great Slave Lake and all the way to Yellowknife on the lake's north shore. Some friends lived there, and it was a chance to see the subarctic.

It took three days to make it the nine hundred miles from Edmonton to Yellowknife, and the road, unpaved north of the 60th parallel, was cold and slippery. Several times I slid off into the muddy ditch. When I crossed the Mackenzie River, the vast and wide watercourse that I now remember drains the deepest lake in the Western Hemisphere for a thousand miles before emptying into the Arctic Ocean, the bugs were so bad they worked their way past my helmet and into my ears. Some even made it through the Velcro of the sealed map holder that's on Jackie New today.

Yellowknife, N.W.T.
21 August 1985

I made it into Yellowknife yesterday afternoon, cold, dirty, and pretty weather-beaten, and I'm now seriously considering calling the whole thing off. I can handle the dirt, the weariness, the pot-holed washboard mud roads, the monotony, and the flies, but the cold is getting to me.

Yesterday's drive was only 350 miles and I kept up a good speed for most of the way, despite much of the road being covered in loose stones that were as slippery as snow for Jackie Blue, or freshly graded earth that forced me to drive in first or second gear as I slipped and twisted along tire tracks, but the cold had set in after only 100 miles and I drove hunched and shivering. The warming sun was continually hidden by low-level rain clouds that poured at regular intervals and I doubt the temperature rose much above 45 degrees.

What could I do? I was numb with no available heat save Jackie Blue's encrusted engine, and no nothing for 200 miles. If I stopped, I shivered all the more and was immediately attacked by a thousand nasty little flies. I'm afraid that I shall always remember the mighty Northwest Territories as a land of trees, rocks, and mud.

No electric vest back then.

I didn't stick around in Yellowknife, though my friends gave me a warm welcome. The miserable ride up was weighing heavily on my stay there, so within the week I dressed as thickly as possible and rode back south, covering nearly a thousand miles during a day and night that stayed warm and dry, before pausing for a few hours of rest in the short period of summer darkness. I had very little money, perhaps a few hundred dollars to last till I found a job, and no credit card, so slept in a bank-machine kiosk.

Fort St. John, B.C.
24 August 1985

Last night was magical. I pulled out of the truck stop and into the vast prairie night; the unending smooth, straight road seemed to unfold at the tip of the dipped headlight while the huge star-filled sky made me feel very small and open on my motorcycle. I could even recognize some of the constellations, easy ones like Orion, the Seven Sisters, and the Plough, which reminded me of the same sky at home.

A gently chill wind cooled my face and its quiet echo in my ears was combined only with the soft background rumble of Jackie Blue's steady, constant, reassuring engine. I drove for miles like that at an unchanging 50 mph, playing light games with the occasional overtaking truck.

Eventually the road began to rise and fall so that I rode through cold, foggy air in the dip and deliciously warm air at the crest. The whole experience seemed unreal even at the time, for I saw several shooting stars up ahead, lightning safely over to the distant west, and, if I glanced over my right shoulder, an enveloping display of the aurora borealis. I was warm and dry, yet open and vulnerable.

The next day I rode north again along the Alaska Highway. The day turned wet and eventually the rain turned to snow and near the high ground close to the Yukon border I pulled in at a campsite that advertised trailers for rent. Motel rooms were at least $50 a night up there and it was far too cold and wet to pitch a tent, so the small trailer was a godsend—I shared it with two other riders, and we split the $15 price among us. The next day I rode down from the snowy high ground and warmed up in a natural hot spring close to the road. From then on, all the way to Alaska, I didn't look back.

Contact Creek, Y.T.
25 August 1985

It seems to me that I seem to keep falling on my feet. The bad experiences have without exception led to good times.

If I'd not stopped for a coffee to avoid yet another rainstorm yesterday, I would not have spent a couple of hours talking to Dave Powell, ex–Egyptian smuggler, Central American gun runner, Arctic cook, and gigolo, who gave me some good advice that I'll always remember:

"When you get old, son, your body will break down like mine and you'll be left with only memories. Isn't it better to be a has-been than a never-was?"

Nineteen years later and it's no different, though I'm probably more cynical about a stranger's claims to having run guns and been a gigolo.

I didn't ride up the Dempster Highway to Inuvik as Kent just has. I headed back south, having crossed into Alaska and gotten most of the way to Fairbanks, but it was late in August and there were already reports of deep snow on the ground to the north. My cash was even more depleted, and I wanted to get to a warmer climate to look for work. Vancouver seemed good.

So I passed the junction for the Dempster and turned east off the Alaska Highway to take a shortcut and vary the route to the British Columbia border along 360 miles of gravel road. There were few settlements along its entire length.

Within ten miles, a rock that might have been an arrowhead sunk its way through the thinning rubber of the rear tire. There was nothing to do but fix the flat myself, stripping everything off the bike to lay it on its side and remove the wheel and tire, put on a new inner tube, and pump up the tire with a foot pump brought along for just this purpose. It was the first flat tire I'd ever experienced, and the persistent bugs made me impatient. By the time the bike was upright again and ready to ride, with everything stowed away, at least a couple of hours had passed. Not a single vehicle had driven by.

A few hours later, after a stop for gas halfway at Ross River and fifty miles or so farther on through the northern wilderness, the tire was flat again. This time everything was at hand and the bike stripped down more quickly, but now I had to patch the hole in the tube, since I'd already used the spare. As well, the foot pump broke and had to be disassembled and repaired. It was another couple of hours before I was back on the road. This was no work of art, a patient soaping of the rim and a leapfrogging of the irons, but a rip-and-tear job hurried along by bugs and sheer frustration.

Thirty minutes on and it was flat again. Still no vehicles had passed. By now the late summer sun was setting, and I could take no more. I pitched my tent beside the road and, having no food or water, slept fitfully until a large animal sniffing at the canvas woke me soon after dawn. The top of the fly was open, and a black bear was on the other side, shuffling around my barren site.

After a long time waiting in the tent to give the bear a chance to leave, I fixed the tire again—a struggle for hours with the sidewalls, which now refused to slide easily into place—and eventually set off into the morning. I was hungry, thirsty, wet, and fed up. And as I rode around a corner of the gravel road a little too quickly, the front wheel slipped and the bike and I flew from the road and down an embankment into a large pool of water. Had it been another flat tire or just the loose gravel surface? I don't know and never will.

The bike fell into the water, and when I jumped off to right her, my ankle twisted and I didn't have the strength to push her out. She was stranded in a couple of feet of water, almost to the top of the engine, with soft mud underneath, a good six feet from the edge of the pool.

I was as stuck as I've ever been and ever want to be.

Eventually, perhaps an hour after I splashed into the pool, a ranger drove past and somehow saw me below the road. He came in and helped push the bike out. She wouldn't start because the electrics were waterlogged. He couldn't offer any more help since I wouldn't leave Jackie Blue behind and his car was too small to carry her.

More time passed, and a pair of pickup trucks drove by, Indian hunters and their families on their way home to Watson Lake, my destination that day. They loaded me and the bike into the back of one of the trucks, fed me sandwiches and whiskey, and eventually provided a sofa for me to sleep on for a week.

Jackie Blue dried out while Charlie at the gas station fixed the tire properly, but my ankle still hurt a great deal. Then the bike just quit as I was riding to Charlie's for a party one evening. Something electrical was fried. My heart wasn't in it anymore and I gave up, arranging transportation for me and the bike down to Vancouver. My dad wired some money and she was loaded onto a truck; I followed behind on a bus.

Vancouver, B.C.
5 September 1985

I feel very much like a bum at the moment, wandering through downtown with my dirty clothes, grimy body, and

dusty hold-all. I'm looking forward to a shower and some
clean clothes.

By the time I knocked on the door of a friend of my sister's, asking for a place to sleep, there was $20 left. Time to get a job.

And here I am now, on this perfect afternoon in Idaho, wondering if I'm up to pitching the tent tonight. What have I become?

CHAPTER THIRTEEN

Idaho

Fʀᴏᴍ ᴛʜᴇ ᴛᴏᴘ ᴏꜰ ᴛʜᴇ ᴘʟᴀᴛᴇᴀᴜ beyond Grangeville, the Pirsigs looked down and saw a road that wound in "a hundred hairpin turns into a desert of broken land and crags." The broken land is there all right, ridges and ripples of folded scrub, but it's not until I'm halfway down the long, straight descent of Seven Mile Hill, past the first of its runaway truck ramps, that the old road's hairpins show themselves off to the left.

This is a new road, built in 1975 to replace the twists of White Bird Grade. That old highway had climbed twenty-nine hundred feet in its fourteen miles with so many turns that if they were placed together they'd have formed thirty-seven complete circles. No wonder the Pirsigs were impressed.

Now it runs through the site of the Battle of White Bird Canyon. A sign at the scenic lookout tells the story of the battle 127 years ago: the U.S. First Cavalry attempted to cut the troublesome Nez Perce off at the pass, stopping their retreat to safety over the Salmon River. But the native warriors were not as tired as the cavalrymen, who had traveled eighty miles in two days, and they fought more skillfully. The cavalry was scattered, and more than thirty of its one hundred soldiers were killed, with no losses among the Indians.

Today the valley is quiet and peaceful. Up here, where the cavalry captain watched the Indian camp and planned his attack, there's just a car parked in the shade of some trees; a pair of small bare feet pokes from the window of the blue Chevy Tracker as the

185

driver sleeps away the hot afternoon. The wind that swept Custer's campground in North Dakota is far away, and the Idaho heat presses against everything.

For me time is slipping away. Without the Sutherlands to slow them down, the Pirsigs made early starts and traveled longer days. Now it's already 4 p.m., and there are another 130 miles to go. I ride down into the valley, near the town of White Bird, where the road follows the canyon floor, running alongside the Salmon River below on the right. This is a deeper, faster-moving river than the Lochsa, and it's not long before there are clusters of rubber rafts floating northward. Some seem to move almost as fast as the few cars on the road. This is the easy part for the rafters. They've just come through the rapids of Hells Canyon.

It might be cool down in the water, but it's oppressive up here. The terrific heat dries my eyes as I head into the sun with just a tinted visor and sunglasses to screen its brilliant light; the walls of the canyon seem white with seared rock and burned grass. It feels hotter than it was in the Dakotas, and when I make it into Riggins, I ask a young guy fixing a rafting trailer if he knows the temperature.

"The sign in town says a hundred and four," he says, "but it's probably hotter in the canyon. Could be a hundred ten out there. Good day to be in the water."

This part of the journey was a slog for the two Pirsigs as well. In *Zen and the Art*, the style changes to little anecdotes seen along the way as the narrator now delivers a lecture on "stuckness" and the mental challenge of not allowing yourself to get hung up on something. It was a lesson Pirsig himself had yet to master.

In the fall of 1968, having come through mental illness, reestablished his marriage and a middle-class lifestyle, earned a local reputation as a handy fixer of small engines and machinery, taken a motorcycle journey, interested a publisher in his thoughts on "a unification of spiritual feeling and technological thought," and turned forty, Pirsig had to sit down and write the damn book.

It did not come as easily as expected and turned out to be the biggest slog of all. He got stuck on many things.

He'd set a target of Christmas for the book's completion but spent most of that fall and winter just organizing his thoughts. Pirsig wrote notes to himself on index cards and by December had accumulated about three thousand of them, categorized as "Events," "People," "Maintenance Broad Fabric," "Zen Broad Fabric," and "Heights." Looking at that daunting slab of cards, he wrote to Jim Landis, suggesting a completion date of September 1969. He sat down each day at Nancy's portable Royal typewriter but had difficulty finding the right rhythm and schedule for the task.

"Writing is like being a lighthouse keeper," he said later. "You've got a job to do. If you say, 'I'll just do it Mondays and Wednesdays,' something's going to go aground."

In the summer of '69, to give himself a break and perhaps to be fair to his younger son, he loaded up the little Honda again and headed north with Ted for another long trip. They rode to Pirsig's aunt's house in Grand Forks, North Dakota, and stayed to watch Neil Armstrong walk on the moon, then continued north just as far as they could go, way up across the Canadian border and into northern Manitoba. When the road ended, they parked the bike and boarded a train for Churchill, the subarctic port on Hudson Bay, and it became the trip on which Ted would catch his first fish. Along the way they befriended a couple from Chicago, the Katzes, and Ted learned to fish and they caught lots of walleye and northern, which Mrs. Katz would cook every day.

"Happy memories. And a lot of staring at my dad's back, and he can be a pretty taciturn person, too," remembers Ted. "Not exactly great company for a kid, but it was interesting."

It didn't help the book to get written, however. It took another six months past that September promise to finish the twists and turns of the first draft. "It's done," Pirsig wrote to Landis. "All 120 thousand words of it, and it contains a story that with patience and luck can be worked into something of real power."

Those words, however, did not include the character of Phaedrus. It was about Bob Pirsig throughout, with too many I's in the narrative: "I did this, I did that." Nancy was mentioned frequently, always negatively. Pirsig knew it wasn't right, and not long after writing that letter he threw away the entire manuscript. Landis never saw it. Quality doesn't come easily.

The heat's too much, so I pull into a treed picnic area in front of an office of the Hells Canyon National Recreation Area. Some deer, grazing in the shade, bounce away, but without much fear. Strapped to the luggage is a Gatorade that I'd found in a store cooler back in Grangeville, and though the bottle's not so cold now, it gives me the lift I need.

Just as the map is spread out under a tree, a pickup moseys down from the office, and the driver leans through its window and asks where I'm from. He's seen the license plate. I tell him and he nods. "Me, too," he says. "I came out here in 'sixty-two on a vacation, and I've been here ever since. You be careful, or you'll stay here as well. It's just too beautiful to leave. I'm retiring soon, so I guess I'm sticking around."

Two sets of neighbors in the same day. Who'd believe it?

"Well, I might try to find somewhere just a little cooler," I say.

He agrees. "Too hot for a motorcycle today. I've got a 'seventy-seven BMW that I want to put on the road when I retire. That'll be fun. You have a good day." And he drives away. The deer, grazing now under some trees a little farther away, lift their heads to watch him.

Pirsig took a three-month break to clear his head and then went back to *Zen and the Art;* he kept the index cards for reference but otherwise started from scratch. He'd decided to create Phaedrus as an alter ego and was thrilled by the creative potential. The fragments of Phaedrus's life that are remembered are just a literary device: in truth, the shock treatments had erased some short-term memory, but his long-term memory had quickly returned. Robert

Pirsig the author could recall everything about Phaedrus just fine; it was Robert Pirsig the narrator who was still delusional.

Once the first chapter was completely rewritten, he knew he was on the right path. "I would go to bed at 6 p.m., get up at 2 a.m. and write until I went to work at 8," he said.

I did that for two years, first at home but then my wife threw me out. I expected the kids to shut up at 6 so I could sleep and she didn't think that was fair. So I got a $12-a-week room at a flophouse. My boss let me come into the office and write early in the morning and I'd show up for breakfast at my own house each day. Writing this book was a compulsive act and whoever stood in the way of it was going to get hurt.

But people *were* getting hurt. The concerns about Chris's mental health that Pirsig had expressed at the Shadehill campsite were warranted, and in 1970 Chris was admitted to the state hospital at Faribault; doctors there wanted to determine the cause of his confusion, which was beginning to echo that of his pretreatment father. Always a jealous sibling, he had been fighting frequently with his brother.

"Chris was not nice to Ted—treated him with a fair amount of disdain," remembers Jim Hayes, Chris's friend. "It was pretty much a one-way street. They'd have some knock-down, drag-out fights, but Chris was always going to win."

Now fourteen, Chris was smoking a lot of dope and even selling it to his brother when the two weren't fighting. And Ted was getting into trouble, too, vandalizing cars, golf course flags, school windows, railroad sheds. When the cops caught him, he was remanded to psychiatric care. Ted was diagnosed as having "a lot of rage," to be treated with group therapy and psychiatric counseling.

Amid the turmoil, Pirsig kept writing. To research his material more thoroughly and "keep his backside covered," and perhaps to find respite from the problems at home, he joined a group of Zen practitioners. After a year he invited Nancy along, and she also became a regular. In January 1972 the group joined with others to establish the Minnesota Zen Meditation Center in an apartment near the university, with Bob Pirsig on its board of directors; a Zen master from San Francisco, Dainin Katagiri, moved into an apartment in the same fourplex.

The Zen may have helped the parents, but counseling was having little effect on Ted. That winter the thirteen-year-old was arrested for stealing a Janis Joplin tape from a Montgomery Ward store. Police found pot in his pockets, and he was charged with both shoplifting and drug possession. Maynard represented him in court and arranged for him to spend two months in a private psychiatric hospital. Halfway through the stay, and against his parents' wishes, he was allowed home for a weekend. He promptly went out for the afternoon with a friend to buy drugs. That evening Ted overdosed in his bedroom on a powerful combination of LSD, speed, and PCP.

"Mom described it to me afterwards," Ted told me in a letter.

She was reading in the living room, Bob was working in the basement, I was upstairs in my room. It was evening, and we'd just taken my friend Paul home a little earlier. Mom heard me come out of the room, then stumble and slide down the stairs. She called out, "Are you all right?" but I didn't respond, and just went back upstairs. A little while later the exact same thing happened again, and she went and got Bob. When he opened the door to my room, I jumped up and tried to get out through the window, smashing it. He grabbed me and wrestled me to the hallway floor, where he pinned me down. Mom said I was screaming every single swear word in the world plus some she'd never heard of. She tried calling the hospital but they said they couldn't help, just call the police. Meanwhile I was writhing uncontrollably and Bob couldn't keep me from thrashing my head back and forth on the carpet, shredding the skin off my jaw. Mom said that when the police came it took a number of them to restrain me and get me to the ambulance, which took me to the Ramsey

*Hospital emergency room, where they pumped my stomach
and stated that if not large for my age I probably would have
died.*

*Me? I remember waking up in a strange hospital room
with restraints on my arms and legs, a chin that hurt like hell,
and I had no idea of where I was or how I got there.*

He went back to the psychiatric hospital, where he turned
fourteen years old. When the medical insurance ran out, he was
sent to another facility, an hour west of home in St. Cloud.

Bob Pirsig, close to finishing his book, wanted a quieter, less
distracting environment, so in the early spring of 1972, with Ted
out of the house and under medical supervision, he left his family
completely, driving their pickup camper to the north shore of
Lake Superior. He went to a campground near Two Harbors,
where his mother was born. The place was closed for the winter
and covered with a foot of snow, but he backed up the camper and
drove as hard as he could into a snowbank, wanting to get stuck so
there could be no turning back. The motorcycle was strapped
inside to provide transportation into town for supplies.

He wrote only during the day because the camper's power
supply was too feeble to create adequate light. But with no distractions, the crucial words began to come together.

"As spring got warmer the lake became more and more beautiful," Pirsig told me in a letter. "One morning I went down to get
water and found the rocks covered with silver fish. I had heard of
the smelt run, decided this was it, and gathered up about a dozen
of them and had what I think was smelt for breakfast for the next
several days. I stayed on there, writing from dawn to dusk until
the regular camping season started in late spring."

And so it was here, on a rock ledge overlooking the lake, that
the final six chapters of *Zen and the Art of Motorcycle Maintenance* were completed in two months of concentrated effort.

Satisfied with the book, Pirsig came home to find that his
younger son was still having problems. Ted ran away from the
facility in St. Cloud and lived on the streets of the Twin Cities for

a month before returning home to face the music. In court, Maynard Pirsig again argued for clemency. He knew what he was doing—as dean of Minnesota's law school, he'd once developed a training program for professionals in delinquency control. It didn't hurt that the judge and prosecutor were his former students. Ted got off with three weeks for "evaluation" in the state lockup at Lino Lakes, which Maynard had helped establish.

Robert Pirsig spent a great deal of time with Ted over the summer and even introduced his son to Zen meditation, but still nothing could get in the way of the book. It was hugely long—more than 200,000 words—and over the year he trimmed and cut it as best he could. It must have been agony. "To get a line that is exactly right, you sometimes have to sacrifice everything . . . ," he said later, "interaction with people, personal comfort, everything. It's that slight difference between a line that's almost right and one that's exactly right."

When he was done, in November, the work was mailed to the six publishing houses that still had an interest in reading it. Five of them turned it down, but Jim Landis was not disappointed and wrote to Pirsig straightaway: "I'm happy, if perplexed, to say that I remain loving the book, which is wise and fun and sad and which taught me some things."

Now it's time for the last push of the day, and I head back onto the road, traveling south. The sun's more tolerable, having sunk below the high ridge to the west of the Seven Devils Mountains. Just another hour or two of riding should get me to my destination with an hour of sunlight to spare. Absolutely no excuse not to camp.

So where was the last place I camped? Probably upstate New York, perhaps near Lake Placid the time spiders came into the tent and I had to pack it up wet in the morning when I might have been enjoying breakfast at a B&B. Yes, that was it. Fifteen years ago.

I once rode a motorcycle with my wife around France, loaded down with sleeping bags and this same tent and poles and pegs, and in the whole ten-day trip we never once pitched camp—it was just too easy and too cheap to stay at motels. The beds were more comfortable and already made, and it didn't matter if it was raining. That was the trip when I asked her to marry me. Not a doubt in my mind. I even had the engagement ring in my pocket, bought in Africa and made of cheap copper; she stopped wearing it because it turned her finger green.

What's she doing now? It'll be after midnight at her sister's farm, too late to call. There was a phone booth in Grangeville and I could have pulled over, but it was getting late and camping tonight was weighing on my mind. I'd told her at the airport that she'd get a call from California on my birthday, and it seems so close now that it can wait until then. That's the goal. Nothing's going to get in the way of that.

As if on cue, a rest area appears, and I pull in to fill the empty Gatorade bottle at the water fountain. There's a family from Washington State in a pickup truck that's loaded with luggage and furniture and a small boy next to the truck already dressed for bed in his Spider-Man pajamas. The boy looks like my younger son, who also has Spider-Man pajamas. He'll be asleep now. Everyone in the family turns to stare, so I leave, feeling guilty.

Maybe Pirsig's right about the loneliness being there only when you're among other people. People are always a reminder of what's so far away.

The pale moon shows through the blue sky as the land rises and turns to flat irrigated fields of grain. The sun softens and the hills on the horizon grow hazy in the gentler light, so different from the fire of the canyon.

Finally I reach Cambridge, the last town for gas and provisions, a chance to fill up and buy a burrito and a couple of cans of beer. Across the quiet street from the gas station are two restaurants featuring "country cookin'," a bar, and a motel with rooms starting at $28. Perfect.

But this really is the last chance. Everything's perfect for camping. If it's not tonight, it'll never happen, and how can I then hope to understand that eleven-year-old boy who loved it so much, who found release from the road in the comfort of nature? Who grins from the photo every time I open the book?

A final kick of the bike's starter for the day. I'm off down the road, heading west again instead of south, to the campground near the Oregon border.

Jim Landis, Pirsig's editor, may have been excited about the manuscript, but the executives at William Morrow were not. It was still very long, and the expense of printing such a work by an unknown author was difficult to justify. However, Landis's enthusiasm and optimism persuaded the editorial board to offer Pirsig a $3,000 advance, and the manuscript was officially sold in January 1973. William Morrow could hardly deny its editor his prize: when Landis presented the book to the marketing department in April, he called it "brilliant beyond belief; it is probably a work of genius and will, I'll wager, attain classic stature."

Over the next year the manuscript was pared down to its final 130,000 words—the publisher had wanted more removed but agreed to the final length in exchange for Pirsig taking a smaller cut of the royalties so that the book could be sold at the affordable price of $7.95. A suitable subtitle was settled upon: *An Inquiry into Values* seemed as good as any, and as Landis wrote to Pirsig that summer, "It's probably as concisely true a few words as any of us is likely to come up with."

The canny young editor shopped it around to some select reviewers and struck pay dirt when George Steiner, the celebrated literary critic, persuaded *The New Yorker* to let him review it. In the opening paragraph of his review, famously titled "Uneasy Rider," Steiner wrote: "Told by the blurb that we have here 'one of the most unique and exciting books in the history of American letters,' one bridles both at the grammar of the claim and at its routine excess. The grammar stays irreparable. But I have a hunch that the assertion itself is valid."

Zen and the Art of Motorcycle Maintenance was published on April 15, 1974, without Pirsig's photo on the book jacket to give the unknown author an aura of mystery. It sold a stunning fifty thousand copies within three months. "There was a supersaturation condition in the country," mused Pirsig that year when asked to explain its success. "All the problems everybody is feeling, what direction our whole national culture is going in, a general feeling of unhappiness about American life—everything from Watergate to the price of bread at the local grocery. I think the book is acting as a seed crystal to solidify ideas about what's going on."

Full-page newspaper ads touted the book's significance; the Book-of-the-Month Club picked it up; Pirsig was invited to apply for, and was awarded, a Guggenheim Fellowship so that he could quit his job and continue to write serious literature—perhaps he had been nominated by Steiner, a fellow three years earlier. At parties, according to John Sutherland, Pirsig clearly enjoyed the adulation that was fed by the buzz. Ted remembers it differently: "His monologues that often rolled eyes at home or in other quarters suddenly were being listened to." In Minneapolis and St. Paul, Maynard Pirsig would stop into bookstores and check for copies of *Zen and the Art,* then tell the clerks with pride that the author was his son. In the conservative Catholic neighborhood in which they lived and stood out as liberal bohemians, Bob gave a copy of the book to one of his neighbors, inscribing it, "Maybe now you'll take me more seriously!"

Interviews were given by Bob and Nancy to the local media and by Bob to the national media. "I'm just sort of trying to stay as cool as I can at this point and see how things happen," he told an interviewer for National Public Radio. "When *Time* reporters come into your living room it just creates a scene that is sharply different from any kind of life you've lived before. I don't know what's going to happen."

Then, in the summer of 1974, when Pirsig might have been expected to take to the road to plug his new book, his publisher withdrew him from the circuit, adding even greater mystery to his persona. The ploy was a success; the book sold better than ever.

. . .

The campground is well signed about twenty miles from town, on the edge of the Payette National Forest. There's a ranger station with some horses grazing alongside, and then there's nobody.

The place is deserted, and all of the dozen or so sites are available. They're very basic, with just a fire pit and a picnic table and a garbage bag under a rock, all in smooth dirt clearings under very tall pine trees. The shadows are growing long, but I ride past all the sites and then go back to one close to the stream and the outhouse. Poor Chris had diarrhea, so it seems a logical choice.

All is quiet when the engine stops. I take the tent bag and the sleeping bag and sleeping roll off the bike but leave everything else packed, and set to, spreading out the ground sheet. The fabric comes next, laid flat on the sheet and formed into a tent with the fiberglass and aluminum poles. I put up the tent fabric and go to the stream to rinse the grime off my hands.

Then the fly covers the fabric and the little vestibule goes at the end and the sleeping roll and bag are laid out inside and everything's fastened to the ground with pegs and it's done. Twenty minutes at the most. That wasn't bad. Used to do it in ten.

Once the tent's up, I can stroll down the path to the campground entrance to place $8 in an envelope and push it into the collection box. Twenty dollars cheaper than staying in town and Pirsig's advice to be honest will keep the rangers away tonight.

This really is idyllic. Chewing on the burrito at the picnic table and sipping the still-cold beer, I read the pink book easily in this place where nothing has changed. This could be the very same site, with a bluff to the west of the stream that rises like a desert cliff in Persia, just as the narrator describes. I read until the sun is too low, then turn the flashlight into a little candle and read some more.

This was a peaceful place for the father and son. They parked, spread their sleeping bags on the ground—actually Bob put Chris's bag up on the picnic table—and fell asleep to the sound of the stream. When all is completely dark, I crawl into the tent, bunch my jacket up as a pillow, undress to my undershorts, and slide into the sleeping bag. I fall asleep as I did in the yurt, listening to the splash of the water nearby.

My night is restless. A root sticks through the bedroll, forcing me to lie on one side. A truck drives past and then another—people going into the forest. The air inside the tent is not fresh and cool but cloying. It would be better out on the table. I drift in and out of sleep.

I'm riding on the White Bird Grade, up and down, and the eagle is swooping down from the sky. Just as it nears every time, the road twists away and the bike turns with it and the huge bird misses and flies away for another pass. It makes no call as it did in the room, but the rush of air between its feathers and around its wings is all around. And from the other side of the ridge, from the new road far away, there's someone else watching us. A woman with dark eyes. I've not seen her before—has she been there all along?

Then I roll onto the root and wake and roll over and dream again, the same dream. And I wake again and listen to the other sounds of the night—the wind in the trees, a bird's call—and, eyes half open, I climb from the bag and carry it out to the table. Back into the bag, now on top of the table, and the breeze clears my head and the splash of the stream continues and sleep comes easily, welcoming, restful, and meditative.

It's cold this morning, but there's no point staying in the sleeping bag. My watch says 8 a.m., but the park is right on the state border, right on the edge of a time zone, so I set it to 7 a.m. and feel good about the early start.

In the book, Pirsig's narrator lay here awhile, watching Chris through the spokes of one of the wheels of the motorcycle, feeling a fondness for him that didn't show itself often. He got out of his bag and dressed and shuffled around, packing the luggage, and then, since Chris showed no signs of stirring and the sun was already over the bluff, walked over to the child. "WAKE!" he hollered in his ear, jolting the boy out of sleep, then began reciting Omar Khayyám:

> . . . *For the Sun who scatter'd into flight*
> *The Stars before him from the Field of Night,*
> *Drives Night along with them from Heav'n, and strikes*
> *The Sultan's Turret with a Shaft of Light.*

What an asshole! It would be kind to give Pirsig the benefit of the doubt and consider the anecdote one of those "changed for rhetorical purposes," to illustrate the narrator's tortured struggle with his alter ego.

I dress quickly, wearing the thin wool sweater that was unthinkable yesterday. There's sunshine high in the trees but not here on the ground. The cliff face opposite is bright from the sun, but here it's cool and still a little dark.

The dry camping gear packs quickly, but before the bike gets loaded there's some time to check her over for the day. That reference to watching Chris through the wheel was a reminder to inspect her spokes, which can work loose over bumps and throw off the symmetry of the turning tire. I work my way around the wheels with a small wrench, tapping each spoke to listen for a difference in the sound of the tap or feel a difference in the rebound of the wrench. All seem fine.

The rear tire is not in good shape, though. It's worn almost flat in the center, leaving very little tread to dissipate water on a wet road. Cornering is riskier with the tire's square profile. With more than a thousand miles to go, it seems to be wearing much more quickly now that the chunky rubber knobs have been eroded. My plan had been to change both tires in San Francisco, but with so little tread left, I don't think the rubber will make it there. Soon

the steel cords will start to show through, and the tire will probably blow.

There's nothing to be done about it here, though, and the bike
loads quickly and the campsite reverts to its original bareness.

I'm thinking of the rear tire as I ride down the campground
road—the rubber's become thin, and any sharp stones or even
pointed roots in the pathway are likely to pierce it. Bloody hell—
there's always something.

Out on the two-laner, the sun warms rapidly, and the pavement
twists away to the west, dropping down the last few miles to the
state line. Soon there's a lake up ahead, and the road turns north to
follow its shore, curving with its shape. No trees here at all, just
scrub and power lines. It must be a reservoir with a dam holding it
back—bare hills, wide water, blue sky.

The road follows the shore for several more miles. Nothing
disturbs the stillness of the morning.

The dam is just a couple of hundred feet wide, and I cross over
to follow the western shore of a second reservoir, much larger this
time. There's no sign, but this must be Oregon. The road's a little
straighter and a little higher. On this side of the dam a boat ripples
through the stillness a quarter mile out in the water, its wake
washing all the way to the rocky beaches on either side.

As I turn left around a hill, there's a T-junction with a stop
sign, and a small town nestled snugly in the folds of the land to
the north. This is where the power station is, and it seems so foreign compared to my own home—no trees, a man-made lake,
miles from anywhere.

Yet there's a sign for a school bus stop and another sign pointing to a picnic area. This is no satellite town built from double-
wides to service the power plant but a self-sustaining community
in its own right, a place to raise kids and go out for dinner and
watch TV in the evening and make lasting friendships.

There are places like this all across America, different from one another but homes all the same. Places to come home to at the end of a long journey. This town is somebody's home, and it could easily be mine.

In the summer of 1974 the sudden attention was getting to Robert Pirsig, and he missed the anonymity of his previous life. Ted remembers coming home one day and seeing a couple of motor-cycles parked outside. "They were up from Chicago," he recalls. "Dad was out of town; no one else was at home; we chatted a bit and then they left, heading out to follow the Zen route. I think they were the first 'Zen Pilgrims.' "

Pirsig would not have wanted to meet them. In *Lila* he recalls a Zen master telling his group that if someone becomes too famous he'll go straight to hell, then recounts his own experience: "You would think that fame and fortune would bring a sense of close-ness to other people, but quite the opposite happens. You split into two people, who they think you are and who you really are, and that produces the Zen hell."

Sometime that summer Jim Landis made a surprise visit to the house on Otis Avenue, stopping over on a flight from California. "Nancy picked me up at the airport and took me to their home," he recalled.

> She called up the stairs, "Bob, there's somebody here to see you." Bob came down the stairs looking somewhat put out and skeptical, which he looked even more when he saw me with my long hair and red beard. Bob was already being sought out by people who were looking for a guru, and I guess I looked like one of them. But then Nancy said, "Bob, this is Jim Landis." So he came right over to me and embraced me which is not, as I've learned, necessarily his Scandinavian way.

The attention soon became overbearing. In a newspaper inter-view Pirsig told of a woman coming up to him in the post office one day and asking, "Aren't you Robert Pirsig?" "That really bothered me," he said.

Then the mail started getting heavy—a lot of people with mental problems. People are calling on the phone. "What motorcycle should I buy?" "You wrote a great book." . . . So one morning I just woke up at three. I told my wife, "I just have to get out of here." We had the camper packed in half an hour and I was on the road. Trying to adjust to the sudden shift of personal situation is probably the worst part of success— certainly it is for me.

That June he drove the old camper across the prairie and back to the high country outside Bozeman, where he could find solitude again and concentrate on writing a second book. His first idea was to write an anthropological examination of American Indian culture, which he wanted to call *Them Pesky Redskins*. "It's going to be very scholarly," he said. "I mean, this is going to be a real dull son of a bitch." Then he planned for a book tentatively titled *Heresy and Insanity*, "a comparison of activity among the people who pressed the Inquisition and psychiatrists." After that perhaps another scholarly work, titled *The Dialectics of Quality*.

A reporter in Bozeman contacted him a month or so later to request an interview, and surprisingly Pirsig consented. He was in town with time on his hands while the brakes were being fixed on the camper and the propane heater replaced. But he had other reasons: "I'm standing here in a phone booth," he told the journalist. "My wife just told me Bantam bought the paperback rights for $370,000 and there's just no one here in Bozeman I can tell that to and have it mean anything."

The reporter drove with him back up into the mountains and interviewed him in the camper. He described a man with gray hair and, at forty-five, deep stress lines around his eyes:

He dresses sloppily: Every day a green army fatigue shirt over a white T-shirt, black slacks and socks and a pair of tennis shoes. He drinks a lot: perhaps a Martini before breakfast, another at lunch, a pitcher of beer in the afternoon, a Martini before dinner and a Scotch after. He carries anthropology books and a clipboard around with him and is constantly making notes to himself: call home, take a bath, buy oil for engine. His favorite expression is "real good," which he uses as a greeting, a farewell and a general exclamation.

Writing was slow, though, with Pirsig stretched out on a mattress in the camper, the typewriter on his lap, half-glasses on his nose, and slabs of index cards by his side. For all his ambitious plans, he spent most of the time trying to clear his mind, not writing a word for hours—days, even—at a time.

Up in the cool high country he shut himself away, and the fabric of his life began to wrap around itself again.

I turn south at the stop sign and head toward Baker City, and there's a sign making it official that I've crossed into the Pacific time zone—although there are still four long days of riding between here and San Francisco. The land is all rippled and scrub, not much good for anything by the look of it except feeding sheep and flooding for reservoirs. I've been going up and down so much that if it weren't for the reading on the GPS, I'd have no idea of the altitude. Three thousand four hundred feet, it says. Within a few miles the fields are greener, and I've dropped a thousand feet.

The year after the publication of *Zen and the Art*, having returned from the isolation of Bozeman to family life in St. Paul, Robert Pirsig agreed to write a review for *The New York Times* of a book titled *One Man, Hurt: A Shattering Account of the End of a Happy Marriage*. Pirsig didn't think much of the book, saying that its author's "atrocious suburban banality drowns out everything else." More than that, he went on to say that the author, some poor sap named Albert Martin, should be able to use his book as an advertisement for a new wife:

> I hope, for his own sake, that his final choice is someone who really appreciates him for the good man he is. Preferably, it should be an Eastern, Polish, Roman Catholic woman, heavy-boned and big-breasted, domineering and authoritarian, from a childhood of poverty like the one he got away from by marrying the little ballet dancer from Texas. She should love him earthily, and also her children and her church discipline and the suburban life, because she finds in these things the meaning of life itself. He deserves it.

Strong words, which were soon turned back on him in a scathing editorial published by his hometown paper, the *St. Paul Pioneer Press*. "Pirsig is a bigot, pure and simple," wrote Andrew M. Greeley, the priest and sociologist. "You don't argue with bigots; you denounce them and drive them out of the mass media. If Pirsig had maligned Jews or blacks, he would never appear in *The New York Times* again or ever have a book published. If he can escape unscathed from such a vicious slander on Polish Catholics, the only reason is the Catholics let him get away with it."

Greeley had been program director of the National Opinion Research Center at the University of Chicago, where Phaedrus had faced off against the committee chairman all those years before. Greeley's fighting words struck a vengeful blow; Pirsig would never write another review. Pirsig nonetheless has said he was unaware of the editorial—he just regretted being so mean in print. "I have always felt bad about that review," he explained years later. "What I wrote was honest and I think true, but I got the same feeling from it that I once got when I shot a deer at close range with a slug shotgun. I looked at the deer, dead in front of me, and wondered, 'Now what did I ever do that for? I didn't need to do that.'"

An explanation for Pirsig's cut-to-the-chase book review may be that the assigned book struck far too close to home. After years of physical separation and emotional isolation, he and Nancy were struggling to stay together. She'd wanted to leave him when he was undergoing shock treatment but had been talked into staying by his parents and his doctors. She clung to the hope that they could rescue their relationship and felt great guilt knowing he'd been too sick at the time to comprehend her thoughts, so she stayed to support him through the years of recovery and "normality." Yet now the great success of *Zen and the Art* was not the cure-all for their relationship that they'd hoped for. The author was not free to enjoy a relaxing and intimate retirement but instead was wedded to his work all the more as correspondence poured in challenging his thesis and questioning his philosophy. Scholars wanted to know why he'd disregarded the works of modern philosophers like Nietzsche, Heidegger, Kuhn, and Sartre. And casual readers just wanted to know what on earth he was going on about.

Nancy and Ted were practicing Zen with him, but the strain of literary celebrity and his efforts to justify the book intellectually were taking their toll. And Chris was back in the state psychiatric hospital at Faribault.

I stop for breakfast in Richland. Outside the café an old guy walking past pauses to look at the bike.

"I used to have a BSA," he says. "What a bike. Used to make my hands swell up from the vibration. One time I was crossing the Golden Gate Bridge and my goggles blew off and I thought I was going to lose it into the Bay. I loved that bike. You're lucky to be able to ride—make the most of it."

There was, at least, the consolation of the money. *Zen and the Art* was a runaway best seller, Hollywood was jockeying for the screenplay, and for a while it seemed Robert Redford would make the movie, although in the end its transition to the screen proved too daunting and Pirsig held out for too great a fee. But there was enough money now to spend $60,000 on a thirty-two-foot cutter-rigged sailboat, and Bob and Nancy began learning how to sail it. He wanted to realize a childhood dream, kindled on his sixth Christmas, when his parents bought him a globe and he first saw how much of the Earth was covered in ocean. They planned to voyage around the world, rediscovering the spirit of adventure they'd found two decades earlier in Mexico. And Nancy was all too happy to quit her job: she now worked long hours, four days a week, as the assistant director of the University of Minnesota's Department of University Relations. "I am looking forward to it," she told the local paper. "I have been dealing with people all my life. I have never spent much time alone—not more than a day or two. This has a terrific attraction."

I'm crossing over the Oregon Trail now, the wagon route of the pioneers, and the road is straight across the parched, rolling scrub. Back on the way out of Richland a sign marked the point where a landslide cut off the old road in '85, the road the Pirsigs would have taken, and the old curving pavement could be seen to the side of the new highway. I paused a moment and tried to imagine the little motorcycle chugging along the broken asphalt with its two passengers and heavy, rope-bound luggage, crossing over the place where I was parked. A straighter, better-built road has taken its place, and I pulled back onto it, heading west.

CHAPTER FOURTEEN

Eastern Oregon

THE *ZEN AND THE ART* STORY pauses awhile at Dayville, where the Pirsigs took a break from the heat underneath some massive cottonwood trees. The gas jockey invited them to rest on his front lawn, opposite the service station, and they fell asleep there for maybe half an hour before waking to the sound of gentle conversation—unhurried country talk between their host and the fire warden, with all the time in the world.

It would be good to find that front lawn. After two days of comparative solitude, this was the Pirsigs' longest conversation. In fact, at this point in the book, father and son are barely even speaking to each other. Chris is hardly mentioned as the narrator gets more and more involved in his all-encompassing lectures, but the boy is always there, riding silently behind or, when they stop, keeping quietly to himself.

There are times on this trip that I feel a bit like Chris, dragged along by the narrator and forced to go the extra miles to reach the night's destination. It'll be a relief to get to San Francisco and take charge again, although it's not clear in *Zen and the Art* just who's in charge right now. The narrator's starting to lose it as they slog along, Chris is shutting down, and always on the periphery is Phaedrus, a nudging, nagging reminder of what the narrator used to be. The closer they get to the coast, the more Phaedrus attempts to assert his personality. The narrator knows Chris is caught in the middle, a pawn between two combatants. He doesn't yet realize that it is Phaedrus who is the most vulnerable.

But here in Dayville there's a chance for a break. Even today the trees are the most distinctive feature of the town, lining the main street and shading it almost completely. They apparently grew so large because the irrigation ditch through town was particularly deep and wide; one cottonwood carries a small hand-painted sign on its trunk that declares, "23 Ft. 6 In. Around." I ride through town, perhaps a mile, and then double back to the eastern limit.

Jackie New doesn't need gas, though she almost ran out before I stopped at Prairie City, going five or six miles on the reserve tank with probably just another ten miles left. I do want a drink, though, and with a sudden pang of conscience remember the oil. Didn't check it this morning at the campground because—well, I don't know why. Hung up on the rear tire, probably.

Now I stop near a water fountain beside a children's playground. When I turn off the ignition and look down at the little oil window on the right side of the engine, I see that the glass is clear and empty. Oops.

I move the bike into the shade of one of the giant trees and, standing on her right side, tip her over as far as she will go before she'll fall. With the bike at forty-five degrees, a film of oil finally slides up inside the engine and coats the inside of the window. The level's very low from all this heat but not so far down that anything's been damaged. These big singles are bulletproof—they'll run on just a pint so long as the engine's not stressed. But not for too long.

This is the first oil Jackie New has needed since the oil change in Lemmon, and I still have the third quart I bought there as well as the original spare bottle brought from home. I take the multi-tool from its pouch on my belt and loosen the hot filler cap on the engine above the level window, spinning it off with gloved hands and placing it carefully on a rock to keep it from the dust of the road. The oil pours in slowly and carefully, without spilling, and the engine takes most of the quart before anything is visible through the little window. About a third down, all told. Not good, but caught in time.

The engine's clean, so there's no leak. Must be burning away quickly in this heat.

After the fix it's time for that drink, and I walk over to the fountain to fill my water bottle. The pressure is very great—water shoots an arc at least two feet into the air—so I put my head under the cool cascading stream, massaging it with my free hand, letting water run through my short hair and over my scalp. It is glorious.

Bob and Nancy loved their new sailboat. They took it out on Lake Superior throughout the summer, learning the ropes and the rhythm of the tides. Nancy hadn't quit her job yet but escaped to the water every three-day weekend. "You get used to the motion of the boat," she said at the time. "You are in that framework. Towns and houses and lawns don't look desirable any more. They just look like responsibilities and the boat looks so free."

It was named *Excellence*, the closest translation of the Greek word *arete* that Pirsig had discovered in that obscure scholarly text when he was searching for other thinkers who cared about Quality. For him, as he wrote later in *Lila,* it was to be "a place to be alone and quiet and inconspicuous and able to settle down into himself and be what he really was and not what he was thought to be or supposed to be." The quest for excellence and the teaching of virtue by the early Sophists had proved to Pirsig that he'd been on the right track after all, and the boat was to be his vindication.

My hair's dry again in moments, and the bike starts easily. She sounds no different from before, fortunately; she's running too well for me to screw it up now.

I ride through the shade of Dayville and follow the roadside ditch to the irrigated fields beyond, but there's a nagging doubt that I've missed something here. Which was the Pirsigs' gas station? Which was the lawn where they rested? What does it matter? But I've come this far and might as well do the job right.

After three miles, impatient to get going but knowing I won't return this way for a long time, I turn around for a fourth trip along the town's main street.

There's just one gas station, and it's part of a general store. Across the side road is an empty lot that might once have been a second gas station—the place Pirsig bought gas because the first place was closed. And across the main street on the north side, under the massive cottonwoods, are a few older houses, white clapboard with small lawns.

I park outside the store and walk inside. There are two women at the counter, one buying and the other serving.

"Excuse me, but do you know if there used to be a gas station across the side street back in the 1960s?"

They frown thoughtfully. "You know, I think there may have been," says the woman behind the counter, and just then an older man walks in, skin brown and hard as saddle leather. They ask him and he nods.

"Yeah, that would have been Grace Laughlin's place," he says. "She ended up owning both places, that one and this one. John leased the garage from Grace—what was his name? Haynes?—but he left town a long time ago. She sold up in the early eighties, when she moved into the nursing home. Probably dead now. That was a Chevron, this was a Shell. There was a time when we had six gas stations in this town, but that's going back some now." And he walks off into the store without another word.

The women are curious, however, and now they're waiting patiently for an explanation. Clearly there's no quick way out of this.

"I'm doing some research—looking to find some places mentioned in a book back then, after the writer came through here."

"You're not the first," says the younger woman, the customer. "We get people like you along every now and again, following that *Zen* book. It was my great-grandfather who was the fire warden talking to John that afternoon."

Her name is Lori Smith; she's a teacher and lives in the white clapboard house immediately opposite. She's a stocky, smiling woman with short dark hair and beautiful eyes, probably thirty years old and comfortable on this hot day in shorts and a T-shirt.

We walk outside and across the street to the house, passing through the low garden gate and onto the lawn. The doors are open, front and back—no need for locks in Dayville—and she goes inside to drop off her bag of groceries, leaving me out on the grass. It could do with a cut and probably a rake, but the DeWeeses would like this place. A hummingbird feeder on the veranda looks mostly empty—it must be a popular stop. A bicycle rests against a porch pillar, below a wind chime.

Lori comes back outside, still smiling.

"I suppose it would have been right about here. He told me about it when I was a little girl. It was my uncle who owned the house, and my great-grandfather was visiting, just walking past. This was a busy place—my uncle had five sons, who all lived here and grew up in this house. They were a handful by all accounts."

All these lives I'd just ridden past.

And what about the "Chinaman's Ditch," mentioned in the book, which supposedly created these huge trees?

"They filled that in a while ago," she says. "It needed maintenance, and the woman who used to live over there"—she points to a similar house next door, with not much paint and an overgrown yard—"didn't look after it. The ditch was blocked and filled in. She had a lot of cats, and the house was condemned. It's a shame."

I comment on the glorious trees.

"There aren't as many as there used to be," she says. "There was the most beautiful silver maple here, but when they improved the road—that would be eight years ago—the town insisted it had to come down. I fought to save it but obviously didn't succeed. But then when it came down, we found it was hollow anyway, so it was just as well. We don't always fight for the right things, and sometimes our hearts don't know all the facts."

"What is good, Phaedrus, and what is not good?" Sometimes those better, straighter roads aren't so bad after all.

Just one more question: Has she read the book?

"You know, there was a copy here when I moved in, and I started to read it but never finished it. I probably should one of these days."

I've already stayed longer than intended. I thank her, and she smiles again.

"You know," she says, "there are some places that change a great deal, and then there are some that stay pretty much the same, just like Dayville. I like it that way—whatever happens, it'll always be home."

Bob Pirsig set sail from Bayfield, Wisconsin, on a Monday morning in August 1975. A couple of students from the Zen Center came along to help crew the boat for a while; Nancy planned to join him soon for a three-week tour through the Great Lakes, after which Bob would continue on along the New York State waterway system, down the Hudson, and on down to Florida. Nancy had to stay at home awhile longer, but she would leave her job at the end of the year, and then they hoped to take *Excellence* around the world. Bob would never live in Minnesota again.

The road leading west out of Dayville passes fertile fields, then approaches a rock that rises straight up five hundred feet above the land. A split in the center cleaves it in two and it seems impossible, but the road approaches and follows the shape of the rock, then darts into the fissure, high stone to either side, total shade within as it zigs and then zags through to the other side. A sign at a pull-off explains the erosion of the volcanic crack. The time frame graphic spans millions of years, and Lori Smith's comment about Dayville never changing comes to mind.

Of course it will change, but we won't be around to care. I'm living in the here and now, and this basaltic rock is making for a great curving road.

The asphalt rises onto the plain and turns back to the west, off through browner land contained by flat-topped buttes, a perfectly smooth highway, freshly surfaced and marked. It's baking hot in the afternoon sun, the rays dipping down, shining in my eyes. I lower my head a little to let the helmet block the glare.

Another half hour passes and this sun's become exhausting, so it's time to pull over with the Pirsigs again. They stopped here in Mitchell for chocolate malteds, and I do the same, parking outside a little café, walking in, the only customer this afternoon, sitting at the bar and picking up the menu. There are no chocolate malteds, whatever they are, so I order a vanilla milk shake.

The woman behind the counter takes a long time to make it, but the wait pays off—it's thick and cold and served in a frosted stainless-steel mixing cup with a spoon and a frosted glass on the side.

A teenager walks in through the back door. "That looks too good, Mom," he says. "I think I'm going to have to have one of those!" And she smiles and makes another, taking the same time and the same care as she took to make mine.

Less than a minute after leaving the café, up to 30 miles an hour on Mitchell's main street and before an audience of young boys, the engine sputters to a halt. I've forgotten—as seems to happen a couple of times each day after a break—to turn on the fuel tap that feeds gas into the carburetor.

I fumble for the tap to let the gas flow as the bike coasts past the boys, knock the gears down into neutral, then swing out the kick-starter and give it a hefty kick. The motor fires to life before the bike can stop moving, and I ride away as Joe Cool.

Nancy took a three-week vacation in October, replacing the Zen Center crew members on the *Excellence* near Sault Ste. Marie. It was not an easy trip—something on the boat broke in Lake Huron, delaying them a week while it was fixed; then they visited with her sister in Detroit and sailed into rough water on Lake Erie. Nancy was wrenchingly seasick, while Bob was unaffected by the constant swell of the churning waves. She took a day to dry out and then flew home from Lorain, Ohio.

It was Chris's turn next. He was living on Otis Avenue again and flew out to Cleveland to join the boat, helping his dad sail it through to Oswego, New York. It was the closest the father and son had been since the bike trip back in '68, and it was the last voyage they'd make together.

Oregon's wearing on. A gorgeous road but a brutal sun that's crouching down now to slam straight into the eyes as I ride west, boring its way through the visor and the sunglasses and ramming its heat full against the jacket's leather.

As well, the hot highway is taking its toll on that tire, which is supporting so much weight. Back at the breakfast café in Richland, after a long look at the map, I'd decided it's time to look after Jackie New.

I'll be staying tonight at Bend, a good-size city that must surely have a good-size motorcycle shop that sells tires. There's no sense leaving it till San Francisco if the tires can be replaced now. It'll be another long ride tomorrow around Crater Lake and on to Grants Pass, 270 miles from start to finish.

But seventy of those miles can be saved, allowing an extra couple of hours for the tire installation, if I cut straight west from the lake. Pirsig screwed up there, not reading his map properly and taking a much longer route around Upper Klamath Lake. Even geniuses make mistakes sometimes.

Back in late 1975 Bob Pirsig was dealing with issues of his own. Chris left the boat while they were delayed by problems with the locks on the Oswego Canal, which set the schedule back several weeks. The delay wasn't a problem for Pirsig, though, who was in no particular hurry and always enjoyed getting stuck. As he wrote in *Zen and the Art*, "Stuckness shouldn't be avoided. It's the psychic predecessor of all real understanding. An egoless accep-

213

tance of stuckness is a key to an understanding of all Quality, in mechanical work as in other endeavors. It's this understanding of Quality as revealed by stuckness which so often makes self-taught mechanics so superior to institute-trained men who have learned how to handle everything except a new situation."

He turned the delay into an opportunity, taking the time out to focus on the approach to his second book, writing away in the small forecastle below deck. And that is where the second book begins: Phaedrus, the main character, who is partly fictional but greatly autobiographical, is on the Hudson River, having finally made it through the Oswego and Erie Canals. Phaedrus has met a number of characters during the trip south, the boaters running into one another as they wait for the locks to clear, and it's here that he first properly meets Lila, the siren of the story. Since *Lila* will be subtitled *An Inquiry into Morals,* it is understood that she's a woman of questionable virtue, and the two of them are already in bed in the very first paragraph.

Bend is even bigger than I expected and has several large motor-cycle shops. I pull over at the first phone booth and find the section in the Yellow Pages that advertises bike shops and rip the pages from the book. What's more, there'll be no sleeping in any half-constructed subdivision tonight, as the Pirsigs did. I'm hot and sticky and need to be ready in the morning to get to the shop.

The Suzuki dealership is in an industrial area and has just closed for the day, but there's a guy out front with a motorcycle tied down in the back of his pickup truck. He's busy doing something in the cab, but I call hello anyway. I want to know if the shop's any good.

"Just a minute," he says, and a small boy looks at me from the passenger seat. What are they doing?

I stroll back to the store and peer through the window. It's a big place, and there look to be plenty of tires in there. After a moment the man walks up to say hello. He's putting something into a pouch.

"Diabetic," he says, and my eye darts over his shoulder to the boy, who's rubbing his hands in the truck. "Can I help you?"

I explain about the search for tires, and just as he's assuring me that this is a good store, a car pulls up and a large man at the wheel greets us both.

"This is Rex," says the man I've been chatting with. "He works here—maybe he can help you."

Sure enough, Rex says it'll be no problem to find some tires for the motorcycle—he'd open the shop and sell them to me now if it hadn't been such a long day. I think both tires should be replaced to keep them well matched, and the front wheel, like the front wheel on all dirt bikes, is unusually large. I need longer-wearing rubber that will get me home from California, not just another pair of knobbies that'll scratch out after two thousand miles. Tires for both asphalt and gravel. Rex doesn't see a problem. "We've got lots of tires—we'll find you something."

With a thank-you and a promise to be back at 9 a.m., I'm off to look for a motel. One block over is the Tom Tom Motor Inn, an older place but convenient, with "Remodled Quaint Rms In Rm Coffee Laundry A/C." Not too expensive surely.

"It's thirty-nine ninety-five—that okay for you?" asks the manager, a vast woman in a floral-print dress settled in behind her computer monitor, solitaire cards showing on the screen. It would be wise to have a look at the room first. She nods and hands over the key.

Inside room 4—a pause. It's done entirely in a kitschy sea theme, with shells and pictures of fish, the lower wall covered in a seafloor mural, a hammock hanging high above the bed, and a fisherman's net draped in one corner. Posters of fish on the wall. More to the point, a TV with a VCR and a little typed note about renting videos from the office, a shower with strong water pressure, a fridge, and a small writing desk. A basket with mints and packets of Rockets. A queen-size bed with fish printed on the pillowcases.

All through the room are more typed notes: one tells how Lilli and Nevada Steele found this place back in '88 and fell in love;

another advises guests to keep the bathroom window open a crack so as not to set off the smoke alarm with the steam; yet another suggests day trips for motorists and motorcyclists. This feels like a bed-and-breakfast, not a motel.

It is hugely different from every other place I've stayed on this trip. Quality—that's what's here. It's more than just clean and functional and anonymous, like the Super 8 in Laurel and the place in Missoula; it's privately owned and individual, like Sidney's place in Oakes, but with a woman's touch. So different from the drab brown dimness of Mike's motel in Lemmon.

I go back to the office. "Not only is your room fine, but it's lovely," I tell the woman. "It's worth a thousand bucks at least."

She chuckles, obviously pleased, and starts doing the paperwork. "We like our place here. And we love meeting the people who come through."

"I thought you might kick me out when you saw me—I need the shower in there."

"No, we like bikers most of all. The ones on the Harleys, anyway. Good, honest people—the worst they'll do is make too much noise, but if we ask them to keep it down, they always do. Are you on a Harley?"

"No, just an old Japanese dirt bike. I found you because I went to the bike shop on the next block to look for a tire, and they'll be putting it on in the morning."

"That's good," she says. "They'll look after you. The only kind of biker I don't care too much for are those BMW riders. They're all too snotty. They like to stay in the chains, anyway, so they don't come through here much. Don't know what they're missing."

I leave my credit card number and unpack for the night. The laptop even hooks up over the phone line, a fast connection, though I notice the little typed note asking guests not to hog the line.

Online I find another message from my wife buried in the spam; she's having trouble getting online at the farm.

"E-mail and phone calls can never make up for actually speaking to each other in person but I hope I've managed to lift your spirits (if they need lifting?) by sending you some shots of the boys," she's written. "We all miss you very much and are anxious to hear how you're getting on."

There's no attachment, no photos of the boys. Damn computers. I really want to talk to her when I arrive in San Francisco on Friday.

Pirsig phoned home from the Hudson River, and Nancy relayed his progress to the local newspaper. The reporter joked in the short published notice: "Robert Pirsig presumably has hit salt water by now in what has to be the Guinness record for the slowest circumnavigation of the world."

Nancy was soon to have much bigger problems of her own, however. Chris was living at home again, but after initially trying hard to help around the house, he'd become demanding and difficult. One day, during a furious argument with his mother, he punched her in the eye, then fought with Ted. It was, in Ted's words, "pretty intense," ending only when Chris left to hide out at a friend's home. His jealousy of Ted had become unmanageable; he spoke of killing his brother. Chris's friend warned Nancy, and Ted began sleeping with a loaded pistol under his pillow.

Ted recalled his father's woefully inadequate advice at the time: "Yeah, you just might have to plug him one."

Nancy went to the police and wanted Chris committed, but Bob refused to co-sign the papers, saying that a limited jail sentence on a charge of assault would be better than open-ended incarceration. After all, he had never forgiven Nancy for signing the papers that committed him to shock treatment, and he'd never forgotten the phone call at his parents' home, when he'd learned that he had a grandfather locked away and forgotten, serving a life sentence in a state hospital.

The choice was given to Chris: serve time or seek help at

Faribault. He chose Faribault. "I remember driving him down there," Nancy wrote to me. "He wanted to drive. I said no, so he started smoking and blowing smoke in my face and trying to burn my hand on the steering wheel until I felt I had no choice but to let him drive."

Upon his discharge, through the influence of his father and Dainin Katagiri, the Zen master, a compromise was reached: Chris would go to California, study at the San Francisco Zen Center, and live at the center's Green Gulch Farm north of the city. It was hoped that the physical discipline of the grueling daily routine—working on the farm, studying at the downtown center, and meditating at the monastic retreat—would turn him around.

In the morning the only thing between the bike shop and the motel is the Tom Tom Diner, which looks like it'll serve a great breakfast while the tires are going on. I ride to the shop and wait for the "Open" sign to flip around, then it's straight inside and upstairs to the tire display.

But I see nothing that will match the bike's wheel sizes. A salesman asks if he can help. When he hears what I need, he looks doubtful.

"We're not going to have a front tire for you that isn't a dirt knobbie, which will wear down quickly," he says. "And on the back—well, let's see." He walks up the aisle and finally pulls out a huge street tire.

"This will be the closest. It's wider than you want, but if you take the chain guard off, it'll probably fit."

This isn't going well. A dirt tire on the front and an overly wide $250 street tire behind is not a good combination, especially on a bike that will be crossing back over the continent in who-knows-what conditions. And with no chain guard there'll be nothing to stop my jeans from getting caught in the whirring links. I say I'll be back if the other shops in town can't help.

"Good luck," he says. "They won't give you the prices that we will."

It doesn't matter how much cheaper his tire is—it'll still be compromise rubber. I go a few blocks down the road to the Honda shop.

This place is even bigger. Behind the counter is a tall and statuesque blonde with plunging cleavage and a large pale mole on her left breast. It's quite hypnotic, and I have to tear my eyes away when she asks if she can help. When she hears the sizes of the tires, she says she'll go look at what's in stock; when I ask if I can look, too, she seems annoyed but nods, and I follow her into the back.

Once again there's a rear street tire but nothing for the front. And the same $250. Not many street motorcycles need such a large front tire. Even so, Jackie New needs a rear tire, and I ask if it can be installed right away. She looks even more annoyed and says she'll ask Marvin, who's riding around on a forklift and seems busy.

After talking with Marvin, she walks away without returning and I wait for Marvin. Five minutes later there's still no Marvin. Maybe she caught me looking at the mole. To hell with this— these people aren't getting my money.

The BMW shop is on the other side of the city, so I go back to the motel and phone from the room. "Geez—a bike like that, for what you want, you'll want a pair of Michelin Anakees," says the BMW guy. "They're a lovely tire—hard wearing on the highway, ride the trails in comfort—I love 'em. And I just put my last set on a customer's bike yesterday. I can get some more in for you tomorrow by noon, but not before, I'm afraid."

Time's not standing still. Staying another twenty-four hours in Bend is not an option if I'm to make it to San Francisco on my birthday.

So the choice is to spend a fair bit of money on a tire that's not right and could make matters worse, probably just to replace it in San Francisco anyway, or keep going and see how it goes—to accept that it's not yet worn out, and it's not a problem right now.

I go outside and look at the tire. There's still rubber there. There's no rain in the forecast. And San Francisco's not so far now—maybe seven hundred miles. I decide to get breakfast.

Lilli's cleaning the rooms and she says she's not in a hurry to get to mine, so I walk over to the diner and enjoy some hotcakes, eggs, and bacon, fruit on the side. This is nearly the coast, after all. Back in my room I check the Internet for a BMW dealer in San Francisco, call through, and ask if they have Michelin Anakees in stock. They don't, but they give me the number of a motorcycle tire shop that will. I make the second call and speak with a sympathetic-sounding woman named Leanne.

"I got 'em in those sizes, but if I hold them till Saturday for you, you'd better not forget to pick them up." She doesn't ask for a deposit.

"Don't worry," I tell her. "I'll be there first thing."

"We're open at seven a.m.," she says. "And I'm here at six. See you then?"

"Well—maybe second thing."

So close now—already making plans to fill the time there. So close I can almost taste the salt air, see the bridge. Its image is clear in my mind.

So close to Friday, to my birthday. It's Wednesday already. So close to forty-two and the meaning of life.

Bob Pirsig sailed through New York State and down the Intracoastal Waterway. It was clear to him then that his second book would be located on those same rivers and canals running to the Atlantic Ocean. During his Christmas vacation, Ted joined the boat in North Carolina, and they sailed for the Virgin Islands but were blown off course and ended up in Puerto Rico. Soon after, Ted returned home to complete his senior year of high school, Bob flew to the Twin Cities to surprise his wife—she'd left her job and was in the hospital recovering from a hysterectomy. When she was fit enough, and once Chris had been dispatched to California, the two headed south to join the boat in the Caribbean.

After years of midwestern isolation and domestic uncertainty, this must have been a writer's dream.

Bob and Nancy spent a few months cruising around the Virgin Islands, then crossed the challenging Atlantic to Bermuda to live the idyllic future they'd hoped and planned for. "I joked about how most kids grew up and moved away," says Ted. "In my case, the *parents* moved away." But he didn't mind staying in St. Paul—at least not at first. "A friend came by on a bike and taught me how to ride it, and the fun of it stunned me. All those years of staring at a large army-shirt-bedecked back; I'd had *no idea* how much fun it was to be out front and in control. So I immediately pulled the Honda out of storage, got licensed, and rode it all summer."

When the weather warmed on the East Coast, the Pirsigs sailed to New York and docked close to downtown—"a huge thrill, I can tell you," recalled Nancy. "Stepping off the boat, on which we had spent every moment for the last six or more days, and onto the dock, we walked a few blocks to a major street, our legs still wobbly from the sea. What a shock to the system! All these people, all this traffic, all this noise, all these lights!"

It should have been a wonderful summer, but it was not, not really. Bob was reticent, absorbed by *Lila,* and they sailed north to New Haven for him to do research at Yale's library. Heading south again as the fall began, they visited friends on Chesapeake Bay and collected mail, only to learn that Ted was having a hard time. He was on his own but ready to move out, and was really too young to manage all this alone. Nancy arranged to fly home.

For some reason—she can't explain why—she packed all her possessions, leaving nothing of her own on the boat. She said good-bye to Bob, who was sailing on south, went to the airport at Annapolis, and boarded a plane for Minnesota. She cried all the way home.

Nothing had been said between them, but Nancy knew it was over. After twenty-three years, beginning with the elopement to Nevada and the interlude in Mexico, through all the struggles and questions, the insanity and resolution, and the successes and final

221

vindication, there wasn't an answer for every case of "stuckness." Their lives were split as permanently and irreparably as Day- ville's basaltic rock. They were both in their forties, their kids had finished school, their relationship was over, and it was time to move on.

I push the bike to the edge of the motel's parking lot and oil the chain. It doesn't need an adjustment, just a lube, and I push the bike back and start loading up. Lilli comes by and we chat. She tells me that business isn't so good at older motels because people think they'll be dirty.

"I've got my standards, and they're higher than theirs," she says. "Just before you arrived last night, two women came in looking for a room. Jewelry dripping right off them, rings and earrings and bracelets. They kept asking if the rooms were clean and I told them to go take a look, but they wouldn't. Just kept ask- ing, that was all. I got sick of it and gave them back their VISA and told them to find someplace else to stay.

"If they want to go stay in a hundred-dollar room someplace, well, it's their money."

The bike's loaded now, and Lilli takes a photo of me and the bike outside room 4. There's a small puddle of oil on the ground beneath the bike. I'm assuming it's from the chain, but it's too far forward for that.

CHAPTER FIFTEEN

Western Oregon

BUTTERFLIES EVERYWHERE, large and dark winged. The air is full of them, fluttering through the slipstream. A few hit the jacket, but most pass by, thrown behind by the turbulence to carry on fluttering to wherever they're going.

I'm headed south through this lava forest to Crater Lake. Trees are on both sides, and the road is full of logging trucks traveling fast. My speed's up to 70 miles an hour just to keep pace. Chipmunks scurry across the highway. Everything's moving more quickly now, everything but the butterflies.

There are high mountains to either side of this straight, straight road, glistening with snow above the trees in the blue sky. Eventually a sign announces the turnoff to the national park, so I turn west onto another long road, straight as the path of an arrow through the trees, wide and clear and climbing to the horizon.

After fifteen miles a sign announces the entrance to the park; there's $5 due to the ranger, and I can ride on in. Some more trees, a little more climbing, up to six thousand feet, and then I'm in the open. The peak's rim is straight ahead, pockets of brilliant white snow not far away. The temperature up here is 70 degrees.

The approach road leads through the Pumice Desert, an area that seems barren but is actually carpeted in tight clumps of tiny wiry flowers, orange and purple and yellow. I pull off the road for a photo, and the tires slip deep into the soft sand at the edge.

Back on the approach road and now I'm riding slowly, almost in reverence, certainly in awe as the road keeps climbing, winding now through the pockets of snow. These are much lower than the snowfields at the Beartooth, nestled into shady ruts and north-facing hollows. Here, too, some visitors are having a snowball fight as I pass. Thin streams of melted ice cross the asphalt to drain away down the mountain's slope.

Finally the road joins the Rim Drive, the paved loop that circles the top. I park in the first parking lot and follow some tourists up a steep, sandy slope. There's a fence at the top, and people are standing there, looking out. I'm not sure what to expect. I've never seen a picture of Crater Lake.

It's not clear why the Pirsigs came here. Bob Pirsig hated tourist areas, skirting Yellowstone and avoiding the Black Hills and many other destinations along the way. God knows what he'd have thought of the world's biggest ball of twine or the Spam Museum. But he came here with Chris that afternoon thirty-six years ago to gaze out over this fence. He parked the bike just where mine is now and walked up this same slope. The two of them could be any of those tourists up there. That man and his son—they could be Bob and Chris.

Perhaps it was a last attempt to interact with Chris, who had little say in the schedule and was retreating into himself as he sensed the growing struggle between his father and his father's nemesis. As their tormented minds tried to find some familiar bond, they came here and walked up the slope to share the sight.

At the fence the rim drops away and the lake shows itself far down in the crater, some six miles wide. It's much bigger than I expected, almost perfectly round, and its deep scree slopes drop a thousand feet to the water's edge. It's much bluer than I could ever have thought, too. Far, far bluer. A dark blue that reflects the blueness of the clear sky, with pockets of brilliant white snow on the icy shore.

Yet it is deep, so very deep, its clear water holding many secrets, this lake that has no rivers or streams feeding into it. It is a sacred place. It takes my breath away.

"Why did we come here?" Chris says.

"To see the lake."

He doesn't like this. He senses falseness and frowns deep, trying to find the right question to expose it. "I just hate this," he says.

A tourist lady looks at him with surprise, then resentment.

"Well, what can we do, Chris?" I ask. "We just have to keep going until we find out what's wrong or find out why we don't know what's wrong. Do you see that?"

He doesn't answer. The lady pretends not to be listening, but her motionlessness reveals that she is. We walk toward the motorcycle, and I try to think of something, but nothing comes. I see he's crying a little and now looks away to prevent me from seeing it.

We wind down out of the park to the south.

In a strange way this feels like my first big break from the spirit of the original trip. Not wandering a few miles off course in Minnesota or staying just one night in Bozeman, and certainly not sleeping in a motel instead of some lousy construction site. It's standing here and being struck by the beauty and the sheer spirituality of this lake when the Pirsigs rode away in their self-obsessed funk.

I can't stop looking at the blue. It's such a beautiful day—such a perfect day—and it's astonishing that my old single-cylinder bike got me here. I walk along the fence line and keep looking down into the caldera at the water and the little island that's close to the shore and at the chipmunks and birds that are scurrying around my feet.

Then a motorcycle starts up and ruins the moment.

It's an unmuffled Harley ridden by an older couple. Every explosion in the cylinders, every gear shift and throttle change reverberates in the air as it rides slowly away. It can be heard for a long time after it can no longer be seen, and then there's silence again.

At a low stone wall I sit for a moment, gazing back down and across the water, scrutinizing the crater's rocky sides and then just letting my eyes lose focus. A chipmunk jumps onto my knee, and I remember a packet of almonds in my jacket pocket. It's been there, unopened, since Minneapolis.

As soon as I hand an almond over, a dozen more chipmunks appear. Birds wheel overhead. I give almonds to more chipmunks and throw almonds in the air for the birds to catch in flight.

Memories come of feeding squirrels with the boys at home and, even earlier, feeding the ducks on the village pond with my wife and first son when he was just a few months old, in his carriage, dressed warmly in blue wool. We were so new at being parents.

More memories come now, all the way back to the start of his life, seven years ago, in that little birthing room—the moment Andrew first drew a breath. The happiness and then the fear as the nurse pulled the cord from around his neck and he was hurried to a side table for oxygen, grunting desperately, but the rhythm of his life soon returned, and he was handed to me to place at his mother's breast, where he lay still and content. It was his fingers that made the greatest impression, tiny and wrinkled, with soft nails torn half away from months of patting at the womb's warm wall.

My life had just changed forever. I knew it, and although it scared me, I welcomed it.

And then his brother, born two years later in a different country, another pair of hands reaching toward me.

The blue, blue water is cold and empty. It's bluer than the sky. Surrounded by chipmunks and birds, I've never felt more alone.

I wind down out of the park to the south; I'm in a funk now from the loneliness, even with so many people gathered there at the crater's lookout. The plan had been to cut across to the west and save seventy miles of riding, but I'm leaving earlier than expected and I might as well follow the route through, so I turn left instead of right and head toward Klamath Falls.

As the road drops, my heart lightens. There's no denying the sheer beauty of the lake—and the playfulness of the animals. And I'm looking forward to calling my family on Friday.

The bike's running well, and the air is warm. Soon, as the trees give way to fields and cattle, my feet are off the pegs and I'm flying again. Just me and the bike rushing through the wind, pressing south to the finish.

Bob Pirsig didn't stay alone on the *Excellence* for long. At a harbor one day on the way down to Florida, soon after Nancy's departure, a freelance journalist named Wendy Kimball came on board to interview him. She was vacationing on another boat at the marina. At twenty-six, she was just a few years older than his sons. She visited a few more times. Then she never left.

After a month or so Bob phoned home. Things had not been going well. Nancy had just spent a week in silent retreat, asking herself questions about her marriage that were still unresolved. She told Bob that she wanted to come to Florida and talk about their future. He told her about Wendy. He told her their marriage didn't have to end. She knew that it did. And that was that.

The GPS has Grants Pass locked into it as today's destination, so when I pull off at Klamath Falls to find some lunch—not having eaten since breakfast, and it's already 4 p.m.—the little computer recalculates straightaway and tries to get me back on the main highway.

As I look in vain for a decent diner, turning down one street after another, the computer keeps recalculating routes back to the main road. Eventually, after the fifth or sixth recalculation, it locks up—just as I've given up on stopping at Klamath Falls and have gotten back on the four-laner.

Now the GPS is completely seized—won't turn off or anything. I pull over and unplug it from the bike's battery, hoping it'll reboot, but nothing happens. The only thing to do is pull out its internal batteries and start all over again. But I have to get off this highway first.

And as I pull away and get up to speed, accelerating quickly into the right lane to rejoin the 70-mile-an-hour traffic, the unit bounces out of its holder, off my leg, and onto the pavement. In the mirrors I see it skittering across the highway, bouncing off the median and then back across the road and into the ditch.

I stop as fast as Jackie New's faded brakes will allow and run back to find it under an inch of water. It's badly scratched, and there's a deep crack along the bottom of the screen, but otherwise it's intact. It doesn't turn on, though. It's busted.

This isn't the place to worry about it. I shove the unit in a jacket pocket and get back on the bike, heading northwest along the opposite shore of Upper Klamath Lake. Now all those little waypoints along the remainder of the Zen route won't be so clearly signed.

I can live without the GPS's route map, though I've depended on it a lot. No, the problem in losing the GPS is that the location of the final scene of the book, in the anonymous field beside the Pacific, will not be easy to find. In fact, since it's just recorded as a map coordinate, it'll be damn difficult.

This is the key to the entire book and the true end point of the journey: the field beside the ocean where the narrator and Chris finally have it out and Phaedrus reasserts himself—the almighty clash of the father, son, and holy ghost. I located this field only because Pirsig later gave a rough description of where it had been, and several Pirsig's pilgrims went there and figured it out.

There's nothing else to think about as I press on along the lake. Do I have the notes of Pirsig's later description of the place? Will the GPS work if it's dried under a hair dryer? My mind is five hundred miles away, along the coast, when the main gas tank suddenly runs dry.

The bike stutters and coughs. I reach down to twist the fuel tap around to reserve and it chugs back to life, but then I look around and realize this is the middle of nowhere—more than fifteen miles from the nearest gas station, back at Klamath Falls. The lake is receding behind me, and there's nothing ahead but trees. I pull over for a check of the map and shut off the engine immediately. The map shows some sort of settlement way up ahead, but there's no guarantee of gas.

The reserve won't get me back to Klamath now. Nothing to do but carry on.

Bob and Wendy sailed down to Florida together and then stalled. They moored the boat in Miami, and Wendy took on a reporting job while Bob concentrated on writing the book. The terrific success of *Zen and the Art,* as well as the continuing debate about his thoughts and beliefs, was an enormous pressure, and the words just would not come.

To clear his mind, he agreed to write a feature article for *Esquire,* published in May 1977 as "Cruising Blues and Their Cure." It was about a subject he knew well: "You can see just so many beautiful sunsets strung end on end, just so many coconut palms waving in the ocean breeze, just so many exotic moonlit tropical nights scented with oleander and frangipani, and you become adjusted. They no longer elate. The pleasant external stimulus has worn out its response and cruising depression takes over. This is the point at which boats get sold and cruising dreams are shattered forever."

But Pirsig wasn't about to sell his boat. He was well and truly stuck now and reveling in the writer's block.

"It sounds strange," he continued in the *Esquire* piece, "but some of my happiest memories are of days when I was very depressed. Slow monotonous grey days at the helm, beating into a wet freezing wind. Or a three-day dead calm that left me in agonies of heat and boredom and frustration. Days when nothing seemed to go right. Nights when impending disaster was all I could think of."

I ride on, slowly and steadily. Of all the pitfalls that could befall this trip, running out of gas is the most stupid and avoidable. I'd reset the odometer at the last fill-up and knew how far I could travel but was too busy thinking about lunch and then the GPS to look at it. This reserve tank will take me only about fifteen miles. Maybe I should have turned around after all, but now more distance has passed and it's definitely too late.

For a while I curse and insult myself and then, since it makes no difference, just settle down to silence inside the helmet, nothing but the muffled chug of the bike's engine as I pass through the national forest and the wilderness.

I feel like a diver in trouble. Don't breathe too deeply—you'll only make it worse.

Everything seems to shut down, mile after mile through the trees as the last of the gas in the reserve tank drains steadily through the feeder tube and into the carburetor, exploding and vaporizing against each spark inside the cylinder.

Nothing else matters right now. A broken GPS could be the least of my worries. I might have to leave the bike behind and abandon all the luggage and walk for gas—don't think about it! It hasn't happened yet. The bike's still running. Forget the technology and all its wonders; just concentrate on the Zen.

Come on, Jackie New. Slow and steady, that's the way.

When riding, just ride. *"Above all, don't wobble."*

And fourteen miles after switching on the reserve tank, right at the limit, there's an outfitter's store in a clearing with a gas pump out front. I don't speak as I park and remove the filler cap, don't even look at the price as the attendant hands over the nozzle and the fuel goes in.

It takes more gas and costs more money than any fuel stop so far, but it feels like a bargain.

When I leave the little station and pass a junction for the small community, there's a sign in the trees: "Next Gas 36 Miles." That was a close call. If I'd had to abandon the bike, I'd have had to push her into the forest to hide her from passersby who could loot the bags as easily as look at them. Even then she wouldn't have been safe.

There I was fussing about a piece of technology while the most basic mechanical need was being ignored right in front of me. Which reminds me—

I pull over and take the GPS from my pocket. I push the ON button, the screen lights up, and the little map appears. It even indicates a waypoint up ahead, where the Pirsigs might have stopped and Chris might have gone for a walk among the giant Douglas firs.

I'd been so focused on the near disaster I hadn't even noticed. These are huge trees, straight and strong; from the bike I can look up their trunks for hundreds of feet. It is a different land now. Tomorrow I'll be in California—I can feel it already.

Bob and Wendy stuck it out in Florida for another year, then weighed anchor to escape the June heat, sailing north to Maine, near Wendy's family.

That summer of 1978 Bob returned to St. Paul to hash out a separation agreement with Nancy. His father presided over the family conference and maintained a poker face when they admitted that they'd never been legally married. It was agreed that Bob would keep all the earnings from his book and the *Excellence* and that the house and its furnishings would be sold, the proceeds split equally. The uncontested divorce papers from their common-law relationship were filed, and the divorce was finalized by August.

This was not a sad time, though. In fact, it was a hopeful, optimistic period for them all. Nancy had reconnected with a labor educator at the university whom she had always liked, and they began living together in October. She was running a small vegetarian restaurant in the Twin Cities while writing freelance articles for newspapers and magazines. Ted had completed a photography course at the Banff Centre and moved to Seattle, where he was working in a shipyard as a welder. Chris was at the Zen Center in California. Back in Maine just after Christmas, Bob married Wendy, and Chris and Ted visited them at the house they were looking after for the winter. The brothers had reconciled most of their differences as they'd grown older and more mature. Zen had turned Chris around; his personality was essentially reborn through the disciplined routine of the monks. The process was constructive, unlike the electric shock therapy that had been used on his father. He wasn't there yet, but for everyone the new year of 1979 held promise.

As I ride away from the tall trees, the heat builds and the road drops quickly, a 5 percent grade for ten miles. A truck towing a boat has a long line of impatient drivers behind it, but I pass easily, accelerating quickly past three and four cars at a time on the downhill straightaways.

As I approach Medford, the GPS shows I'm down to fifteen hundred feet, the lowest point of the entire trip, lower even than my home. The sun is in my eyes again, and the heat's built rapidly since I've left the forest.

I want to stop for something to eat, but it barely seems worth it now, less than an hour from my destination. Besides, this doesn't look like a good place to stop. If it weren't for the mountains, everything would be the same as any drive to work: three lanes of traffic going into town, mile after mile of strip malls, car dealerships, Taco Bells and McDonald's, Food 4 Less stores and Comfort Inns.

Eventually there's a sign that says "Welcome to Medford," which seems ridiculous since the town appeared to have started ten minutes ago.

I take a drink from the water bottle and then ride on toward Grants Pass and a comfortable room. The Pirsigs stayed in a motel there with a heated pool, their first night in beds since Bozeman.

It's really hot, though, and humid as the coast approaches. The bank sign says 100 degrees, and there's not a cloud in the sky. I'm paying down here for the perfect weather at Crater Lake, six thousand feet higher up.

Worst of all is the sun, lasering straight into my eyes as the road heads west. Every scratch on the tinted visor is intensified; every splattered bug is another film of guts and fluid to distort the light.

The highway turns to interstate, and traffic is heavy. Every driver alongside me has the sun visor down and is sitting a little higher in the seat to shield the eyes, but there's no such luxury on the bike. I can't even relax or look away, thanks to the press of vehicles all around. This is commuter traffic, the first since leaving Minneapolis last week. Everybody's sitting in air-conditioning, listening to the radio and thinking only of getting home.

That sun. That heat. It's too much.

After another thirty miles, I'm seriously afraid for my stability on the bike. I should have stopped back at Medford. I can't see well, and I'm beat. There's a rest area up ahead, and I pull in, circling around the access road to find some shade. Once the bike is parked, I take off the helmet and jacket and lie there on the grass, eyes closed at last, regrouping, listening to the voices all around.

There's a family nearby rearranging their luggage on a roof rack. I caught a glimpse before lying down and closing my eyes. I keep my eyes closed now and listen. There's a mom and dad and two young children, a boy and a girl. The girl wants to run in the sprinklers that are soaking all the picnic tables, and the boy just wants to sit in the car and play his Game Boy.

The mother makes the boy get out for some exercise, but she doesn't want the girl to run off and get wet. The father keeps saying that he's almost done and they're almost there, wherever there is.

In the end the little girl gets wet anyway, and as the mother is scolding her and looking for a towel, there's the sound of a car door closing. That will be the boy, sitting inside now with his Game Boy. Andrew would be doing that while Tristan gets soaked.

I lie there for who knows how long, motionless. They drive away at last, and afterward, with a long stretch to fight off stiffness, I open my eyes and get on the bike and ride the last few miles into the blinding sun.

In August of 1979, perhaps to make a break from the familiarity of Maine and to kick the writing of *Lila* into another gear, Bob and Wendy Pirsig took the *Excellence* on its most challenging voyage yet, across the Atlantic, to a berth in England. It was not an easy crossing. The weather turned savage when they were three hundred miles from England; a freak storm slammed into the Fastnet yacht race between England and Ireland, part of the Admiral's Cup series. Force 7 winds hurled several hundred racing craft about the ocean in what witnesses called a "great fury." "It's an experience that I do not think anybody would want to go through again willingly," said sailboat racer Edward Heath, the former British prime minister. "It was a raging sea with enormous waves and one of them picked us up and laid us on our side." Fifteen yachtsmen died in the turbulent waters, from drowning or hypothermia. The Pirsigs were terrified as the center of the storm passed right over them. But *Excellence* was a slow and steady Norwegian double-ended Colin-Archer-design boat, her hull filled with seventy-five hundred pounds of lead for stability, and they reached safety at the tiny Scilly Isles off the coast of Cornwall as a second storm came in.

The signs for motels at Grants Pass are unreadable—the sun's too dazzling. I take the first turnoff, and there's a Best Western. Fine. They only have upstairs rooms. Sure. It's $95. Whatever. Just let me in out of the sun.

The room is large and comfortable and bland. All my gear has to be carried up a flight of outside stairs to the upper floor and into the room, three trips, as always. When the bike is unpacked, I see clearly that a pool of fluid has formed beneath her. She's parked with her side stand on a metal drain cover so the stand won't sink into the asphalt, and with little room to maneuver I just wipe the oil from the ground with an old shop towel. Check it out later.

The shower is cool and does the trick. That was as close to heatstroke as I've come on this ride.

I go back down with another shop towel and look at the bike. There's a fresh pool of oil underneath her. She's parked close to a pair of Harley-Davidsons, nestled in the last shady spot, and there's no oil under them. Getting down on hands and knees, I look straight up from the puddle and realize the fluid is not coming from the engine at all but from the shock absorber.

This is much more serious. Engines can be fixed with gaskets and compound and, if all else fails, by chucking in more oil. I once had a Honda 350 with a blown head gasket that I rode for weeks by topping off the oil every hundred miles—I wore high leather boots, from which I could easily wipe the hot splashes coming off the cylinders. This shock absorber, though, is a sealed unit. It carries a precise amount of fluid and cannot be refilled without being cut and welded in a shop.

Back in the room, I pull out the thick manual that was sent to the cottages at Gardiner. Sure enough, a diagram shows that the shock is not rebuildable; it can be fixed only in a shop.

I purse my lips, pick up Pirsig's pink book, and head next door to the family restaurant for dinner. Time for a steak.

The problem with a leaking seal is that it can only get worse. Now that there's a rupture in the main rubber seal of the shock absorber, a single mono-shock unit that supports the entire weight of the back of the bike above the wheel, it'll only get bigger with every bounce and bump. Oil's not going to squeeze back in; it'll only squeeze out until the shock cylinder is empty. The worn-out tires are secondary now.

The main part of the shock, though, is not the oil but the spring. The oil damps the spring, steadies it, and calms the extremes of movement. With no protective fluid and all that luggage, the bike will begin to resonate, and the spring will eventually break.

Where will that leave me? Not stuck beside the road, although it could throw me into a ditch if it breaks on a corner. No, the bike can still be ridden. Hell—some choppers don't even bother with shock absorbers on the back. Won't be much fun, though.

The waitress takes the order. It's an interesting challenge to see this problem through. It's not going to stop me from getting to San Francisco in forty-eight hours, although it might stop me from getting home again.

Best-case scenario? It drips a bit more oil and then mysteriously seals itself, maybe from some kind of kinetic rubber bonding. Yeah, right.

Worst-case scenario? I park the bike in San Francisco, remove the shock absorber, and take it on a bus to a shop that has the precision tools to fix it. Would probably set me back a few days, but that's all.

Actually, no. The worst-case scenario is that I crash. Or that the spring breaks and I limp to the Bay and have to replace the entire shock absorber. And you can be sure I won't easily find one for this old motorcycle. A new one, if it's even available anymore, will probably need to be shipped from Japan and will cost hundreds of dollars. It's too old for an easy replacement but not so old that there's no technology involved—this can't be fudged with a farmer's tractor spring and forgotten with a visit from the farmer's daughter.

The waitress brings a beer, very cold in a frosted glass. At this moment, I have a cold beer and a working motorcycle—life can't be so bad, can it? So what's to be done about this problem?

I think of the miles Jackie Blue covered, loaded down with her suspension absorbing the weight. A sip of the frosted beer and the light comes on. Of course—that shock absorber is still on Jackie Blue, back at home in the garage. She's not using it now. But how to get it here?

There's nobody home—but my neighbor is a mechanic. If Tim

knows the code to open the garage door, he can pull off the shock absorber in a flash. If he does it tomorrow, it could be couriered overnight to the hotel in San Francisco, and it would arrive on the weekend, Monday at the latest.

If he's going to do that, he can probably pull off the clutch, too, which has much newer plates and springs, and send that along as well.

The clutch has been working fairly well, still slipping under load and on the uphill climbs but always coming through. Getting home again, though, back over those high mountains, will be a challenge.

There's always a way, provided Tim's at home. It's too late to call now, so I'll phone in the morning, before he leaves for work.

The waitress brings the steak, and I dig into it happily. There's still a qualifier here—provided Tim's at home—but it's a good plan, thought through from beginning to end and solving the clutch problem, too.

At this point in *Zen and the Art,* Pirsig's narrator is ready to give up. He's talking about selling his little Honda in San Francisco and sending Chris home on a bus while he checks into a hospital. The struggle with Phaedrus is spiraling into a schizophrenic depression and dragging Chris down as well.

This is another place where Robert Pirsig probably took artistic license. In a letter in which he answered my question about his route home from California, he wrote that the two of them actually traveled on to stay with a friend in Hollywood before returning home through Utah and Nebraska.

This doesn't matter. After San Francisco—in fact, after the field beside the ocean—it will be time for me to travel my own road at last.

CHAPTER SIXTEEN

Into California

THE WARM BED IN THE COOL ROOM gives a restful sleep. No eagle tonight, no eyes watching, nothing—like staring at a blank wall and relaxing into emptiness.

The alarm goes off early so I can call Tim before he leaves, but the curtain across the window keeps out the morning and it's easy to hit the snooze and stay asleep.

Waking at nine, I make the call and speak to Tim's wife. No problem, she says. He'll be home soon—he's working a short day. She'll send him over to pull the shock and the clutch off the bike.

It's ironic that the shock absorber should go here, at Grants Pass. When the Pirsigs rode in, the chain protector on their bike came loose, and Bob spent the morning getting its broken bracket welded back into shape. That made for a shorter riding day, just 170 miles. I'd forgotten that.

Packing up, I find the key to room 4 of the Tom Tom Motor Inn. After that long good-bye, I never did return it to Lilli, but I'll mail it back this morning. And as the numerous plastic bags go back into the saddlebags, the mysterious gift shows itself again, resting securely near the very bottom. Still no clue as to its contents—just a small square box wrapped in tissue, sealed in a plastic freezer bag. At this time tomorrow it will be revealed.

I ride through town to mail the key at the post office. The bike is definitely bouncier, hitting a bump and jumping up and down like a pogo stick, but she's not uncomfortable. While I'm out, might as well see if there's anyplace that might be the Pirsigs' motel or the Laundromat Chris went to or the welding shop. Nothing's obvious. The Knight's Inn Motel? Right age but no pool. The Rogue Laundromat? Who knows? The Muff Shop and Welding? Doubt it—looks too new; the old guy who owned the place Pirsig went to was already in his sixties or seventies. Back then he danced his torch and the filler rod across the guard's thin metal to produce a work of art, much as Tom did for me in Bozeman. But I can hear the radio playing in the Muff Shop. Pirsig would have avoided such a place.

I head back to the hotel to load up Jackie New, surely squeezing out a few more drops of shock absorber fluid with each heavy layer I strap on, then over to last night's restaurant for breakfast. It's hot again—82 degrees already—but there's time this morning for a leisurely start; the state line is just forty-four miles down the road. No sense hurrying the moment.

The waitress is a different woman from last night, but she points the way to the same table. After she brings the coffee, she starts chatting with an older couple who are obviously friends.

"I'm off to see him on Monday for a little visit," she says. "Portland's not so far away. It'll be really great to meet him at last. When we finally spoke on the phone, he sounded so strong but he listened to me as well. He's forty-one with his own computer business, and I'm thirty-four, so I think it's a good match. He cares for his parents and he's a Christian, too."

Her friends aren't speaking, just listening.

"I was with this dating club here, but all they wanted me to do was go to church three times a week and read the Bible every day. He's not like that. Every time he told me something about himself, I just kept thinking, 'Man, you're pushing all the right buttons.' "

She has a pretty face, the waitress, though everything about her seems homely, and her figure can't be seen under her uniform.

Another lonely person surrounded by people. Funny that—

Pirsig thought his own waitress to be lonely that long-ago morning, with a beckoning gaze. Not enough love, probably. Some things will never change.

When the sea had calmed and the furor had died away, Bob and Wendy sailed to the English mainland, finally mooring *Excellence* on the Cornish coast, in Falmouth's deep, still water. A visitor's visa and a generous income from the royalties of *Zen and the Art* would allow them to stay over the winter, writing and reflecting. The voyage had left them shaken, and they were in no hurry to recross the ocean.

A few weeks after their arrival in Falmouth, however, Bob's mother died, and he flew home to attend her funeral. The entire family was there—the siblings she'd traced long ago after their placement in foster care, and other relatives from her large extended family and many friends, everyone going to Maynard's house afterward for coffee and sandwiches. Nancy was there, for she'd always been close to the family. Ted came from Seattle and Chris from San Francisco.

It was the last time any of the family would see Chris alive.

A late departure and onto Route 199, which feels like the final stretch, though there are many miles still to go. It's a two-lane highway edged by coniferous forest, hot but not as hot as yesterday. The sun is high in the sky.

At 1 p.m. exactly, there's a break in the woods and the sign appears, a large blue sign with looped yellow writing beside a picture of a yellow California poppy: "Welcome to California." Just beyond is an inspection station for trucks, closed today.

I roll up to the sign, park, and silence the engine. I feel as if I could kiss the ground. The road is quiet, with just the occasional logging truck going by. Most of the traffic south is over on the interstate, fifty miles inland.

There are no drips of oil under the shock. That's it, then—completely empty. When I sit on the bike, she sags a few extra inches but starts again readily and sounds good. Snicking her into first gear, I ride slowly into the land of milk and honey.

I ride awhile on the road through the tall trees, and then there's a sign for Crescent City, just ten miles away. More important, it's also a sign for San Francisco—359 miles—the first to be seen on this quest.

Here's the final drop down to the ocean, with a bank of cloud pressing against the coast, plunging the temperature into the low 60s. The sun is obscured completely, and all turns gray. Looking in the mirrors, I see blue sky above the cloud, but that's behind me now. It was gloomy in *Zen and the Art,* too—wet and cold and gray.

With the cool air comes the smell, that salty smell of water and fish and seaweed.

And finally the ocean, colorless beyond the town. I've been here before. This is where the coastal road from Oregon meets the road from Grants Pass. At last I'm not just retracing the Pirsigs' route from thirty-six years before but my own, on the same bike, from nineteen years ago. Feels like the same bike, anyway. But the dull sky and dismal water are an anticlimax after so many days of travel, depressing on this cold afternoon after the light and warmth of the forest road.

I want to touch the ocean, as everyone does when completing a trek across the continent. There are signs to the Battery Point Lighthouse, and I ride as far as possible before parking above some steps down to the cold, sandy beach. The luggage will be safe here for a while.

Down the dozen steps, across the sand kicking at the washed-up plants, and the water's right here, about to cover my boot. That's done, then. If the weather's this overcast here, it'll be the same all the way down the coast while the sunshine stays inland.

The heat that was such a curse yesterday seems alluring now. I'll take another look at the map and see about other routes south from here.

When I turn to walk back up the sand, there's a young boy watching, maybe eleven years old. I ask if he'll take a photo, and he shrugs okay. He knows how to work the camera, and I step out onto a small rock in the water and dip a finger into the salty ocean.

He snaps the picture and grins when he sees the image on the small screen.

"Are you from here?" I ask.

"No, mister," he says. "I'm from Logan, Utah. It's nine hundred eighteen miles from here. We're visiting my grandfather—he lives nearby."

"Did you drive here?" Stupid question surely. A foghorn sounds in the distance.

"Yes, mister. We brought our pickup truck so my grandfather could have it. He's going on a mission and won't be back till November. He's got to take a dredger home. We're going home in his car—it's a little car, so I don't know where we'll sleep. When we came out here, we had a big old mattress in the back of the pickup, and whenever we needed to sleep, we just pulled over and slept on that mattress. It was awesome."

He says his name is Landon, and although he loves Logan, Utah, which is apparently in a valley and very pretty, he also loves it down by this beach. I'm thinking that under this cloud bank Crescent City seems like a resort town in the off-season and there's no reason to be here or anywhere near here. The rapid drop in temperature from the extremes of the past few days makes it seem like a different country in a completely different year.

We go back up the beach together, and he takes a look at Jackie New. He asks if I have kids, and when he hears about Andrew and Tristan, he asks if they'll be coming to visit here. No, they're far away. "That's too bad," he says. He looks like he needs a friend in this lonely town. If only they were coming here to visit—I'm missing them very much now.

There are palm trees in the park beside the parking lot, the first I've seen, but they look low and sad under the cloud. A huge wooden play fort is surrounded almost entirely by a long wooden fence. My kids would love that fort, whatever the weather.

My warmer Gore-Tex jacket is needed over the leather jacket for the damp and the chill. When Landon sees me pull out the map, he asks where I'm headed and I tell him San Francisco and say that I'm looking for another route south that's a bit warmer.

"It's a long way inland to get to the interstate, mister," he says. "But you don't want that route anyhow. This is too beautiful to miss. . . . I love driving along the coast—we don't have roads like this in Logan. People come from around the world to drive this road. You can't come as far as you've come and not ride along it."

This is cute. What does he know about motorcycles, anyway?

"I wish I could come along with you, but my grandfather wouldn't let me. I'd love to ride on a motorcycle—never have. Sat in the back of the pickup, but you can't see what's up ahead then, and it's what's up ahead that counts, right? Maybe if I was older I could ride your bike for a ways; maybe you could ride on the back and teach me. But I'll have to get older first, right? Well, I'm working on it!"

And with another grin he jumps on his bicycle to pedal off and tell his grandfather about the guy he just met. I'm left shaking my head at his presumption and his youthful wisdom. I put the unopened map back in my jacket pocket, fire the motorcycle to life, and ride away on the road along the cool coast.

In *Zen and the Art* the Pirsigs pass by Crescent City on this road and stay at a nameless motel about an hour south, riding through thick fog and arriving long after dark. The narrator wanted to get to within an easy day's ride of San Francisco, but poor Chris, cold, wet, and bored, just wanted to go home. Before falling asleep, he told his dad that he missed the way they used to be, how it was once fun and now this grown-up just sits and stares and doesn't do anything. For a careful reader of the book, this is an indication that Phaedrus may not be the evil ghost that the narrator portrays him to be. The end is coming, and it's coming soon.

Chris Pirsig was twenty-two years old and back in San Francisco when his dad and stepmother were moored for the winter in Cornwall. He was a philosophy major at San Francisco State College but still studying at the Zen Center near Haight-Ashbury, searching for comfort and meaning while living down the best-selling description of a whining, challenged kid and his real-life reputation as a psychiatric train wreck.

He'd bought a secondhand motorcycle, perhaps to retrace the route home to St. Paul the next spring and exorcise the demons that lived along that road. In an encouraging letter to his dad, he wrote, "I never thought I would ever live to see my 23rd birthday." On Saturday morning, November 17, 1979, he bought a ticket to England so that he could visit his father on the *Excellence.*

That evening around 8 p.m. he left the Zen Center to walk the short distance to a friend's house. According to witnesses, he was stopped by two men who tried to rob him; one held him from behind while the other threatened him with a kitchen knife. They emptied his pockets and found nothing. Chris was uncooperative and mumbled something to the thieves that angered them. The man with the knife plunged it into his chest, and the two of them drove away, never to be caught.

Chris propped himself against a parked car as he struggled to breathe, then staggered down the road seeking help. Underneath a streetlamp just a block away, less than two weeks before his twenty-third birthday, suffocated by the blood that filled his lungs from a slashed artery, he collapsed and died.

Two miles south of Crescent City the coastal road is more than four hundred feet above the beach and in the clouds. Sometimes I catch glimpses of people down below, bundled up and walking on the sand and throwing sticks for dogs and whatever else they do.

Nineteen years ago I stayed the night at a motel in Eureka for $13, sleeping in the sleeping bag on top of the bed's grimy sheets. The door locked and the TV worked and the electric light went on and off with the switch, so all was well.

I want to find that $13 motel to see how much it costs now. Maybe even stay in the same room, preferring to retrace my own journey rather than the Pirsigs'. But when Eureka appears after eighty-five miles of cool forest and cold ocean beaches, I'm still in the grayness of the cloud and the whole town looks like a dump. The first bank sign says it's 56 degrees.

Here's a place that might have been the motel. Rooms from $35. There are trucks and battered cars in the lot, women with kids smoking to one side and men smoking on the other side. This isn't a good place to stay, next to the bail-bond offices and liquor stores. And here's the reason: the county jail, right in the center of town.

I don't remember that from before, but then it was already dark. Must not have noticed.

I ride around awhile on the one-way streets and finally double back to the Super 8, which seems safe and clean. The first priority is a working phone from which to call my family tomorrow. And after all, nobody wants to wake up on his birthday in some fleabag dive.

The woman behind the counter is old and humorless. Her name's Betty, and she says a room with a queen-size bed and HBO will cost $74. Thanks, I tell her; I'll come back. "Okay, I can give you a discount to sixty-two dollars," she says without a moment's hesitation. We look each other in the eye, neither blinking. Sure, I say. That'll be great.

She hands over the registration form; her hands are slender and stitched with veins, but the fingers are delicate. Her nails are at least an inch long, painted with silver moons and stars. I comment on their beauty, and she smiles, not so dour now—in fact far from it.

"You should park your motorcycle right here under the office window," she says. "There are transients who use the alley over there, and I can't be sure of its safety unless it's here in the light."

Three journeys back and forth and the bike is unpacked. I call Tim, and he confirms that the shock and the clutch are already on their way to the hotel in San Francisco. Took an hour, he says. Should be there tomorrow. *Thank you!* I'm so grateful, but I don't know what else to say.

There's still a chill from the day's cool ride, but instead of running a shower or bath, I change into swimming shorts and walk over to the small indoor pool. Beside it in a separate room is a Jacuzzi. No one's around.

The Jacuzzi is very hot and bubbling quickly. I sit in it for a long time, perhaps an hour, thinking of nothing at all. Absolutely nothing.

When sitting, just sit.

CHAPTER SEVENTEEN

California

The eagle is there again, calm now, watching from a cliff high above the trees as I ride the curving highway, ocean to one side, fields to the other. I'm riding to the crest of a hill, where a woman is waiting beside the road. She turns to look at me as I approach, and her eyes are as dark as the bottom of the sea.

I ride toward her but never get closer.

Now it's slipping away, and I can't remember.

Come back!

And it's gone.

So this is it, the big day. Open an eye and look at the bare off-white wall of the motel room.

Maybe this will finally be a birthday to remember. What happened last year, for my forty-first? Oh, yes—we were at a cottage beside a lake, and I lay in a hammock and finished reading *Zen and the Art of Motorcycle Maintenance*.

I get out of bed and shuffle over to the drawn curtains. Peering between them, I see it's gray outside but not raining. The plan is to phone at 9 a.m., when my wife will be waiting, so there's time now to shower and pack.

Everything is tucked into its place. At last the mysterious gift is no longer in the saddlebag but waiting on the bed, out of its waterproof bag and ready to be opened.

Soon it's 9 a.m. and time to make the call. The phone connects and Wendy—my own Wendy—answers on the second ring. She sings "Happy Birthday" and asks if I'm in San Francisco yet.

"No, I'm not supposed to be there till tonight—there's another three hundred miles to go. But I'm on the California coast."

"Have you climbed your mountain yet?" she asks. I'm not sure of the answer to this one.

"I've been over a few mountains, but there are still some hills to go."

But I don't want to talk about mountains—I want to open my present. She's pleased when she hears it's still wrapped and tells me to go ahead. Now's the moment.

The tissue comes off the small, square box and the cardboard opens and the gift falls into my hand: a black wooden yo-yo—something small and light, something playful. Something that no matter how many times it's thrown down will always return, spinning and whirling to perform tricks and stunts, always coming back to my hand. *Yo-yo* means "come-come" in its inventors' language—had she thought of that?

"Can't say as I did," she admits over the phone so far away. "I just knew you wanted a toy and it had to be small, and you used to be pretty good with a yo-yo. How about that?"

Wendy gets the boys, and I speak with Andrew and then with Tristan. It's difficult to tell them apart; they're growing up so fast. They tell me about their vacation and the animals on the farm and the places they've visited, and we talk and talk about the minutiae that are important in childhood—the worms in the ground, the stars in the sky, the ride on the airplane. I'm happy just to hear their voices. They know this is an important day, and we haven't spoken properly since I waved them good-bye at the airport and they faded into white. Their days have flashed by; mine have climbed mountains.

Finally I speak with Wendy again, and we say how much we love each other. We don't say it often, but I'm saying it now.

"How *are* you?" she asks. I tell her I'm at peace but it's a lonely peace. I want to talk about Crater Lake but don't know where to begin.

"How are *we*?" she asks. We're stronger than we've ever been, I tell her. We talk about her visit with her sister and my ride and her family and my near completion of this quest, and the loneliness goes away.

I'm spinning the yo-yo with my left hand as the long call finally ends. After we've said good-bye, I take a deep breath. Many people go their entire lives without enjoying a bond like ours; others find it and then lose it. I've not lost it, not yet. I hurl the yo-yo toward the door. It flies away and comes straight back, looping around my ring finger and flying away again. Then it comes straight back and settles in the palm of my hand.

The senseless, brutal murder of Chris devastated his family, of course. Maynard telephoned the Falmouth marina, and Bob took the call at the dock phone; Wendy was with him, and he told her they had to get back to the boat quickly, before the shock hit. On board *Excellence*, they cried and cried and cried.

Ted was the first to arrive in San Francisco, flying down from Seattle. His brother had already been formally identified by friends from the Zen Center, but the body was still on the slab in the morgue and he asked to see it. Later he wrote about the experience:

> Brown eyes, brown staring eyes, eyes that didn't move, eyes that were open, that stared vacant, death's eyes, the mouth, the slightly opened mouth, the dried blood below the nose and around the mouth, the slight stubble of a beard, a reddish beard that would never need shaving again and really that's all I could think, looking at that stubble and wondering if it still grew but no it must've stopped growing, dead less than 24 hours there in the city morgue and everyone so quiet, three of us living ones in that room, two people I didn't know, that

thick glass wall that kept him cold and kept us warm and it was so important for me to be there and I'm crying now as I write this, so important for me to see his body, to make it real, to see my dead brother, to see that it really was him murdered last night.

When Nancy arrived at the morgue to claim his belongings, she was asked if she wanted to view the body but couldn't bear the thought of doing so. "I feared that that vision of Chris would be the one I remembered from then on," she explained. "I hold to the belief that after one dies, what's left is not the person but just the body, the shell, so I saw no point in looking at this thing that was not Chris."

Ted's experience was enough:

There was nothing, no feeling, just close observation of the way the eyes were set, the way they stared so blank and I just looked and looked and it burned into my memory and I *wanted* it to burn into my memory and Mom and Dad never came, Mom didn't want to and Dad didn't arrive from England in time and so they both asked me about what he looked like, and I described as best I could the dried blood, the staring eyes, but not the stubble—no—I kept that to myself.

Chris was cremated the following week, and a funeral service was held at the Zen Center, where Dainin Katagiri gave the address with tears flowing down his face. Bob bought an old pickup truck and drove with Wendy back to Minnesota, carrying home his son's few belongings and half his ashes.

Bob and Wendy drove east on many of the same roads Bob and Chris had ridden, snow covered now. They stopped at Bozeman— Gennie DeWeese has a photo of Bob walking in the meadow on that sad visit, head bowed and mood contemplative. In St. Paul, Chris's things were stored in his grandfather's attic. The ashes that had been carried there were given to the Mississippi and Minnesota Rivers, at the point where the two waters meet.

Then it was back to California, where, after the forty-nine days dictated by Zen custom, Chris's remaining ashes were buried on a hill at Green Gulch Farm. It rained during the ceremony, and a sudden gust of wind blew through, strong enough to turn the attendants' umbrellas inside out. "That's Chris!" said Bob. "That's his spirit!"

Bob and Wendy flew back to the *Excellence* in England, stunned.

My bike is covered in giant squashed bugs, some of them at least an inch long, from yesterday's damp ride through the cloud. They are scraped from the headlight with a piece of cardboard, and the luggage is loaded, the bike sinking lower on its suspension spring with each layer. Finally, wearing a sweater under the jacket in the 50-degree morning chill, I ride out of Eureka, past the cheap motel with its smoking residents still in the lot, past the jail, and head south toward San Francisco.

The road soon leaves the coast and climbs inland toward the redwood forests, where the cloud lifts and the sun warms the air. For a while I ride behind a BMW motorcycle with German license plates, a big 1,150-cc Adventurer with a huge gas tank and rugged aluminum panniers. Its rider, an older bearded guy, doesn't acknowledge me when he finally pulls over.

I'm looking for any sign of a motel that might fit Pirsig's description as the place where they stayed, but other than mentioning some apple orchards at the bottom of a slope, he didn't provide much to go on.

Signs beside the highway point to the Avenue of the Giants. The Pirsigs stuck to the main road, but I want to ride alongside it, through the narrow clearings between the huge redwoods. Besides, it's still morning, and there's plenty of time. I pull off at the first sign and enter the forest.

The trees tower above the winding strip of asphalt, which curves and twists its way around their huge trunks in deference to their bulk. This is a state park, protected from commercial encroachment, and these are the world's tallest trees, some more than three hundred feet high, having sprouted several hundred years ago from seeds no larger than a tomato's, weighing five hundred tons at maturity, their bases as wide as the widest cottonwood in Dayville and their bark like armor, a foot thick. It's cool and mossy down here as I thread between them, pausing to read the signs by the groves. It's no wonder this place is called a cathedral.

Traffic is light on this Friday morning, and I press on, swinging the bouncing bike around the bends of the road, as narrow as a driveway with barely room for two vehicles to pass. I come out from the forest's shade at Weott, where the Pirsigs had breakfast, but there's no place there to eat, just a group of wooden buildings under renovation. The workmen don't look at me, but through the window of a house across the street an old man stares my way. I wave, but he doesn't respond; perhaps he's a mannequin. As I ride away, his head turns slowly to follow my track.

I find the trees depressing now, no longer majestic but oppressive, claustrophobic. Nothing seems to move beneath them; they're still and silent. I pass through Miranda, a little place with a couple of stores, and decide to ride through the next stretch of forest and then leave for good, getting back on the highway and rejoining the Zen route to the coast. My speed builds past 40 miles an hour, and I'm ready to break through from the trees and into the sunshine when I lose all control of the bike.

It's slewing to the other side of the road. I'm going 45 miles an hour, and I can't steer. Must be a flat on the front tire. Christ—front flats are uncontrollable.

The overloaded bike swerves and wobbles, slews and dips on the narrow highway through the trees. The handlebars pull to the left as the wheel rim touches the asphalt, then bounce back to the right as the tire rubber slips underneath and runs flat against the ground. There's no other traffic, thank God. The bike's slowing quickly but still headed toward the trees. They wouldn't move for this road, and they're not going to move for me. There's no time—to think, to pray, to see life flash by. Here it comes. . . . But then, as I brace for impact, the rim slips again against the tire rubber and the motorcycle slides back to the left and my feet can paddle against the ground. The bike judders left and right, but she's going slowly now. I ram both feet hard against the road and somehow keep everything upright as Jackie New stops. The front tire is completely flat. This bike's going *nowhere.*

I walk her over to a nearby pull-off, close to a path leading to a grove of redwoods. She's difficult enough to balance just being walked. My hands tremble for a few minutes when I realize the closeness of this escape. How ever did I get away with it?

I push her up into the trees to shield her a little from prying eyes and try the cell phone, but there's no signal. There's also no spare tube or tire irons or pump among the heavy luggage. There is an AAA card, however. I'd thought about this before setting out from home and decided to leave some of the repairs to the Triple-A guy and save the extra tool space.

This is not as bad as in Oregon, when I nearly ran out of gas in the forest. Parked so close to a pathway, the bike will not appear to be abandoned; the front tire does not look flat from afar, and most people will assume that her rider's gone for a walk and will reappear at any moment. My things should be safe for a while. Even so, I remove the GPS and the pink copy of *Zen and the Art* and push the bike behind a tree, giving her a little pat on the tank before walking away.

There aren't many options right now.

A car is about to drive away at the other end of the pull-off, and the couple inside, a middle-aged man and woman, are happy to offer me a ride back to Miranda. The woman volunteers to sit in the rear while we drive the two miles to town. They're from Los Angeles and going to a wedding in Eureka, taking the scenic route between the redwood groves. "It's so inspiring, isn't it?" she says. "It proves there has to be a God."

Miranda is even smaller than it seemed before: two stores and an auto-detailing shop. I go straight to the auto shop, where the owner is about to close for lunch. He can't repair the tire, but he's happy to provide a phone and I make the call to Triple-A.

But the woman at the other end is not helpful when she learns it's a motorcycle that needs assistance. "We can't repair your tire, and we cannot tow a motorcycle," she says. "We can deliver you compressed air. Would you like some compressed air?"

"That's just going to come straight out the hole in the tube, isn't it?" I ask, not quite believing what she's telling me.

"Well, yes, if you haven't fixed it," she says. "Would you like me to mail you a copy of our motorcycle repair policy?"

I flash back to the guy asking my name in Bill's newly computerized motorcycle store in Miles City, but none of this is helping, so I end the call and look hopefully at the auto guy. His name is Eric.

"Nobody here can fix a tire," he says, "but I can recommend a towing service that can take you to a bike shop not too far away. Want me to make the call?"

Of course—I'm helpless here. Eric makes the call and says the truck will be along soon. It's coming from Garberville, maybe fifteen minutes away. It'll meet me here, and then we'll go pick up the bike.

Eric closes the shop and drives away for his lunch. The sun's out, heating the street. It's too warm now to wear the jacket, so I sit on the stoop and wait.

And wait.

And wait.

Time passes. There's little going on here. Next door is a souvenir store, but few people are shopping. Across the street there's a general store and supermarket with a gas pump out front, and people come and go every few minutes. Half an hour passes and the tow truck's nowhere to be seen.

Why hadn't I checked the AAA policy before leaving? If I had, I'd surely have packed tire irons and two spare tubes. With them in the tool kit, it would have been simple to make the Triple-A phone call, go straight back to the bike, remove the front wheel, and be ready when the repair guy showed up with the compressed air. Come to think of it, it would have been even easier just to pack a miniature spark plug pump or a couple of small compressed-air cylinders, and then there would have been no need for AAA.

Time passes. Still no tow truck. The only sounds are the occasional muffled conversations of people going in and out of the stores and the insects and the birds. What was the name of the towing company? I can't remember, but it'll be in the Yellow Pages. There's a phone booth across the street—I'll call from there to find out what's happening. But in the phone book in the booth the pages for towing services have been ripped out. How can anyone be so selfish? And then I remember the bike-shop pages from Bend that are still in one of the saddlebags back in the forest. I dare not even go into one of the stores, in case the truck comes.

An hour goes by. This is ridiculous. Everything of importance to my quest is on that motorcycle, vulnerable to thieves. And God knows how much this repair will cost—I'm at the mercy of the tow truck guy. A couple of hundred dollars easy, maybe more. And who knows how long it will take to fix the tire? All this way on schedule and then thrown at the last moment, so close to the end. It'll take all afternoon, and then it'll be too late to reach the final, crucial point of this journey, the resolution at the coast, the scene of the famous climax, whose coordinates are keyed in to the GPS.

So much for San Francisco tonight. So much for anything. I thought this was going to be fun, and it isn't any fun. I'm sorry I came. Right now somebody's probably snipping the cable that's holding the laptop to the bike. So much for my birthday and the meaning of life. It's the helplessness that's the crusher, to be so dependent on others. It didn't have to be like this. God, this is a hell of a way for the trip to end.

There's a sound from the woods to the right, music of some sort, and soon a small car drives into the sunshine. As it comes out of the trees and into the town, the music from its open window grows louder and louder until it's as loud as it can be, some kind of rock guitar, but then it fades away at the end of the track. A young woman is driving the car, a blue Chevy Tracker, and the stereo is probably worth more than the vehicle, for the sound was clear and musical even at full volume.

A pickup truck backs out from the store's parking lot, and the Tracker comes to a halt to let it pull into the road. The music has ended now, and the silence is more pronounced because of it. The pickup drives away.

And then a voice comes from the Tracker with no music behind it, clear as can be. It must be the next song on the CD, but it's so loud it's as if it's all around.

BE NOT AFRAID—THIS TOO SHALL PASS.

And as the voice speaks, the young woman turns and looks directly at me. Her eyes are very dark, almost completely black.

Silence. She looks ahead again and drives off to the south, toward my stranded motorcycle. As the Tracker pulls into the forest, there's the sound of rock guitar starting up again and disappearing through the trees.

The hairs on the back of my neck are standing up. I'm waiting for a gust of wind to blow through.

And here's the tow truck, pulling into the parking lot, its driver looking all around and then waving this way.

"You look like you need a tow!" he calls. "Get in and we'll go rescue you."

I gather my jacket and throw it into the truck—there'll be time to think about this later. Settling into the seat, I look down at my hand and see that it's trembling again.

"Sorry it took a while to get to you—I was in the middle of another job," says the driver. "Eric told me you're a long ways from home and need a friend. Well, we'll see what we can do for you."

It's a big truck that looks like it could tow a house, and we sit high above the road as the driver, Ross, double declutches around the curves of the Avenue of the Giants. We reach the bike in just a few minutes, and she's untouched, exactly as I left her. "This shouldn't be too difficult," he says. I start to unload the luggage, but he says to leave it in place. He wants to pick up everything just as it is.

Sure enough, he backs up to the bike, lowers the boom, and busies himself with some straps and chains. He lifts the boom and the bike swings up a few inches and to one side, so he lowers it again and makes some adjustments. A couple more lifts and tucks and the bike is secure and straight behind the truck, hanging three feet from the ground.

"You're a guy who takes some pride in his work," I say.

"Thank you," says Ross. "I appreciate that. It's good to know somebody notices." If a job's worth doing, it's worth doing well.

He suggests a motorcycle-repair shop in Redway, a place that's honest and apparently owes him a favor, so we return to the highway at Miranda and head south. Along the way Ross is chatting happily about how much he loves the area, and I'm thinking about the woman in the Tracker.

"It's not too far," he says. "I can take you there for fifty bucks. Does that sound okay?"

"That's fine—thanks." I'm listening to the voice and looking into the woman's eyes, dark as coal. Of course he's not overcharging me; in fact he's undercharging me because he's a decent guy. *"Be not afraid."*

We pull up at Rooster's Motorcycle and 4x4 Superstore, a small prefab building on the edge of town, and Ross explains the situation to the owner. "Our motorcycle mechanic is out for a few hours," says the owner, "but you're welcome to use our space." He's got tubes for sale and tire irons—I'm happy to buy them and do the job myself. In fact, from now on I won't travel without them.

Ross drives around back and drops the bike carefully, and we shake hands as he bids me well on the journey. I'm about to push the bike under the shade of a tree when one of the car mechanics invites me inside. "No one's using this bay and this jack, so you're welcome to it," he says. "Here's the compressed air, and all the tools are in this drawer."

It is unheard-of for a mechanic to invite you to use his tools and his work space, but the offer is there and I'm not about to turn it down. The bike jacks up, still loaded with all her luggage, and the front wheel pulls off quickly. There's no sign of anything puncturing the rubber. The tire irons are good ones, long and strong, and I leapfrog them around the rim until the tire's bead breaks easily.

I pull out the old tube and find the hole, then look for the cause. There's nothing to be found. Nothing at all. No hole in the tire itself at the point of the hole in the tube and no debris or foreign object inside the tire that could have rubbed its way through. No reason for the hole whatsoever, except perhaps age and a weak point in the rubber. If that's the case, it could have gone anywhere, at any time—climbing the Beartooth Pass, speeding beside the Lochsa River, out on the baking Oregon plain. Maybe even when the wheel hit the huge pothole in Montana, just before the pickup truck rounded the corner coming toward me.

But it didn't. It happened in California, close to a friendly tow truck driver and an obliging motorcycle shop. *"Be not afraid."*

I clean out the tire anyway, blowing it clear with the compressed air, then push the new tube inside carefully, taking the time to make sure it settles into position and is not pinched. I find some soap and run it on the edge of the tire to lubricate the bead, then inflate the tube to just a few pounds and deflate it again to help it settle against the inside of the tire, then inflate and deflate it a second time just because I can.

Finally, happy with the way it looks, I inflate the tire to the correct pressure, hold the wheel up between the front forks, and push the axle through cleanly with a dab of grease to help it slide. It tightens with a few turns of the mechanic's socket wrench, and I'm done. For good measure while it's up on the jack, I check the pressure on the rear tire and lubricate the chain.

The bike's ready for the road, and all it cost was a total $75 for a tow, a tube, and a pair of tire irons that I needed anyway. It's 2 p.m. *"This too shall pass."*

I think about the voice and its message. For a start, there's no such thing as voices. Tom in Bozeman told me that he'd heard a voice clearly while driving a pickup truck somewhere near Mount McKinley in Alaska: it recited a poem. He turned to his passenger and asked if he'd heard it, but the passenger had heard nothing, so Tom pulled over immediately and wrote the poem down as best he could remember it. He even recited it for me, and I smiled supportively when he said he couldn't explain it. Tom had looked like the kind of guy who'd appreciate some mushrooms once in a while, anyway.

But this voice was completely explainable. It must have been gospel rock and the timing pure coincidence. It was just a woman driving a Tracker, looking my way as she waited for the pickup truck because she had to look somewhere. I was looking at her, after all.

I'm not a religious person. But riding south now toward the turnoff for Highway 1 and the coast, I feel like a heretic who's recanted.

CHAPTER EIGHTEEN

Pacific Coast

CALIFORNIA'S HIGHWAY I climbs up and up from its northern junction at the Redwood Highway, twisting and cambering over the Coast Ranges in the tightest series of turns yet. Many of the curves are marked for just 15 miles an hour, and there's no point in hurrying. It reaches eighteen hundred feet above the Pacific, and the edges of the road drop away through the evergreen woods to points far below.

As the road finally descends and the coast approaches, there's a bank of cloud moving through the valley down in the trees. It's going to be cold down there. In *Zen and the Art,* Chris didn't want to go on, not with this man in control of the motorcycle, and the two of them stopped and argued along the way, waiting each other out to see who'd give in first.

There's no giving in for me, though. As the road falls into the wet cloud, the route begins to straighten and leads directly west to the ocean. Once again there's salt in the air and seagulls on the wind. The gray sky is obscured by the ceiling of cloud, and when the first coastal cliff face breaks through the trees, there's water everywhere, but no rain.

I pull over and stare awhile at the choppy ocean, not sure what to think. Just a short ride south and the quest will be over. Is that good or bad? Don't know. The road hugs the coast, sliding down sometimes to the beach and rising up along the cliff, always under the cloud. There are very few vehicles. Is that the farmhouse that Pirsig mentions, the one that's poor and weathered with broken fences? Probably. Even here, twenty-seven hundred miles on my odometer from Minneapolis, the journey stays honest. When he says there's a tree, there's a tree.

Due south now, no place else to go. No roads leading east, just the deep, deep ocean to the west. Here's a town with strange trees overhanging the road, humble houses outnumbered on the hillsides by architects' marvels with high fences and strong gates.

I'm through Fort Bragg and approaching Caspar at last, where the Pirsigs stopped for lunch and the narrator tells Chris he's going to send him home on a bus. Chris cries at his father's desertion, clutching at his stomach. The narrator has no sympathy. He recognizes something in Chris over which he has no control. He finally sees that Phaedrus is winning the boy, that his son feels betrayed and is wrestling his own demon; that before long, if nothing changes, the son will ride with the father into madness.

Echoing Goethe's "Erlkönig" all those miles ago in South Dakota, Phaedrus has been carried this far just to prove that Chris plays the role of the father and that the narrator, after all, is the pursuing evil.

They pay up and get on the little motorcycle for a short ride to find a private place beside the ocean, to have it out at last. The meeting of the father, the son, and the ghost.

I ride into Caspar. Due south now, no place else to go.

Still trying to come to terms with the death of his son and the void that the loss created, Bob Pirsig left England when his visa expired in the spring, sailing with Wendy to Europe. The Dutch authorities gave them a sheltered mooring on an abandoned branch of the sea canal that leads to Ghent. *Lila* was a slog and many years yet from completion. A page here, a rejected few paragraphs there. Many days nothing happened.

Then one day Wendy realized she was pregnant. She and Bob were shocked—a pregnancy had not been planned, nor was it welcome. Bob was fifty-one years old, too old, he thought, to become a parent and nurturer again; a child would surely live only to prove his failing as a father. They decided the child should be aborted, and Wendy dutifully arranged for the procedure.

The exact site of the climax, when the narrator pulls the motorcycle over at "a high point that apparently juts out into the ocean but now is surrounded by banks of fog," was later identified by Pirsig as Point Cabrillo, close to the lighthouse at Caspar, about seven miles south of Fort Bragg.

The GPS guides the way with some difficulty to a waypoint near the local bar in Caspar, for there's a short one-way road off the highway that complicates the route. This doesn't seem right. There's a field here that runs down to the sea, and I park the bike by the store and walk around with the GPS. A pathway is beaten through the grass past some blackberry bushes and pussy willows, but no—this isn't it. Doesn't stick out enough.

I look around for likely places. Standing in the field still, peering everywhere, I'm hemmed in by the high grass but unrestricted by fences and properties. The few houses are all on large plots of land, an acre or more each, and there's nothing between me and the sea. To the north are woods and an expensive-looking ranch. To the east is the Caspar Inn, standing in its own brown field of grass. That must have been the GPS waypoint. And to the south, on the other side of the inlet, is a development of large houses with manicured lawns, filling the high promontory that juts out into the ocean—

That's it—that's Point Cabrillo! I'm on the wrong side of the bay. I shove the GPS into my pocket and run back along the path through the grass to Jackie New. She starts with the first kick, and I head quickly back along the one-way road—more of a track, really—to the highway and then west down to Caspar Beach. It's cool and gray, but some people are on the sand, a family building sand castles, the children in their bathing suits, the parents in shorts.

The road leads around from the beach and up to the headland. Another road branches west onto the promontory and into the development, and there's a large sign at the entrance, surrounded by a low wooden fence.

"Caspar South—Private Property," it reads. "No Trespassing, Hunting, Fishing or Ocean Access without Written Consent of Property Owner. Violators Will Be Prosecuted."

But there's no gate blocking the way. I haven't come this far to be stymied by a bunch of wealthy property owners. What would the DeWeeses say? Prosecute and be damned!

There's no one at home anyway in the dozen or so large houses that lead out to the land's tip, perhaps a quarter of a mile west of the beach. I ride in on their smooth, fancy road and take a look around. Now this seems right.

Thirty-six years ago there would have been no houses here. There would have been fog obscuring the ocean that's splashing perhaps a hundred feet below against the sheer cliffs of the promontory. And the small road that leads to the lighthouse climbs toward this spot and then passes nearby, the road on which a local truck driver made his way through the mist and asked the Pirsigs if they needed a lift.

They did not. They needed each other.

Not every property is developed, and there's a wide gap between two houses, facing north onto Caspar Bay. It's a field of dry grass, perhaps a half acre, grass not so high as across the bay, but the place is clearly waiting to become the site of someone's home. It looks north across the water at the field where I first stopped, and then beyond it, visible through traces of mist from the ocean, is the large ranch. There are others there, too, low and partially hidden by trees.

I park, then walk into the low golden grass of the field and look out long and hard at the ocean.

This is it. After the plains and mountains and now down at the water, this is where Chris collapsed. This is where he lay with his head in his hands, rocking back and forth on the edge of sanity, and Pirsig's narrator considered his own abject failure as a father and a person. Where he thought about running off the cliff, drowning himself in the cold, dark, cleansing ocean. But he hung on for just that extra moment as Phaedrus pushed through the billowing curtain of the narrator's mind and began to speak directly to Chris, for the first time in years. "I haven't forgotten you," he tells his son, who recognizes the old voice immediately. "How could I forget you?" he says, and "We'll be together now."

And as I gaze at the ocean, I see the young face of the boy in the photographs in my book finally clearing and smiling at his reclaimed father. In his eyes is a light of innocence and happiness and excitement for the future.

I slip my hands into my jacket pockets and feel something there. The yo-yo. I take it out without looking at it and loop the string onto the second finger of my left hand, then hurl the wooden toy toward the water. It flies away and comes straight back, looping around and flying away again. Then it comes back, and I hurl it again and again, flipping it all around, up and down, somersaulting it through the air for circle after circle, freewheeling it on the end of the string and laughing out loud before I finally slow the speed and catch it to let it settle in the palm of my hand, solid and safe.

I'm alone out here and far away on my forty-second birthday, but there's no reason to be afraid—this too shall pass, and it's time to go home.

Talking it over one last time before the scheduled abortion, Bob and Wendy Pirsig looked at each other and were overwhelmed. "Wait. Stop. Something's wrong," said Bob, hanging on for that extra moment as it became clear that this was no unwanted stranger. This child was a reinstatement of a part of Chris, returning in his own way from wherever his essence existed to enrich their lives with a feeling now that had not been there before.

The appointment was canceled, and later that year a daughter, Nell, was born.

"What is seen now so much more clearly," Pirsig wrote later, "is that although the names keep changing and the bodies keep changing, the larger pattern that holds us all together goes on and on."

It was a joyous motorcycle ride at last for the father and son from here down to San Francisco. Chris and Phaedrus rested and talked for a while, then got on the bike and headed inland, helmetless and carefree, away from the evil narrator left behind in the mist. The sun came out and Chris stood up on the pegs, finally able to see past the driver and all around, and the book ends with its most famous line of all, Phaedrus talking now: "We've won it. It's going to get better now. You can sort of tell these things."

A huge weight lifts as I pocket the yo-yo and fire up Jackie New, her spring still holding and her rear tire not yet worn through. I ride out of the development and past the beach, where the family is packing up their things and leaving sand castles to be washed away by the evening tide, and I wave at them as I pass. They wave back and smile, too, happy for the contact.

There are two routes the Pirsigs could have taken to Ukiah, but I take neither of them, breaking away completely for the first time to follow my own route, staying on the cool coast awhile longer. The road passes by inlets where birds skim the still water to hunt fish and where sea lions bask on rocks, calling into the wind. On the right, out across the deep, deep ocean, there's a silver light far on the horizon where the late sun shines past the edge of the cloud.

I turn in at the Navarro River and wind through a state park, again filled with redwoods, and as I come around a corner, there's a bright patch of sunshine on the road ahead. The bike bursts through among the trees and into the light and the cloud is behind me now and the sun is warm on my back. Down toward Philo and its vineyards, the grass on the folded slopes between the vines shines golden in the soft light of early evening.

Is this what riding a bike is all about? Is this the reason I came here? Surely this is the most beautiful place on earth, the Promised Land. It's natural and inspiring—the DeWeeses would love it; so would Mike's wife—so different here from the prairie and the steppe.

So many people I've encountered along the way, people searching for a place to live and be themselves: the mother at the motel in Laurel, setting up a new home for her daughter in North Dakota with a man she barely knows; the lonely waitress from Grants Pass, heading up to Portland to meet her Christian beau; Lacy and Jenny, bored in the bar in Lemmon.

And me, riding away from my family about as far as I can go, whirring now on the end of the string, ready to return and be a proper dad again. Phone calls aren't enough: even in this beautiful place, I can't wait to see Wendy and Andrew and Tristan again. We're related to each other in ways we never fully understand, maybe hardly understand at all, but my family is pulling at me now as, at forty-two, I come to realize the meaning of my life.

There have been so many more people who love their homes: Bill and Bonnie, both fighting his Parkinson's to live out their dream in Montana; Sidney Berreth, proud of the rich soil of Oakes; and Lori Smith, of course, content for Dayville to never change.

And then there have been the people who are traveling around the country for what time they can spare, exploring and meeting others but happy to return: Kent the Harley guy, heading home from Alaska; Jim and Nick, breaking away for a couple of weeks to see the ocean; Vince the farmer, who's visited every state but Maine and always wants to come home.

Home is where you make it. Even the French author proved that, flying in his mind to Atlantis and to castles in Spain while lying motionless in his hospital bed, trapped by a broken body but allowing nothing to hold him back. I have no such limits, and I'm making the most of it now, bouncing past wineries and meadows, flying on the motorcycle. People who care and people who care enough for me to give me a home—*they* are Quality.

266

The Pirsigs raised Nell for a while in Norway and Sweden, but when she was four years old and their money was running low, they returned across the Atlantic to the northeastern United States, to the familiarity of spoken English and family nearby. They dry-docked the *Excellence* and have lived in content New England seclusion ever since.

Lila sold for a rumored $2 million and was published in 1991; it has sold more than half a million copies. Its philosophical arguments still cause many readers to scratch their heads in puzzlement, but it expands on Robert Pirsig's thoughts far more thoroughly than *Zen and the Art of Motorcycle Maintenance* and has found favor with a small but enthusiastic academic audience.

At the Pirsig home, Bob built a special room with a sound-proof floor. Nothing in it except a chair and some windows that look out onto a beautiful valley. It's a place for him to sit and think for hours at a time. Outside in the shed the old Superhawk sits unridden; Bob's license to ride it expired with the move east, and he flunked the state motorcycle test. But he and Wendy go for a drive in the car every morning to share time and talk.

Not far away is the home of Jim Landis, the editor who saw the vision and understood the meaning of *Zen and the Art* from the very beginning. The editor and the author became close and trusted friends as Landis rose to become editor in chief at William Morrow before eventually quitting to write books himself. They still visit regularly, and their families share every Thanksgiving. Bob Pirsig took Landis out to buy a computer when he decided, reluctantly, to switch from typewriters. He's better known now as the novelist J. D. Landis.

Recently Bob gave his friend a signed copy of *Lila.* "For Jim Landis," it's inscribed, "who made it all possible."

And this summer of 2004 the Pirsigs finally completed the restoration of *Excellence,* making her ocean-worthy again. As I gazed west today across the calm Pacific, they were out on the rolling swells of the Atlantic, sun in their eyes and wind at their backs, gulls swooping all around. Nell was with them. She's twenty-three years old now—the age that slipped away from Chris.

The winding road ends at Cloverdale just as the sun drops behind the western ridge, and the rest of this ride will be on the interstate, fast and direct, straight to the hotel in San Francisco.

I turn south toward Healdsburg and shift on the padded seat, getting comfortable for the final hundred miles. My feet come off the foot pegs to skim the asphalt, and I lean into the slipstream. I don't turn to look, but there's a feeling that off to the right a regal bird is flying alongside, sharing the wind.

San Francisco

San Francisco, Calif.
5 February 1986

The final drive into San Francisco, riding across the Golden Gate Bridge with my hair streaming in the wind, felt as triumphant as I had hoped. I made my way to the top of the Twin Peaks and gazed out in the sunshine at the city, the mountains, the bay, and the ocean and felt, not for the first time, that I had really achieved something.

I arrived in San Francisco after dark and checked in to my tiny hotel room close to the Haight district.

The desk clerk knew I was coming: waiting were half a dozen birthday cards from family and friends; a bottle of wine from Franz and Gregor, the German Harley riders who'd passed by just a week before on their own Zen trip; and perhaps most important, a heavy package containing Jackie Blue's shock absorber and clutch.

It was good not to travel to a new place each day, packing the bags every morning and leaving no trace of my presence. Leanne was waiting early on Saturday, as promised, with a pair of new Michelin Anakee tires, and as soon as the bike was ready, I headed over to the final stop of the Zen journey. Originally I'd wanted to stay at the Zen Center, but it was closed to outsiders this week. A retreat was taking place, and no one could be disturbed. No matter. I parked the bike outside the main entrance of the large, three-story redbrick building and peered through the dimpled glass of the large wooden door. The hallway inside was cool and airy.

Inside, the adherents would be meditating on the wisdom that had gotten me here, peeling away the layers of the world like an onion to discover that there is no world after all, just layers. Recognizing that one of Zen's greatest lessons is to live as if you'll live forever, but also to live each day as if it were your last.

Then I backed down the steps and walked to the corner, crossing the road and continuing a block south along Laguna Street to Haight. Was this the way Chris came that night in 1979? Was this where he was jumped and his assailants emptied his pockets to find nothing? Was this where they argued and he was stabbed?

I walked the final block to the corner of Octavia and Haight. He crossed the street to collapse and die beneath a streetlamp. Was this the lamp?

The houses along the gentle slope of Haight and southward down Octavia were just as they would have been twenty-five years ago: fine three- and four-story buildings with ornate bay windows, mostly converted to apartments, with cars nudging into each other for parking spaces on the road outside. But across the street the entire eastern side of Octavia was ripped up and dug deep for a new development, perhaps offices or condos or maybe just to widen and straighten the highway. It's next to the Central Freeway after all, the multilaner that connects to the interstate and carries cars more quickly and efficiently into the city's downtown.

Perhaps the streetlamp was on that side of the road. If so, it's gone now, in the name of progress.

A short walk back to the bike and I was about to ride away when the wind picked up, blowing an empty paper cup across the sidewalk and onto the road. I looked up again at the heavy wooden door of the Zen Center. Again I climbed the steps and peered through the dimpled glass. Nothing had changed, but it was easy to imagine that a ghost might live there, entombed within its structure, within its soul.

Afterword

Last summer, riding home from the Sturgis Motorcycle Rally on a borrowed bike, I stayed a night in Lemmon, South Dakota. I called the number Lacy had given me during that drunken evening in the Trail's End bar, and to my surprise, she was there at her parents' home. We arranged to meet over pizza that evening— no alcohol this time. There were no sparks, either, when we saw each other, of course. Both of us had made it clear that this was only a social meeting between two people with common interests. She was curious to hear about the rest of my journey, but I wanted to know how her life had progressed in the three years since we had first met.

She told me it had been rough. There'd been more drinking and more debauchery with Jenny, more trouble over the following year, and it had all ended in a police car chase, arrest, and imprisonment. She'd spent forty-five days in a psychiatric ward, which had forced her to dry out, and she hadn't touched booze since. Now she was at the university in Spearfish, back into her studies to become a psychologist.

She couldn't tell me anything of Mike. His motel had closed the previous winter, and nobody was sure what had happened to him. Apparently, he'd just walked away from the place, giving it to the bank. When I went to the motel, it was empty, abandoned. Nothing was locked, and I walked into room 28, where the bed was unmade and the window blind still had a tear through its fabric. In the main house, keys were strewn across the reception desk

271

as if the place had been looted but there'd been nothing to take. Among the dismal, thin-walled rooms behind, one was clearly the little girl's room, with brightly colored crayon drawings of princesses still taped to the wall. It wasn't until just a couple of months ago that I finally found Mike. He's living with a new girlfriend in Chicago and had been driving trucks across the country; he'd been diagnosed with cancer and was undergoing chemotherapy and radiation treatment; his ex-wife and her daughter have a new life in a new city in the Midwest. South Dakota is a hard place to live: the Trail's End was boarded up; the store down the road with the "Kennedy's car" sign was bolted shut and its parking lot overgrown with weeds. Change is inevitable, but it strikes hard when it seems to end in emptiness.

There was no emptiness, though, in Gennie DeWeese's life. She died from lung cancer last November after eighty-six years of creative existence. When I called Tina and Tom to express my condolences, I also had to ask the inevitable question: Did Gennie ever get to hear a wolf howl in the Valley of the Flowers? No, said Tina, but she and Tom spotted one a couple of years ago, sitting up high on the ridge. "He was a mangy thing—not a lot of hair on his body. We didn't see him again but kept running across his tracks. We think he came down from the Gallatins and found a home at Ted Turner's ranch. My mom never saw or heard him, but she knew about him. She was so pleased."

On that trip home from Sturgis, I met again with Ollie Foran and made sure that the Sutherland motorcycle was still safe in his garden shed. And I enjoyed dinner with Sue Nemitz and John Curry in the old Pirsig house, and personally thanked them for their help with this project. John Sutherland was not at home, but he's still well, a little deafer but just as feisty as before.

Bill Bergeron is not doing so well, but he's toughing it out. He developed aspirated pneumonia that took away much of his muscle strength, and now gets around with an electric wheelchair and a pair of crutches. It was difficult for him to read the manuscript I sent because he would shake so much; he could read for only short periods of time. He still has the Harley trike, though he can no longer ride it. Instead, he gets around his subdivision on an Arctic Cat four-wheeler with side-by-side seating, a gas pedal, and a steering wheel. I'm not sure if the four-wheeler gives way to the planes coming in to land on his driveway or the other way around, but I have a hunch I know which gets its way in the end.

During the four years of this book's preparation and writing, I stayed in touch by e-mail with most of the people involved. Robert Pirsig himself preferred the regular postal service for the half-dozen letters we exchanged. He was always courteous but progressively became less forthcoming and more protective of his privacy as my questioning continued until the publication of this book was a certainty. Then he wrote me a long and supportive letter of congratulation: "ZMM also took four years to write—two years to write the first draft, three months to throw it away and never want to see it again, and two more years to write the final draft. So now you know what it's like."

He read and commented on two versions of the manuscript: in the first, where his story was barely told, he wrote that reading it made him feel like a ghost at his own funeral. He preferred the second version, which fell back on a great deal of the biographical material he'd provided over the years to curious members of the media, much of it found on the Web sites of Professor Henry Gurr (ww2.usca.edu/ResearchProjects/ProfessorGurr/Main/HomePage) and Ian Glendinning (www.psybertron.org/pirsigpages .php). Both Henry and Ian provided me with invaluable assistance from the very beginning of this project, and I cannot thank them enough for their help. I also benefited from the Web pages of Anthony McWatt, the first person to earn a PhD from a thesis that explores Pirsig's philosophy. At his site (www.robertpirsig.org), you can now order a DVD that includes interviews with Pirsig, John Sutherland, and others. The most authoritative site of them all, www.moq.org, provides "a forum for discussion and study of the Metaphysics of Quality as proposed by Robert M. Pirsig" and is recommended for those who wish to pursue Pirsig's philosophy more deeply.

I also sent the second manuscript to both Nancy James and Ted Pirsig. No one had ever asked them for their version of events, and they filled in most of the blanks that Robert Pirsig had been reluctant to discuss publicly and answered my many questions with care and precision. This story could not have been told properly without their patient cooperation.

I offered to provide a manuscript to Jim Landis, who told me wonderful stories of his days in New York publishing, but he declined the offer. "All these years later, I still have a fear of people showing up with manuscripts," he wrote. "I doubt there's anyone as eager to read your book as I; just the finished product, its pages glued."

Of course, when it comes to patience, no one has proven more understanding than my wife, Wendy, and our two boys, Andrew and Tristan, who let me shut myself away and write, and who encouraged me to continue during numerous revisions and the search for a publisher. I've retired Jackie New to a more sedate life of local exploration, and now she shares my garage with a Harley-Davidson Low Rider named Lucy. Andrew is now eleven, and he and I will be riding places this summer on the cruiser while we plan to make a cross-country trip next year. Robert Pirsig's remarkable book changed my life in numerous ways. I hope that you'll seek it out and give it an opportunity to change your life, too.

Mark Richardson
March 2008

ABOUT THE AUTHOR

Mark Richardson is the editor of the automotive section of *The Toronto Star.* He lives near Toronto with his wife and two sons. He can be reached at www.zenandnow.org.

A NOTE ON THE TYPE

The text of this book was set in a typeface called Times New Roman, designed by Stanley Morison (1889–1967) for *The Times* (London) and first introduced by that newspaper in 1932.

COMPOSED BY CREATIVE GRAPHICS, ALLENTOWN, PENNSYLVANIA

PRINTED AND BOUND BY BERRYVILLE GRAPHICS, BERRYVILLE, VIRGINIA

MAP BY DAVID LINDROTH, INC.

BOOK DESIGN BY ROBERT C. OLSSON